A Notorious Woman

A Notorious Woman

ANNE ROYALL in Jacksonian America

ELIZABETH J. CLAPP

UNIVERSITY OF VIRGINIA PRESS

Charlottesville & London

To David

University of Virginia Press

Printed in the United States of America on acid-free paper
First published 2016

9 8 7 6 5 4 3 2 1

Library of Congress Cataloging-in-Publication Data
Clapp, Elizabeth J. (Elizabeth Jane), 1960–
A notorious woman : Anne Royall in Jacksonian America / Elizabeth J. Clapp.
pages cm
Includes bibliographical references and index.
ISBN 978-0-8139-3836-3 (cloth : acid-free paper) —
ISBN 978-0-8139-3837-0 (ebook)
1. Royall, Anne Newport, 1769–1854. 2. Royall, Anne Newport, 1769–1854—Public opinion. 3. Royall, Anne Newport, 1769–1854—Political and social views. 4. Women journalists—United States—Biography. 5. Women travelers—United States—Biography. 6. Sex role—United States—History—19th century. 7. Journalists—United States—Biography. 8. Newspaper editors—United States—Biography. 9. Travel writers—United States—Biography. 10. United States—History—1815–1861—Biography. I. Title.
E340.R88C55 2016
973.5092—dc23
[B]

2015034546

Contents

Acknowledgments

This book has been some years in the making and in that time has undergone a number of changes. As the book has grown, I have accumulated many debts, both academic and personal. I am delighted to acknowledge now the help of those people and institutions that have assisted me.

First, I would like to thank Melvyn Stokes, who introduced me to the "Grandmother of the Muckrakers" and suggested that I might investigate Anne Royall as an antidote to the Progressive Era women reformers of my first book. She has certainly been different. I thank him for the idea, for reading and commenting on the early drafts, and for his continued encouragement in my academic career.

The University of Leicester has been my academic home during this project. I have been fortunate in the support I have enjoyed from successive heads of school, my colleagues in the School of History and the Centre for American Studies. I am especially grateful to Professor Roey Sweet for her encouragement and support. I am pleased to acknowledge the periods of research leave the university has granted me, and the financial help I have received from the School of History, which has assisted in the funding of research trips to the United States. In the busy life of a British university, the commodity in shortest supply is time. For this reason, I am particularly indebted to the Arts and Humanities Research Council for its help through the Research Leave Scheme enabling me to complete the first draft of this book.

The community of British American Nineteenth-Century Historians has been a source of intellectual stimulation—their enthusiasm and scholarship a great strength. I have presented papers on Anne Royall at several conferences and seminars on both sides of the Atlantic—the comments I have received on these occasions have helped to focus and shape my ideas.

A number of people have read parts or all of the manuscript at various stages. I would particularly like to thank Richard Carwardine and Martin Crawford, as well as the anonymous readers who provided comments on earlier articles that now form part of the book. Julie Roy Jeffrey has read a number of versions of the manuscript, and our discussions have been invaluable. Her friendship has meant a great deal to me. I am grateful to Anne Boylan for her help at a critical point in the final stages of the manuscript. The criticisms and suggestions of the anonymous readers for the press have been extremely helpful in revising the manuscript. Dick Holway, my editor at the University of Virginia Press, deserves special thanks for his encouragement, advice, and persistence. I am indebted to him and to his editorial staff for their guidance and professionalism in bringing this book to publication.

Sections of this book have previously appeared in the *Journal of the Early Republic* and *American Nineteenth Century History*. I am grateful to the editors of these journals for giving me permission to reuse some of the arguments and materials from my earlier articles.

In the course of the research for this book I have visited many libraries and archives on both sides of the Atlantic. Without the help and advice of the staff at these and other institutions this book would not have been possible. I would like to thank the University of Leicester Library, Library of Congress Manuscript Division, American Antiquarian Society, Historical Society of Pennsylvania, Library of Virginia, Albert and Shirley Small Special Collections Library at the University of Virginia, the David M. Rubinstein Rare Book and Manuscript Library at Duke University, Newberry Library, Huntington Library, Boston Public Library, Massachusetts Historical Society, Houghton Library at Harvard University, and New York Public Library. I am particularly grateful to John Vandereedt for helping me to track down materials at the National Archives, and to Carol Brydge who finally located Box 235 at the Augusta County Circuit Court in Staunton, Virginia. I also gratefully acknowledge all of the institutions who have granted me permission to publish quotations from their collections.

Friends and family members have been unwavering in their support during this project. Susan-Mary Grant has been a good friend throughout. Theresa Kaminski and Elizabeth Dunn have helped in many ways. I have enjoyed meals and good conversation with many academic friends, most notably Dan and Kitty Preston, Carol Lasser and Gary Kornblith, Stacey Robertson, Don Ratcliffe, Chris Clark, Charles Joyner, Connie Schultz, as well as Julie and Chris Jeffrey. My brothers and their families have shown interest, offered their hospitality, and kept me grounded. I am greatly appreciative of the company provided by my sister-in-law, Margaret Evans, on a number of research trips to the United States. My parents, Richard and Susan Clapp, have always given me their love and support. I am forever grateful to them.

Without my husband, David Wykes, a fellow historian, there would have been no book. He has listened patiently to my ideas about Mrs. Royall, driven me to out-of-the-way places in the search for illusive archive materials, acted as my amanuensis, read countless versions of the manuscript, all with stalwart good humor, but above all he has given his love. I dedicate this book to him as a small measure of my gratitude and love in return.

A Notorious Woman

Introduction

William Morgan's disappearance in 1826 from the Canandaigua town jail in New York State, and the alleged involvement of Freemasons in his kidnapping, prompted an outcry against the Masons throughout the United States. With Morgan still missing in July 1828, the editor of the *Carolina Observer* of Fayetteville, North Carolina, printed a shocking revelation: "*Morgan found at last.*—The editor of the Darien Gazette has made the important discovery, that the famous Wm. Morgan has been playing *possum* with the good people of New York, by perambulating the country in petticoats, and that he and the equally famous Mrs. ANNE ROYAL are one and the same person!!"[1] Other newspaper editors and writers had similar ideas, for at much the same time, the New England author and literary critic John Neal described Royall in equally unfavorable terms: "She is no woman at all but a stout, saucy, swaggering, two fisted chap, with a skull of his own, who having a mind to live an easy life and be impudent with safety, has turned author, and equipped himself in petticoats for protection."[2] In like spirit, both men agreed that these comments would probably provoke a reaction from their subject, and they concluded lightheartedly that they would in all likelihood be "skinned alive, or roasted or barbacued in the next edition of the Black Book."[3]

By the time these opinions were voiced in the summer of 1828, Mrs. Anne Royall was a well-known public figure. As the author of *Sketches of History, Life and Manners in the United States* and *The Black Book,* she was familiar to newspaper readers across the United States, for she frequently appeared in their pages. By 1828 she had gathered a formidable reputation as a result of the books she had written. Among other materials, they were filled with often unflattering descriptions of the places she visited and the people she met, including the newspaper editors. In an age in which short tempers and sensationalism characterized much of the editorial matter in their columns, newspaper editors felt little compunction in retaliating in kind.[4] But if her descriptions of people and places were confrontational, so too were the methods she used to market her publications. Royall maintained a public presence as she traveled through the United States in order to collect materials for her books, but also to sell them. She generally sold them by subscription, and her method of doing so was highly personal. She quickly became notorious for her habit of intruding into people's homes and demanding their patronage. To many this was an affront and an invasion of their privacy, but they were still more irritated to discover that should they refuse, they were lampooned in her next work.

Although her sales methods caused widespread annoyance, her vigorously expressed views proved still more controversial. As a travel writer, and later as a newspaper editor, Royall wrote extensively about the religious and political issues of her time. She was highly opinionated, and the themes she discussed, as well as her style, were contentious and pertinent. In both politics and religion she took an actively partisan line, forcefully attacking the agents of the evangelical revival, their followers, and aims, as well as the Bank of the United States, corruption in government, and other political subjects. Her opinions were frequently extreme, directly challenging the authority of those who were trying to shape the religious and political culture of the early republic. Moreover, her attacks were persistent, and they attracted an audience of like-minded people. Insecure in their own hold on public opinion and wishing to safeguard their target audience of women, evangelical ministers and their supporters reacted by trying to marginalize her. Repeatedly they expressed their response in gendered terms, arguing that Royall's behavior unsexed her, even that she was a man in petticoats.

In the eyes of these commentators, Royall did not conform to conventional and appropriate forms of womanly deportment, but exactly what this meant was not always clear. For in the first decades of the nineteenth century, as Americans responded to upheavals in their long-established ways of living, ideas about a "woman's place" and her "proper behavior" were keenly debated and contested. A variety of groups, among them evangelical ministers, politicians, and newspaper editors, as well as women themselves, shaped and reshaped their understanding of the role of women in the new nation. These debates were especially marked in the 1820s. During this transitional period, women's religious and political involvement came under scrutiny by competing groups, each trying to convince Americans of the superiority of its own ideals. The outcome was not a foregone conclusion. The issues were often complex, but an examination of Anne Royall's life, and the reactions to her public career and behavior, provides a lens through which to identify and explore some of the factors influencing these discussions in the early nineteenth century.

The responses to her behavior and opinions are important for what they reveal about the deep divisions in the social and cultural life of the early republic, but Anne Royall's own story is significant and should be studied. Royall was a notable figure during her lifetime. Many of her contemporaries tried to dismiss her as a crazy and eccentric old woman who had nothing to contribute to national life, but their efforts to diminish her in this way belie her contemporary and historical significance. Audiences were attracted to buy her books and newspapers because of her descriptions of the United States and its people, and the particular style of writing she developed, which included "pen portraits" of individuals. Through them she reached a popular, national audience, and presented them with her opinions and views on a variety of subjects. Although her ideas were not especially sophisticated, they were forceful, and they spoke to a readership sympathetic to her opinions. She lectured her readers on the importance of maintaining and protecting American liberties, and of being watchful of those who sought to undermine them, espousing a form of patriotism that looked back to the principles of the Revolution. Her roles as an anti-evangelical, anti-Sabbatarian, and Jacksonian sprang from this sense of patriotism. In this, she stood apart from many contemporary women. Her political and religious views were contrary to those usually associated with women, being much more concerned with the protection of the civil liberties of American citizens than she was with the moral issues of the day.

Royall was significant as a woman with a public voice able to attract audiences and supporters, but she appalled many others. Her opinions on a wide variety of subjects, together with her public presence, meant that she created enemies. Her public views, and the reactions to her, serve to reflect and highlight the anxieties that many people at this time had about new developments in the social, political, and religious life of the nation, and particularly their concerns about the part that women should play in the new United States.

Anne Royall was born in 1769 and died eighty-five years later in October 1854. Her life stretched from the years of the American Revolution to the crisis years before the Civil War. This was a period of profound social, economic, cultural, and political change as the United States developed as a new nation. The nation also expanded westward as territories were opened up for white settlement. It was in these new settlements that the waves of religious revivals known as the Second Great Awakening began and then spread to the rest of the country. But it was in the more established regions in the years after the War of 1812 that the beginnings of an industrial revolution became apparent. Gradually the northern states began to focus on manufacturing and commerce, whereas the southern states developed an economy based on the "peculiar institution" of slavery. These political, economic, and religious changes were fueled by and encouraged multifaceted social and cultural transformations as Americans adapted to these upheavals. In these circumstances, ideas about men's and women's roles in the new republic were discussed, negotiated, formed, and reformed, as competing groups fought for the ascendancy of their ideas.

Traditionally scholars of the early nineteenth century have seen this as a period when women's lives became more rigidly confined by the ideology of separate spheres for men and women. More recently, however, historians of the early American republic have challenged notions that women of the period were defined and restricted by domesticity, or that they literally inhabited a private sphere. Studies have discovered women in all kinds of situations, private and public: in their families, workplaces, churches, charitable organizations, and reform associations. These analyses have meant that older frameworks for understanding women's experiences are no longer useful, and they have sought fresh lenses through which to view women's lives in the past. Increasingly scholars have focused on gender as a social construction, one that is dynamic and that affects and interacts with other social constructions such as race, ethnicity, class, and region. The nature of women's role has therefore come under scrutiny, and historians have recognized that men's and women's understandings of femininity in the early republic were diverse and complex.[5]

Some of the recent focus on women's involvement in areas of society that have traditionally been seen as men's preserve is of particular relevance to this study. Historians have questioned whether women, even middle-class women, were absent from the economy and politics—what in the past had been referred to as the public sphere. Developing from an interest in politics in its widest sense, scholars have sought to establish women's relationship to the state in the early republic and the ways in which they could influence and shape the direction of public policy.[6] From the 1790s onward, women entered into what has been characterized as "civil society" in increasingly large numbers. In its great variety of forms, contemporaries understood civil society as gatherings of private citizens meeting together and explicitly engaging in the formation of public opinion. Through the elite salons and tea tables of the late eighteenth century and the voluntary associations of the antebellum period, women took every opportunity to construct public opinion and engage in cultural uplift and reform.[7] Moreover, women's associations, particularly those for temperance, moral reform, and the abolition of slavery, allowed women to exercise considerable power as they insisted on their right to contribute to the great reform causes of their day and to shape the wider political culture.[8]

While some historians have been concerned with female involvement in civil society, others have examined women's activism in areas outside civil society or domesticity. The assumption that in the early United States women were formally barred from politics narrowly defined—from voting, electioneering, and participating in governmental institutions and formal governing activities, as well as from party organization—has been closely scrutinized. Recent research has shown that far from being totally excluded from electioneering and party politics, women were often an important presence, at least in the first few decades following the Revolution. Although they were not voters, party leaders encouraged women to participate in political rallies and party activities, sometimes on the streets. In New Jersey, certain women were able to vote in elections and were involved in electoral politics in the same way as men, until the privilege was removed in 1807.[9] In the antebellum period, too, political parties encouraged women to become involved in their activities and identify themselves with a particular party, lending their supposed moral superiority to partisan rallies and events.[10] Women also exercised influence on the political process by reading about and discussing politics, among themselves but also with their male family members. Historians have discovered that at both state and national levels, women were interested in and sought to influence political opinion in ways that an insistence on the separation of spheres previously obscured.[11] Far from being excluded from the political sphere, women were active in many areas of political and public life.

Women's entry into civil society and politics did not go uncontested, and there were specific moments when the level of female political involvement came under close scrutiny.[12] As the United States underwent vast social and economic instability during the first decades of the nineteenth century, certain groups sought to redefine women's roles in reaction to these changes, and they were often single-minded in their endeavors to do so. These efforts were not always immediately successful, however, and no one group's notion of womanhood was easily able to attain dominance. The 1820s were noticeably a period of transition as both the agents of the evangelical revivals and political leaders tried to rethink women's relationship to religion and politics, and to impose their ideas on the wider society. Evangelical ministers especially looked to the emerging middle class to adopt and promote their values, and they saw middle-class women as important allies in their efforts to gain ascendancy in American life. Thus they sought to convince these women of their "natural" affinity for religion, and to shape their political identities not as voters or as political partisans but as religious activists working to ensure the cultural ascendancy of Protestantism. The evangelicals tried to persuade middle-class women that their only route to respectability and fulfillment was to embrace this intense association with religion.[13]

It is in this context that Anne Royall's story is important. For the evangelical mission was by no means certain of victory. As a result, evangelical leaders tried to contain and marginalize any opposition to their attempts to christianize the United States and particularly their efforts to convince women of their key role in this project. During the 1820s, just as Royall was traveling throughout the United States at the height of her celebrity, the evangelical movement was developing its campaign to secure the loyalty of American women. Royall's sustained public attacks on the evangelicals, denouncing their methods, their money-making activities, and especially their emphasis on converting women, were anathema to these evangelicals. The reactions to her public career, even more than to her writing, highlight the powerful response of many evangelicals to any threat to their authority, particularly from a woman. Their accusations that her behavior was not appropriate for a respectable woman, their insistence on her irreligion, and their attempts to curtail her activities all parallel many of the responses that historians have emphasized in their studies of women such as Frances Wright, the Grimké sisters, and Peggy Eaton.[14]

The 1820s were a period of change in politics too, as women's ability to participate in party and electoral politics gradually contracted. In the face of a party politics that became increasingly organized, and political leaders who concentrated their attention on white male electors, women were pushed out of politics. But as Royall's experience shows, this too was contested. Women who remained actively and publicly engaged in politics faced widespread criticism, but nonetheless a significant number of women maintained an interest in party politics albeit away from the public gaze.[15] During the antebellum years, many newspaper editors began to censure women who were openly involved in party politics, dubbing them "political women" and intending it as a term of abuse. For Royall, however, the epithet was merely a description of her activities, and she ignored such criticism. Throughout the 1820s and beyond, she remained a highly individualistic political participant. Exploiting the developments in print culture to express her political opinions, she did so with little regard for attempts to exclude women from partisan politics. As a newspaper editor she openly supported Andrew Jackson as president, but insisted on her independence when Martin Van Buren was anointed as his successor. She used her newspaper as a forum to express her political views, assuming her right to do so as a member of the body politic. She had no interest in promoting the kinds of causes that many other women were involved in at the time, and violently opposed women's rights.[16]

Royall became one of the "celebrities" of the Jacksonian era, and as such, her experiences were not typical of other women of her time. The period of her national fame, however, was only a relatively brief episode in her long life. It was not until the summer of 1826, when in her mid-fifties, having published her first book of travels, that she became a "public woman."[17] Before that she had lived in obscurity in the western regions of the United States, as a daughter, wife, and widow—roles that were shared by many other women. The loss of her husband's estate prompted her to leave the western regions, and for about five years, from 1826 until 1831, she toured the United States and wrote about what she saw and experienced. During this phase of her life, Royall was the subject of countless articles published in newspapers up and down the country, many of which condemned her writing and behavior as inappropriate and intolerable from a woman who expected to be accepted into polite society. Equally there were editors of newspapers who held her in some regard, even celebrated and courted her, suggesting that notions of female respectability were fluid and were perceived differently depending on who was passing judgment.[18] In the final chapter of her life, while Royall occasionally acknowledged the limitations imposed on women's involvement in politics, she developed into a thoroughly political woman engaged fully in the partisan politics of the period. By contrast and at the same time, she sought to use traditional discourses of female dependence to campaign for a pension as the widow of a Revolutionary War officer.

Responses to Royall were frequently colored by regional and class prejudices. Described as an "illbred and independent backwoods-woman" by one New England editor, Royall's behavior seemed to him the height of vulgarity, although other observers were much less offended.[19] Her childhood in the backwoods of western Pennsylvania and her limited education meant that she had gained few of the trappings of gentility or refinement which the eastern middle class, to whom she sought to sell her books, expected to find in a respectable, middle-class woman. Female manners that might have been acceptable in frontier society were often considered brash and rude among those who regarded themselves as part of a more sophisticated social milieu. For this type of display of independence in thought and action reflected a quite different set of values. To many in the East, unaccustomed to women from such a background, Royall appeared impudent and even vulgar.

Royall's conduct and experiences highlight the extent to which notions of appropriate gender roles were contested in the early republic. For while she might have believed herself to be a respectable woman, and frequently insisted that her position as the widow of a Virginia gentleman gave her an inherent respectability, she was not perceived as such by many who met her. Her impoverished state and her consequent need to earn a living made her class position ambiguous, but this alone does not explain the reactions to her. Royall found herself caught up in the debates and negotiations of an increasingly influential group in early-nineteenth-century society who sought to define new roles for women and tried to dictate their viewpoint to others. On occasions Royall was ostracized or the subject of violent attacks as her critics condemned and abused her, denying her the respect and protection they would give to a woman they regarded as a member of the middle classes. For in the eyes of her critics, respectability equated to a set of values that defined the emerging middle class—values that included an emphasis on female piety and morality, as well as absence from the public sphere. Royall generally found these values objectionable and had no hesitation in saying so. For some she became a byword for a certain type of "public woman" who was oblivious to the social expectations implied in the term "respectable womanhood."[20]

Royall drew a good deal of attention during her lifetime, but it was not until the early twentieth century that she attracted her first in-depth biographer. Since then there have been several accounts of her life. Each of these works has attempted to unearth the details of Royall's life and to argue for her historical importance. Some have seen her as an eccentric who operated on the peripheries of Jacksonian society, while others have portrayed her as some kind of proto-feminist, representing her as a woman writer and journalist, even a women's rights activist, who pioneered the way for other women. Still others have depicted her as a crusader against the evangelical preachers and campaigner against government corruption. The most significant of these are based on thorough research and have sought to dispel many of the abiding myths about Royall's life and origins.[21] Historians too have taken an interest in Royall, but not to the extent of an in-depth study that examines her career and works in a wider context. Her books have been cited to gain insights into the social relationships in a New England town, and as a witness to women's presence at the debates during the Virginia constitutional convention. Her crusade against corruption in the federal Post Office has also received coverage, but she has yet to gain the serious attention of a modern historian.[22]

Yet Anne Royall deserves the recognition of historians and is certainly worthy of study, for her career helps to illuminate much about her time, and she is of intrinsic interest. Understanding her is not straightforward. In many senses she was a woman who existed on the margins of respectable society, and her behavior ensured that she continued to do so. Nor is she very easy to like—she was often irascible, quick to condemn those who disagreed with her, and overly fond of singing her own praises. Getting to know and understand what motivated her is difficult, as much of what we know of her is through the pages of her books and newspapers. These give a self-consciously limited insight into her personality. She was careful not to reveal much about her origins, and consequently we can learn very little about her early or private life. We have to look to other sources to gain hints at another side to her personality. Diary and letter writers, while often expressing irritation about her demeanor, also occasionally suggest some sympathy, and newspaper editors regularly remarked on her good humor and intelligence. She inspired loyalty in her friends and perhaps, too, some admiration—aspects of her personality that are not always immediately apparent in her public persona.

One of the problems scholars have faced in trying to explore Royall's career, or that of many other women with obscure origins, has been that of sources. Although Royall left a considerable body of work in the form of travel books, a novel, and a newspaper, none of these aimed to be memoirs of her life. There are letters, too, but the majority of them are business correspondence created for very specific purposes. Nonetheless, Royall left more of a trail than many other women, and we can gain some insight into her life from these fragments—notably through court records, and late in life through the Revolutionary War pension files. Above all, it is through the newspapers that we can learn most about her as a public woman. Few other women of her time received such widespread attention from the press as she did traveling around the country, and editors were quick to pass judgment on her and create stories about her early life. But each of these sources produces its own problems. Her books give a carefully controlled version of her experiences and the reactions to her, the court records and pension files are often formulaic, and the newspapers reflect particular points of view. By placing her in her historical context and piecing together the sources we do have, we can begin to understand her and probe beneath some of the myths that surround her.

The myths continue to fascinate and can offer us some further insight into her character and impact. As befits a woman who was so well known in her own lifetime, Royall holds a place in the popular imagination. On several occasions the *New Yorker* and *Washington Post* have carried a story about her that was said to be a favorite of President Harry Truman's.[23] As a journalist in Washington, Royall had for some time been trying to obtain an interview with President John Quincy Adams but had been consistently refused. Discovering that he regularly took a morning swim in the Potomac River, she lay in wait for him. She watched as he divested himself of his clothes and plunged into the river for his swim. Quickly she gathered up his garments, sat on them, and waited patiently on the river bank until he returned. Seeing Royall sitting on his clothes and refusing to move until he agreed to be interviewed, Adams had to submit to her interrogation. Thus he stood naked in the Potomac until he had finished answering her questions. Only then were his clothes returned, and he could recover his sense of dignity. Mrs. Royall finally got her story.

The tale is apocryphal, but it has had wide circulation since at least the early twentieth century.[24] Like other stories about her, it reflects enough of her characteristic traits—her brazen manner, persistence, and willingness to trample on another's dignity—to make it believable. Biographers have, however, dismissed it as untrue, observing that Royall had no need to go to such lengths because Adams was a friend and would have gladly given her an interview.[25] But a similar anecdote appeared in several newspapers during her lifetime, which although slightly different suggests the origins of the more modern story:

> Mr. Everett was standing alone one morning on the Washington side of the bridge built across the Potomac, as early as four o'clock, when he was suddenly accosted by Anne Royal, with a request that he would favor her with an introduction to the President, the executive chair being at that time filled by his friend John Quincy Adams. "Would you wish to see him now ma'am," replied Everett. . . . As was perhaps expected, the lady at once replied in the affirmative, when Everett immediately took her towards the railing of the bridge and told her to look over. She did so, and in a few moments the chief of the Republic appeared in the waters of the Potomac, kicking and plunging from under the arch, where he was quietly enjoying the comforts of a cold bath, a refreshment of which he is said to be very fond. This was Mrs. Royal's first formal introduction to President Adams.[26]

Perhaps having more grounding in historical reality than its twentieth-century adaptation, the earlier account nonetheless captures many of the same qualities—the sense that Royall ambushed Adams in a situation that could only lead to his discomfiture. But both versions also portray Royall as indelicate and lacking the modesty expected of a woman of her time: she is shown as unfeminine and concerned only with getting her story, or introduction, and hence oblivious to social conventions. Royall could display all these characteristics, but neither the perception of her behavior nor the reactions to it were straightforward. Moreover, although she was an independent and forthright woman, Royall took some pains to project herself as an honorable, virtuous, and even submissive woman who would have remained in quiet retirement had not misfortune and the danger in which she believed her country to be forced her to take a more public role. She took this position deliberately in order not to alienate those who sympathized with her. The reactions of contemporaries to Anne Royall and the reputation she gained in some sections of society reflect the complexity of early nineteenth-century social conventions, and in doing so, expose the concerns and methods of the agents seeking to shape the society in which she lived.

1 · A Frontier Childhood

While visiting western Pennsylvania in late 1828, Anne Royall reflected on the differences between the people in the west of the country and those of the older Atlantic states to the east of the Appalachian Mountains. One striking feature of the people of the West she discerned was "a native and inbred sense of honor." Elaborating, she suggested that "the children of the west greatly exceed those of the old states, in size and manliness of expression, and the capacity of the mind seems to be in proportion to the size of the body. But besides this, they have an independence of manners, and an elevation of thought unknown in the latter." To Royall the superiority of the people of the West was self-evident and a source of strength and hope for the future of the United States. She was making a political point, for one of their number, Andrew Jackson, had just been elected president in the face of widespread personal criticism by genteel eastern newspaper editors who portrayed the president-elect as a rough and uncivilized frontier outlaw. Royall asserted a quite different viewpoint: "This high sense of honor is our surest safe-guard, and is worth more in a republican government than all the learning of the boasted schools of the old states. These principles will soon give a preponderance to the people of the west, and accordingly we find them now at the head of the nation."[1] Like Frederick Jackson Turner several decades later, Anne Royall contemplated the character of the frontier regions and concluded that the people who lived there were more independent, more immune to European influences, and possibly more "American" than those of the older states. While lacking Turner's wider perspective on the frontier's significance, Royall nonetheless identified the West, as she understood it, as the home of American virtues and a haven of liberty.[2]

Her point was certainly a political one, but she had other motives besides. Royall's remarks about the distinguishing features and superiority of the western people prefaced a lengthy passage in her travel narrative in which she reminisced about her own childhood in the frontier regions of western Pennsylvania. Her intention was clearly to associate herself in the minds of her readers with the sense of honor and independence that, she claimed, characterized all the "children of the west." This self-portrayal was already familiar to many of those she had met on her travels, but this was the first time in print that she had revealed much about her background. For despite her reputation for verbosity and boastfulness, and a willingness to express forthright opinions on many subjects, she was largely reticent about her childhood, early adulthood, and married life. The carefully selected details of her formative years spent in the backwoods of Westmoreland County, Pennsylvania, during the Revolution, therefore served an important purpose in reinforcing the image she had been crafting for herself, but the account she gave was far from complete.

Besides the fragments of her life history Royall related directly to her readers through her books and newspapers, the editors of rival newspapers printed their own accounts of her early life. These narratives, the editors maintained, were based on conversations they had had with her as she passed through their towns. Very few of them were much more enlightening than Royall herself, but occasionally they cast a more romantic light on her past: "It appears from her account of herself, that at the age of five years, she was captured in her native state of Maryland, by the Indians, and not ransomed until she was twelve years old; that at the age of fifteen, she was married to Major William Royall, a distinguished officer of the Virginia Line of the army of the Revolution, and lived with her husband, on a plantation in western Virginia until the year 1812, when he died."[3] Royall did not, apparently, contradict such interpretations of her early life, and indeed she may well have been the source of them. They served to reinforce her own account of two aspects of her history: her childhood on the frontier and her marriage to a Revolutionary War officer. Other facets of her life before she traveled to the eastern seaboard were passed over in silence, and she seems to have been at some pains to keep them hidden. But to comprehend

Royall's assertions in the 1820s, we need to have some knowledge of the circumstances and influences of her earlier life.

Anne was probably born in Maryland in 1769.[4] It is difficult to establish who her parents were, beyond the fact that they were named William and Mary, and that the name Anne was using at the time of her marriage was Newport. It seems likely that this was the family name rather than that Anne was a widow at the time of her marriage to William Royall. Her mother came from Annapolis, but neither her background and family connections nor those of William Newport were discussed by their daughter.[5] For while she did not wish to appear secretive, she gave very little away. She did not set out to write an autobiography nor were her works intended as memoirs. The hints about her past she did divulge were prompted by specific places or events, causing her to reminisce in the pages of her travel books and newspapers. Nevertheless, her revelations were not random. As scholars who have examined the nature of autobiography and personal narratives have discovered, such texts are shaped by both memory and the imagination to serve present needs. The omission of certain episodes can therefore be as informative as the past events that are included. While Anne Royall's determination to shape her history may not always have been conscious, her choice of incidents to recall, and the absence of any details regarding her adolescence or married life, suggest that she was fashioning a usable past for herself.[6] It was, moreover, a past that served her present purposes well. It established her patriotic credentials, showed her in a favorable light, and explained what might have seemed a lack of refinement to an eastern audience who mocked her for her uncouth manners.

Anne's recollections of her frontier childhood therefore served the dual purpose of excusing any deficiencies in her behavior while suggesting that civility was not the monopoly of society in the East. In reporting the comments of a female benefactor in Boston, Royall intimated that many people recognized her native gentility: "I had a number of questions to answer respecting my country, education and childhood. Having to her apparent astonishment, understood that I was reared in the woods, without the benefit of schools or society, she surveyed me earnestly, for some time, and asked 'if any more such flowers grew there?'"[7] These anecdotes aimed to counter assumptions about the inhabitants of the frontier to which Royall was subject. Such notions dated from the late colonial era when travelers in the "backcountry" commented that these regions were uncivilized, their populations backward, barbarous, and immoral.[8] These attitudes were not easily dispelled. Even when the West became a symbol of opportunity as migrants flocked there in the years after the War of 1812, many in the East continued to regard its inhabitants as vulgar and uncultured.[9] Thus, Royall sought to establish her own gentility in the face of critics who insisted on her lack of refinement: "She is said to have been reared among the savages, and she certainly has not done discredit to her tutors. She retains their rude independence of character, and their scorn for the forms and dandyism of what we are accustomed to call civilized society."[10] Her detractors added to their portrayal of Royall by emphasizing her unkempt appearance and even claiming her use of a pipe, implying that she did not match eastern ideas of femininity.[11] In the choices she made of childhood memories to relay to her readers, Royall contrasted the harshness of the environment in which her family lived with their kindness, hospitality, and insistence on honor, and their own idea of what constituted "civilized society."

In this context, her parents' background was of little relevance. It may well have been that, like many other migrants to the Pennsylvania frontier, they were of humble origins, but Anne's later recollections skirted around such issues. Her failure to write about her father can be contrasted with the comments she frequently made on the manliness of western men and the considerable emphasis she placed on the heroic nature of her husband's Revolutionary War exploits. The memory of her father's death may have been too painful for her to recall, but it is significant that she did not mention his part in her early life. Was there something about her father that she wished to conceal? Throughout her writings, the connections she made through her marriage appear much more important and relevant to her than those of her own family. She seems to have internalized early-nineteenth-century ideas that a woman took her social status and identity from her husband.[12]

One of the earliest events Anne recalled was her family's migration to the frontier in about 1773. Her parents left Maryland and moved to western Pennsylvania when she was three or four years old. She did not remember much about the journey: "When I was a child, my parents removed from Maryland to the frontier of Pennsylvania, and settled in the woods at the mouth of the Loyalhannah, now in Westmoreland County. I can just remember passing through Tanny Town." She also recollected that the trees were covered with snow, and that they had companions on the journey.[13]

The Newport family's move most probably occurred in the years after the easing of restrictions on settlement on the frontier—Anne remembered that "it must have been about the beginning of the revolution." Their motives for removing to the frontier were not unusual; like those of many other families, they were almost certainly economic—a desire to improve the family's prospects by acquiring land or establishing new trading opportunities.[14]

In the years after the end of the French and Indian War in 1763, many families migrated to the Pennsylvania backcountry. They came from a diverse range of backgrounds, including thousands of Germans and Scots-Irish who had recently arrived in the country. English and Welsh settlers who had more established roots in North America also joined the movement westward in search of new land and opportunities.[15] Permanent settlement in the country around Fort Pitt, the area to which the Newports moved, began after 1758 when the British defeat of the French and their capture of Fort Duquesne enabled them to secure control of the upper Ohio River. Although the British attempted to restrict settlement in the hope of maintaining good relations with the Indian peoples in the region, there was little the British could do to prevent squatters establishing themselves on lands away from the forts and main roads. In 1768, the British authorities removed restrictions and settlers began to pour into the region. One observer suggested that as many as four to five thousand families moved into western Pennsylvania between 1768 and 1770.[16]

Like the Newports, most of these families journeyed from Maryland or Virginia, some also coming from Pennsylvania. They traveled toward the area around Fort Pitt along well-defined routes—the roads cut through the country by General Edward Braddock and General John Forbes proving as helpful for the peacetime movement of families as they had been for the rapid deployment of soldiers during military campaigns. Although not on the same scale as the nineteenth-century trans-Mississippi movement, this westward migration was significant. As people spread out across the land to the west of the Appalachians in the 1760s and 1770s, they set a pattern for later families seeking to improve their fortunes by moving west. They also hastened the loosening of British control in North America, as settlers established their own sources of authority with little reference to the colonial power.[17]

The absence of British authority and the jurisdictional disputes between several colonies meant that many of the families who moved to the area around Fort Pitt had no legal claim to the land on which they settled. Instead they squatted on vacant land without first obtaining warrants or surveys.[18] The Newport family seems to have adopted the same strategy, living briefly in what Anne later described as "the camp" before building a cabin of their own on the land they had chosen to settle. Their cabin was on the edges of the settlement, the last "between there and Pittsburg."[19] It was not entirely isolated, for the Newports followed the practice of others and settled as part of a group, forming a community of people from similar backgrounds and with common interests.[20] In other respects, too, as far as can be told from Anne's later hints, the Newport family functioned in much the same way as their fellow settlers.

The contributions of all members of the family were essential to the success of the frontier enterprise. Many historians have assumed that women were reluctant migrants to the frontier, for women had much to lose in leaving the settled areas of the East. During the eighteenth and early decades of the nineteenth centuries, it invariably meant permanent separation from family and friends, as well as the loss of existing exchange networks. Moreover, the frontier did not represent independence for women in the way it did for men, since they remained dependent on their men.[21] But while the final decision to remove was usually that of the male head of the family, it seems likely that the majority of women had some say in the discussions. Women exhibited a wide range of emotions in leaving familiar surroundings and family members for the uncertainty of the frontier. No doubt some refused to go west and were able to convince their husbands of the folly of the enterprise. Others may have tried to persuade their husbands not to uproot the family but failed to do so, and as a consequence moved west only reluctantly. But for some the chance for adventure or the opportunity to improve their family's fortunes was undeniably attractive.

Women's labor was crucial to the family's survival in the new settlements, and they entered a life of hard physical labor and often primitive living conditions. In many of the communities on the early trans-Appalachian frontier, men spent at least part of the year on hunting trips or on long journeys back to the East or down the Mississippi to find markets for their goods. Their wives had to carry the burden of running the household and the farm, and it was often women's work that made men's hunting and trading possible.[22] As women shouldered these dual responsibilities, their perceptions of themselves as dependents of their husbands likely changed, fostering a sense of self-reliance and even autonomy, whether welcomed or not.[23]

The Newport family was typical of many other frontier families in that much of the work was divided along gender lines, but with her husband frequently away from home, Mrs. Newport had to take responsibility for his duties as well as her own.[24] Thus, like other backcountry women, she had to balance the domestic duties she had been used to in the East with the need to deputize for her husband on the family farmstead. She did so in fairly primitive living conditions, where she had few material possessions to lighten the burden. Royall described the cabin where her family lived as "very small—not more than 8 or 10 feet." She also listed the furnishings and household goods: "One bed, four wooden stools, with legs stuck in them through augur holes, half a dozen tin cups, and the like number of pewter plates, knives, forks, and spoons. . . . Besides these we had a tray and a frying pan, a camp-kettle, and a pot." But though there were no refinements, such as a tablecloth, there was a table made of puncheon, and skins to lie on, "and our cabin was considered the best furnished on the frontier."[25]

In these circumstances, Mary Newport had to clothe and feed her family, as well as keep the cabin clean and rear the children. With no access to manufactured goods she, like other frontier women, would have to spin, weave, and sew the family's clothes. Typically her daily work would involve fetching water and chopping wood, alongside her household chores, and at certain points in the year, preserving food for the winter. In her husband's absence she had to tend the livestock and crops to provide the family with cornmeal and bread. There were seasonal jobs too that took her away from the immediate vicinity of the homestead. In the spring she worked with other women of the community making sugar from the sugar trees, and occasionally she used her spinning skills in other households.[26] Few women on the frontier had much domestic help except that of their daughters and the tasks they shared with their female neighbors. When their husbands were away, they looked to other women for company and protection—a not infrequent occurrence, as Royall noted: "One of the next neighbors, a female (the only one we had, except the Peery's) came with her, as she frequently did, when my mother was alone: and, in turn, my mother would take us children, when their husbands were absent, and spend the night with her."[27]

When Anne and her sister, Mary, became old enough to help, their mother instructed them in household tasks. Thus they learned to feed the animals and cook, and were occasionally lent by their mother to assist their neighbors. The girls were also taught to be hospitable to strangers and to take pride in their housekeeping.[28] But this was not a cozy world of domesticity such as Anne might have experienced in the more settled eastern colonies. As she was later at pains to tell her readers, it was a life which required resilience and fortitude to endure its many hardships: "The presant generation have scarcely any idea of the privations and trouble of settling the country—no such thing as salt had we for three months at one time, and as for sugar we could make enough of that from the trees, but for tea we drank the johnsworth, and pinned our clothes (when we had any) with thorns."[29] Deprivation of goods considered standard to civilized life was not the only difficulty she encountered, for the family lived in the woods, which were filled with their own perils. They were, as Anne hastened to add, "alive with snakes, and every species of wild beasts and game."[30] Still more hazardous was the ever-present danger of Indian attack. Soon after moving to the frontier, the family fled from their original settlement to escape Indians and settled closer to their neighbors for protection. Over the next few years they lived at a place called Moor's, as Anne recalled, "if it could be called living." For the state of the country was such that she and her family spent little time there, having to seek refuge in better protected houses since "the country was much harrassed by the Indians, and for greater safety, many families used to live in one house."[31]

Anne's childhood experience of life on the frontier was certainly not unique, but she was highly selective in what she recounted to her readers. Many of her memories were wrapped in a rosy glow, emphasizing the kindness of neighbors and the sense of community, rather than the horrors of Indian warfare. There was a purpose in her nostalgia. Juxtaposing her recollections with comments on the present state of society, it allowed her to evoke a sense of the superiority of the earlier time, when people helped each other in adversity notwithstanding the hardships and dangers they faced. As she commented to her readers, this was in sharp contrast to many of those she had encountered in the present, who despite their much more comfortable positions refused to help those in need.[32] Such memories of her past could be made to highlight the humanity of the frontier settlements and her own association with them, setting her apart from what she depicted as the heartlessness of the present day. The highly selective manner in which she recalled episodes of her childhood served to reinforce the self-image she wished to promote to her readers.

Although Anne provided few details of Indian raids, they were endemic to the area where she grew up. They were to become part of the wider imperial conflict between Britain and her American colonies, but initially they were of a more local nature. In western Pennsylvania a running dispute over boundaries and jurisdiction between Virginia and Pennsylvania escalated into what is often known as Dunmore's War, and this occupied the attention of the settlers; so too did continued disputes with the Indians. In 1774, the clashes intensified into a state of near war around Hannastown and Fort Pitt, the area where the Newports had settled. Further to the west of Fort Pitt, encroachments on their lands provoked Indians in the vicinity to attack settlers from Virginia, producing panic among many of the inhabitants of the region, who as a consequence fled back to the East. Eventually the state of alarm was quieted when Arthur St. Clair, the Penn family's chief agent in the region, succeeded in putting down the Indian uprising. The uneasy relationship with the Indians remained unresolved, however, for as the colonizers moved further west and established themselves in ever greater numbers, the Ohio Indians became increasingly fearful about the intrusion of white people into their territories. In anticipation of further raids, St. Clair organized a company of rangers to protect the frontier, while the population around Fort Pitt began to erect forts and blockhouses for protection against attack.[33]

The backcountry's involvement in the wider imperial dispute began when reports from Massachusetts raised fears about British intentions toward all the colonies. In response the inhabitants of Westmoreland County met in a convention held at Hannastown on May 16, 1775. They drew up a series of resolutions that committed the men of Westmoreland to form a defensive military association to protect their liberties should Parliament not repeal "their late obnoxious statutes." The participants affirmed their loyalty to the king but, like many of their fellow colonists, by mid-1776 they had rejected his authority. Soon after the signing of the Declaration of Independence, the region descended into chaos and violence as the British and Indian peoples fought to regain land from the settlers.[34]

Anne's own memories of this period of her life are vague and fragmentary, sometimes contradictory, and they are scattered through her later writings. Uninterested in giving her readers a narrative of events, her focus was on the uncertainty and privations caused by the Indian raids. She emphasized the settlers' bravery in the face of danger, and by associating herself with them, suggested that she shared such characteristics. It was a chance too to show her patriotism, remarking less on her animosity toward the Indians than the perfidy of the English, the common enemy of all true Americans. As she told her readers, her experience of the Indian raids on her childhood home had given her, like many others in the West, "a strong aversion to the English, which is natural enough, from their hiring the Indians to murder our women and children."[35]

Exactly what happened to the Newport family during this time Anne did not recount, and the story has to be pieced together from the snippets of information she did provide. Unconcerned with relating the full story of her childhood, the episodes she related speak to the suffering of the times but rarely in personal terms: "Oh, ye wealthy of those times, little idea had ye of what the poor frontier settlers suffered. Often running for our lives to the forts, the Indians pursuing and shooting at us. At other times lying concealed in brushwood, exposed to rain and snakes, for days and nights without food, and almost without clothes!"[36] Her anecdotes instead served to reinforce her own self-presentation as the representative of a better and hardier generation who suffered for American liberties.

When the hostilities first began the Newports were still living where they had initially settled, but rumors of British spies and fear of Indians compelled them to leave this isolated spot. They moved to the same neighborhood as the Denistons, a family of settlers from New Jersey, where the houses were closer together and they could gather for protection. At times of heightened tension Anne and her sister were placed with other families: "My parents used to leave us where they thought we (only my sister and myself,) would be safe, and would go to their farm, but very often called to see us—my sister at this time was at some other house." This practice enabled Royall to comment pointedly, "The people in those days were kind and affectionate to each other, much more so than now."[37]

As the raids became more frequent, the country was in a constant state of alarm forcing frontier families to seek a safe haven when an Indian raid threatened. According to Royall's account, the settlers were brave in the face of danger and established routines to deal with an attack and ensure everyone's safety. As she later recalled, "Hannahstown was five miles from hence, and contained a fort; and we were continually running either to it or Shield's, the latter a little over a mile from the former." Other homesteads too acted as places of refuge from the Indians, "it being the custom in those days for several families to assemble at one house."[38] The raids became such a regular occurrence, however, that "the people never thought of fleeing to the forts in those days till the Indians were within a mile or two."[39] Occasionally, a misjudgment meant the settlers were not able to make it to the forts, and they had to hide as best they could in the brushwood.

Gradually the situation worsened, and the Newport family moved to Hannastown, retiring to the fort for protection and abandoning their home and possessions to the destructive forces of their attackers.[40] The evidence suggests that Anne's father died at about this time, making the family's position still more difficult. Royall was not usually reticent in demanding the sympathy of her readers, but she was surprisingly unforthcoming about her father's death or the circumstances surrounding it. The only reference she later made to it was the assertion when visiting the area in 1828, that this was the "place where I first learned the nature of care." Her father may well have been amongst those killed during the Indian attack on Hannastown in July 1782 or in one of the other raids in the surrounding countryside that immediately preceded it.[41] According to one witness, the assault on Hannastown was particularly devastating: "Such wanton destruction I never beheld, burning and destroying as they went. The People of this Place behaved brave; retired to the Fortt, left their all a prey to the Enemy, & with twenty men only & nine guns in good order, we stood the attack till dark."[42] The Indians killed about twenty people and captured others, mostly women and children. The whole town was destroyed, with all but two of the houses reduced to ashes, "exclusive of a small fort which happily saved all that were so fortunate to get to it."[43]

The attack on Hannastown was so disastrous that the commander of the fort felt forced to report to his superiors: "The situation of the Inhabitants is deplorable, a number of them not having a Blanket to lye on, nor a Second Suit to put on their Backs."[44] As a consequence, the army permitted the "distress'd Inhabitants" to draw rations from their supplies for two months. The state of affairs stayed confused for some months after the destruction of Hannastown, as people remained anxious that there would be further raids. As the threat receded, those who had homes to return to slowly did so, while others tried to rebuild their lives, and still others left the area entirely.[45]

What happened to the remnants of the Newport family in the period that followed is unclear. Many years later, Anne stated that she had not seen the town "since the burning of Hannah's town by the Indians" forty-eight years previously, suggesting that she left the vicinity shortly after the raid.[46] But if Anne left the Pennsylvania frontier, she did so without her mother and sister. Whether this was because she had become separated from her mother in the confusion caused by the raids, or, as had happened on previous occasions, she was placed deliberately with another family for safety, it is not possible to conclude.[47] Now a widow and with the possibility that the Indian raids would continue, Mrs. Newport would have needed to employ a number of different strategies to ensure the survival of her family and her remaining resources. To attach one of her daughters to another person or family who were leaving for a safer place might well have seemed prudent in the circumstances.

Certainly Anne's mother and younger sister stayed in the neighborhood, for less than three years later, Mrs. Newport applied for a warrant on a piece of land several miles to the north of Hannastown. The tract of land was on a "small run that empties into Crooked Creek above Anne Jamison's survey in the County of Westmoreland" and had been "improved," that is, it had been cleared and farmed. Her application for a warrant on the land accompanied those of several of her neighbors, each seeking to legitimize their claims to the land they had farmed for several years. This was the consequence of the passage of laws in 1784 giving preference to squatters in the purchase of land they had settled, before it was opened for general sale.[48] Like Newport, a number of the other claimants were widows, testifying to the tenacity of women in this frontier region who, despite the deaths of their husbands, persisted with the family homestead.[49] In May 1787, Newport sold the tract of land to James Stuart, a Philadelphia merchant, and at that point probably left western Pennsylvania and remarried soon afterward. Anne's sister remained in the area, later marrying and bringing up a family on the land where the Newport family had first settled.[50]

Anne was among the refugees who left the devastated area around Hannastown and headed for the Great Valley of Virginia. The wagon road along the Shenandoah Valley was a well-established pioneer route and an obvious one for refugees to follow. At its southern end, particularly in the more settled area around Staunton, migrants could shelter well away from the immediate danger of Indian attack.[51] She found a refuge and spent the remaining years of her childhood in Middle River, Virginia, close to Staunton. Thirty-six years later, when passing through the place, she recalled these years as happy ones, certainly in contrast to the intervening years: "An absence of thirty-six years, embracing a thousand (nay, ten thousand) vicissitudes, rendered those objects melancholy pleasing. The river, the house (Col. Anderson's,) the gate, all were familiar, and inspired feelings such as I shall ever esteem the most exquisite of my life. . . . My feelings became overcharged with a thousand tender recollections, so much so, that I dared hardly trust a glance toward the house of my infant years."[52]

These years in Colonel Anderson's gentry household ended in the late 1780s when Anne moved from Augusta County to Sweet Springs, Virginia. Anne did not divulge to her readers in what capacity she lived in the Anderson household, nor why she moved to Sweet Springs. There was little reason for her to do so for her situation contributed nothing to the image she wished to portray. Her social status at this point in her life was ambiguous—the daughter of a man of modest independence yet with her father dead and her mother living in a different state, she had no immediate family connections in the vicinity.[53] She was dependent on the good will of others, and because she was without independent financial means and only a limited education, she had no prospect of marriage among the gentry families with whom she had been living. Consequently, as she grew to adulthood, an unmarried and propertyless woman, she had to find some means of support. For most rural southern women this meant paid employment using traditional feminine skills, none of which were well paid or high status.

It would have been unusual if Anne had not learned domestic skills while living at Anderson's, and the most likely place for her to find employment would have been in another woman's household. Other options were limited. Some women found work in taverns and shops, while others used domestic skills such as sewing, weaving, and spinning to earn a living. Still others found work in the households of wealthy planters, where they offered their services as children's nurses and housekeepers. Each of these occupations drew on widespread assumptions about women's abilities, and was viewed as an extension of women's "natural" roles as housewives and mothers.[54] The likelihood is that until her marriage, Anne filled a succession of such jobs, perhaps moving to Sweet Springs to work in the developing resort town.[55] There in November 1797, at the age of twenty-eight, she married the considerably older and wealthier Major William Royall.

Royall was the younger son of Richard Royall of Amelia County, Virginia. He was born and grew up at City Point on the James River, where the family had been established for several generations. They were related to many of the leading families of Tidewater Virginia, among them the Eppes, Ishams, and Worshams. Although not as wealthy as some of his neighbors, Richard Royall owned a considerable number of slaves, signed himself as "Gent.," and had acted as justice of the peace and sheriff for Chesterfield County.[56] It was a father's duty to make provision for his sons' economic independence, and Richard apportioned his lands between his sons, Joseph and William. These arrangements were disrupted in 1774, when both Joseph and his wife, Rebecca, died. Richard died shortly after his eldest son and within a few years so too did William's mother, Elizabeth. Consequently, William inherited his father's lands in Chesterfield, Prince Edward, and Cumberland Counties, together with the residue of his father's estate and his mother's dower rights.[57] William was not present to administer the estates though, for even before his mother's death, he had enlisted in the Continental Army. He saw service in the Revolutionary War for a full seven years and four months, first as a lieutenant and eventually promoted to captain, though in his later years he was generally addressed as "Major."[58]

Rather than settling back in Amelia County at the end of the war, William decided to move his household west, having bought lands in the mountains at Sweet Springs, Botetourt County. His wife later claimed that he decided to do so because of his admiration for the bravery and independence of the Augusta County backwoodsmen. Anne's pleas for the superiority of frontier men aside, it is probable that hard economic realities encouraged William to uproot, rather than romantic notions of frontier fortitude. In all likelihood he bought lands in the western parts of the state as a speculative venture or in order to replace an estate in the low country depleted by soil exhaustion.[59] Such strategies were common among members of the Tidewater gentry at this time, as was Royall's decision to diversify into general farming and herding. With economic opportunities deteriorating in the Tidewater region and tobacco prices declining, the relatively cheap land available in the Shenandoah Valley could help to improve his fortunes. He was to keep horses, sheep, and cattle on his estate at Sweet Springs. These changes in farming practices also affected the slaves he owned and took with him to the new plantation. Less reliant on their field labor than he had been on his Tidewater lands, Royall continued to exploit their labor to work around the house and farm, or, when it seemed more profitable, he hired them out.[60] As he had done in Amelia County, Royall played a prominent part in the community, acting as a member of the Grand Jury, though he was apparently not involved in many of the local disputes or attempts to develop the locality.[61]

Even though William was a younger son, he might have been expected to marry while he was a young man. By the mid-eighteenth century, as life expectancy rates in the Chesapeake began to increase and the chances of reaching adulthood improved, marriage became the expected duty of both men and women. It was also the means by which eighteenth-century Virginia gentry families consolidated their membership of the ruling elite and helped to create a close-knit and self-aware class.[62] An advantageous match was the goal of all gentry parents for their children. Moreover, the gentry considered marriage to be a necessity in order to provide men with the respect and comforts expected of their class. William Royall's failure to marry while in his twenties or thirties was therefore unusual, and might have been due to the deaths of both his parents and older brother, followed by the interruption of the Revolutionary War. It was exceptional and increasingly unacceptable for men or women of the gentry class to remain single. Women who failed to secure a husband often became objects of suspicion, but Virginia society viewed men who avoided matrimony with some contempt.[63]

William Royall's marriage to Anne Newport was outside the normal pattern of gentry marital alliances, for she was a woman from a lower social class and had no property or other dowry to bring to the union. The advantages to Anne were manifold, for it brought her social status and an escape from the need to support herself that she had not previously enjoyed. As Royall's wife she took on his class standing as a propertied gentleman and slave-owner, according her the respect due to her as a married woman of the gentry class. Independence, especially among women of the lower social classes, was highly suspect in a society which increasingly emphasized the ideal that white women should be the dependents of white men. Those who did not conform might be cast outside assumptions of feminine virtue and could be open to suspicions of sexual impropriety.[64] Her marriage placed Anne above such suspicions, but it also meant that she was expected to embrace the dependency and domesticity of that status. Anne was later accused of being William's concubine before their marriage, although the allegation was made as part of a lawsuit. The suspicion might have stemmed from a more general distrust of self-supporting white women, but Major Royall's relatives deeply resented her lowly origins and suspected her of marrying him for his money and status. The charge of sexual misconduct and coercion was useful as a means to cast doubt on Anne's character in a court dispute to overturn a will.

The privacy generally accorded to marriage and family life during the early republic meant that Anne wrote very little about hers in her later writings. She also had good reason to be reticent about this period of her life. For the Royall marriage was the subject of gossip among their neighbors, and some disapproval, especially after William's death. This was not something Anne wished to resurrect. In his last years, Major Royall's behavior became erratic as he developed a problem with drink, and this did not accord well with the picture Anne painted of him as a Revolutionary hero and upright member of society, nor with her own status as the widow of such a man. Her conduct toward her husband was also the subject of criticism. While there were witnesses in the lawsuit over William Royall's will who said that they "never saw any thing but good kind treatment from her to him in his sickness or affliction even to the day of his death," some neighbors claimed that Anne treated him with contempt and even cruelty when he was intoxicated.[65]

Anne did give her readers some insight into certain aspects of her marriage, although, as with so many other facets of her earlier life, these were highly selective. In the early years the couple entertained guests frequently, especially when the court was sitting at Sweet Springs. On these occasions Anne sat at her husband's table as his hostess. It was not just those who had business at the court who visited the Royall household, but strangers, including the English botanist John Bradbury.[66] There are other hints at William Royall's hospitality and generosity, which Anne herself did not mention but which appear in court records. Anne's niece, Anna Malvina Cowan, came to live with the couple, and Major Royall paid for her education. Similarly, Anne's mother, now a widow again, and her half-brother, James Butler, lived with them for some time. Some of William's Tidewater relatives even came to visit, suggesting that this was not the shameful marriage hostile neighbors and relatives subsequently portrayed it as. If William later became irascible, frequently drunk, and possibly senile, with Anne in turn frustrated and rather isolated, this was in contrast to the earlier years of their marriage.[67]

This was a marriage that rested on a considerable level of wealth. At his death, most of William's property was tied up in real estate, but four adult slaves with a combined value of $1,500 were also listed in the inventory prepared for probate. The house in which they lived was furnished with several bedsteads, bookcases, and desks, and Anne enjoyed such refinements as fine white counterpanes and tablecloths. As befitted a gentleman of his status, the household also included among its material possessions several sets of china, looking glasses, silver plate, and considerable numbers of books. A gig and harness as well as several horses revealed that the Royalls lived in comfort and even some style.[68]

On the occasions when she did write about her husband, Anne spoke of him in terms of admiration and respect, and he was clearly a significant intellectual influence on her. Although her father had first taught her to read, and she had gained the rudiments of an education at a small log cabin school in western Pennsylvania, she credited her more sophisticated understanding and reading to her husband. As she observed, "Had I not fortunately fell in with a person of learning, I should always have delved at *little histories.*"[69] Her education was not a conventional one, however, and she later emphasized that there were significant omissions: "It is understood I never have, nor am I capable, of dressing out my subjects in learned phrazes or bold images or any of the elegances of style." Nonetheless, she did not see this as a handicap in her later writing: "Judging of others by myself, I seek only to give such descriptions of things as may bring them as near as possible before the eyes of those who have not an opportunity of seeing them, and that in my own homespun way without regard to style or rules of composition, which I know nothing of, and care as little as I know."[70]

The education she acquired through her husband's tutelage undoubtedly lacked the finesse that might be expected of a genteel lady, but it was more extensive than some of her later disclaimers implied. It is difficult to identify exactly what the nature of her education was, but through her reading of books, conversations with her husband, and the visitors they received in their home, as well as newspapers, she gained a familiarity with the classics and natural philosophy, as well as works of travel and history. Many of the beliefs that she articulated in her own books would suggest that her reading reflected the Enlightenment ideas which were pervasive among the colonial elite of Virginia and had influenced the colonies' break with Britain. Although missing some of the refinements advocated by those who debated the need for women to be educated in the new republic, Anne's reading fulfilled some of the purposes these educators demanded.[71]

The anecdotes and scraps of information about her early life that Anne Royall gave to her readers did little to enlighten them as to her origins, nor was it her intention that they should. Neither her travel narratives nor her newspapers were intended to be vehicles for extensive autobiographical writing, but they did enable her to create a past that served her current objectives. Undoubtedly her primary aim was to present herself in the best possible light and to gain her readers' sympathy and support, but she was also concerned to portray herself as a defender of American liberties against those who, in her eyes, sought to undermine them. Her emphasis on a childhood disrupted by British-sponsored Indian raids on the frontier and her marriage to a Revolutionary War veteran bolstered her credentials in this respect. Similarly, by stressing the privations and hardships of her early years and the lack of finesse in her education, she could shield herself against the condescension of those eastern commentators who regarded her as vulgar and unworthy of the attention of civilized society. In recalling only carefully selected aspects of her childhood and marriage, and imbuing them with a nostalgia for a more charitable and heroic past, Anne Royall portrayed herself, like other "children of the west," as the safeguard of the future.[72]

2 · The Widow and the Court Case

William Royall's death in December 1812, and the events that unfolded thereafter, changed Anne Royall's fortunes profoundly and set her life on an entirely new course. Anne offered few insights into this period of her life in either her books or newspapers. Instead, she passed over these years by stating that "sundry unforeseen events," of which she was the innocent victim, had changed her circumstances and prompted her to become a writer. The reality was more complex.[1] Over the decade following William's death, she was embroiled in a series of court cases over his will that almost ruined her financially and threatened to destroy her reputation.

As William's wife, Anne had enjoyed the social and financial status among her neighbors that his position as one of the wealthier men in Monroe County accorded her. She might have expected this comfortable situation to continue throughout her widowhood: Major Royall had, after all, accumulated considerable landholdings in Monroe, Greenbrier, Botetourt, and Kanawha Counties, as well as being the owner of livestock and several slaves.[2] But within a few years Anne had been stripped of the property, slaves, and material goods that supported her station in life, and her position as a respectable widow had been brought into question. Rich widows who lacked powerful connections could be vulnerable, but Anne's reversal in fortune can only be partially explained in these general terms. Of much greater importance was the animosity of William's relatives, the attempts they made to blacken her character, and their eventual success in overturning his will. She was not an innocent or passive victim in the affair, for the testimonies given in the court case revealed a quite different side to her marriage than the one she hinted at in her later writings. In bringing charges of fraud against her, the family's legal proceedings concerning the validity of her husband's will brought Anne's character and reputation under rigorous scrutiny.

Anne's status as a wealthy widow seemed to be confirmed by William's will. Dated November 4, 1808, it gave her a life interest in all of his estate both real and personal, except for one legacy to Anna Malvina Cowan, Anne's niece. On the death or remarriage of his widow, the estate was to go to William Archer, son of John Archer, one of William Royall's cousins. Anne was named as an executor of the will to act alongside William Archer.[3]

There was nothing particularly unusual in the terms or form of the will. The manner in which men divided their estates and provided for the execution of their wills at their deaths tended to reflect wider social concerns and demographic factors. Thus, while the high rates of mortality and family instability in the seventeenth-century Chesapeake had prompted many men to leave large portions of their estates to their wives and name them as their executors, by the late eighteenth century the situation had changed.[4] Whereas in the unstable conditions of the seventeenth century widows could often enjoy considerable independence in organizing their affairs, as the Chesapeake became more settled, and family life more stable, the autonomy of widows narrowed. Men's wills also began to reflect emerging assumptions about gender roles. During the eighteenth century, as patterns of labor and authority began to form along gender lines and women concentrated increasingly on domestic activities, there was a gradual trend among male testators to leave their property to adult children, rather than to their wives. Widows were also less likely to be named the executors of their husbands' wills and were therefore much more limited in their abilities to control or direct the distribution of their husbands' estates.[5]

Since William Royall had no children, it was natural for him to leave his estate to his widow, though his provision that her control over his estate should be limited to her widowhood was more restrictive than some scholars have suggested was generally the case in the early nineteenth century.[6] Nor was it unusual for William to name his widow as co-executor to his estate, even if this practice was no longer as common as it had been in the seventeenth and early eighteenth centuries. Then many men had named their wives as sole executors, and the courts had appointed widows as administrators where there was no will. By the late eighteenth century, as financial affairs increased in complexity, most male testators turned to male relatives and lawyers to act as their executors, and there was a sharp decline in the number of widows appointed. Where a man did name his wife as executor, he tended to nominate a male relative to act with her. By the early nineteenth century, in the more settled areas of Virginia, many husbands, especially those with large estates, had begun to question their wives' abilities to handle such business matters. An area like Monroe County was rather different because it was so remote from the more developed centers of Tidewater Virginia, meaning that older patterns of appointing wives as sole or co-executors persisted. Practical considerations may have been another factor, for William Royall had no male relatives living in close proximity to Monroe County.[7]

In taking on the role of executor of her husband's will, Anne assumed economic responsibilities and a legal status usually reserved for men. Her attendance at the Monroe County Court seeking probate for her husband's will was the first of the new roles she had to perform. Court days had become increasingly masculine occasions during the latter part of the eighteenth century, and although women had business in the courts as litigants and administrators, gradually they had become marginalized and pushed out of the county courts as the dockets were filled with cases related to commercial transactions. Specifically female business was often excluded, and women tended only to appear in court in connection with family business. Prominent among the women in court were widows, who entered the courthouse to obtain probate for their husband's wills—a process that was often complex and time-consuming.[8]

On March 16, 1813, Anne Royall appeared before the Monroe County Court to prove her husband's will—the first step in securing probate. She brought with her the two witnesses to the will: Mary Butler, her mother, who had been living in the Royall household intermittently for the past fifteen years, and James Wylie, a neighbor. The court questioned the witnesses under oath and declared the will proved. The clerk of the court later claimed that there was some hesitancy on Wylie's part in recognizing his signature on the will, but if this was the case, it was quickly overcome.[9] The court then proceeded to accept Mrs. Royall as the sole executor of her husband's will, as William Archer had declared himself "unwilling to take upon himself the Burthen" of the execution of the will. Archer's repudiation of the role was not considered significant by the court for he lived on the other side of the state, more than two hundred miles from Monroe County. He appeared satisfied to allow the widow to sort out the intricacies of the estate from which he would eventually benefit. Having established that all was in order, the court granted Anne a certificate to obtain probate for the will on condition she posted a bond—usually set at about twice the supposed value of the estate. Two days later Anne duly posted the bond of $9,000, as required by law.[10]

The role of executor was an important one for it involved managing the estate, dealing with daily business transactions, collecting and paying debts relating to the estate, and settling taxes, as well as distributing the legacies. Executors were not only in a position of considerable influence but they were also allowed to take 5 percent of the estate's income in payment for their services. They had little freedom of action in administering the estate, however, for all transactions were accountable to the court.[11] The widow who acted as executor was thrust into a world of business with little training for it, and this sometimes meant that she was vulnerable to sharp practices by others wishing to exploit her inexperience and naivety. But despite widespread early-nineteenth-century assumptions that women had little understanding of business or aptitude to make financial decisions, many widows proved the contrary.[12]

Anne's experience of business was limited. She had some knowledge of William's land deals, since court officials had questioned her as to her willingness to relinquish her dower rights in them. Besides such formal involvement in the court, Anne had also acted as her husband's deputy during his absence from home on various occasions during their marriage, and she would have learned a great deal about the business of the plantation simply by observing his activities. As a widow with considerable assets at her disposal, she quickly seized the opportunities that her independence and position as executrix gave her. She showed little hesitancy in discarding her supposed dependency.[13]

For many early-nineteenth-century widows, the deaths of their husbands meant a loss of financial and social status, as well as robbing them of their husbands' maintenance and protection. Yet widowhood could also bring a new independence, and for some women it represented new opportunities.[14] In the first years after William's death, Anne sought to accomplish what many other widows aimed to do—to manage her husband's estate and establish her own independence. Having proved William's will and secured her appointment as executor, Anne set about administering the estate. This was not a simple matter: there were debts to pay, debtors to chase, and titles to land to clear. There were also a number of legal cases, begun by William, which had to be guided through several different county courts. The commissioners completed the inventory and valuation of the Monroe County estate in March 1813, but William had also invested in lands in other western counties, and these too had to be accounted for and managed. While some of this business could be transacted by letter, or by using agents, much also required the presence of the executor, bringing the widow-executrix more fully into the public sphere. In a bid to establish her new independence and with few ties to keep her there, Anne quickly determined that she would no longer live in the isolation of William's Sweet Springs plantation. She soon made preparations to move to Charleston in Kanawha County, western Virginia.[15]

Anne's motives in moving to Charleston are unclear, but she claimed William had already begun to make preparations for the move before his death, and he had made investments in land there. The testimony presented to the court during the will case suggests other reasons. The land on which the Sweet Springs plantation was built was of poor quality, and many doubted it could produce a reliable income. Moreover, her neighbors were unlikely to give her much support, for she had provoked their hostility for reasons that became clearer during the court cases.[16] Charleston presented more favorable prospects. Like many widows, Anne may have felt that a town, even a small one, offered more opportunities for society and economic ventures than the plantation in the mountains. In the years between 1800 and 1815, Charleston experienced something of an economic boom as the salt industry on the Kanawha River began to develop and expand. The availability of suitable marriage partners for Anne's niece, who lived with her, might also have been a consideration. Having no experience of the more settled areas of Tidewater Virginia, she moved west.[17] With the authority vested in her as executor, and with William Archer's approval, she advertised the plantation for sale and asked local merchants Andrew and George Beirne to act as agents for her and look after her interests at the sale. Since the estate owed the Beirnes a considerable sum, it was reasonable to expect that they would take an interest in the sale and ensure that it secured a sufficient return to pay off some of the estate's debts.[18]

William Royall, like many of his neighbors, had accumulated considerable debts at the time of his death, but his neighbors, relations, and business associates also owed him substantial sums. This reflected a more general pattern of credit and debt among Virginia planters both great and small, for this was an economy where cash was in short supply. Reliance on the single cash crop of tobacco, the shortage of cash in the economy, and an enthusiasm for consumer goods made many Virginia planters dependent on the credit extended to them by British merchants in the years before the Revolution. Their indebtedness did not disappear with independence from Great Britain, because the peace treaty included provision for British creditors to collect the debts owed to them. For some planters the desire to escape their accumulated debts prompted them to leave the Chesapeake and move west, where land was cheaper and they could live in comfort for less. For many this meant moving to Kentucky, but lands on the western side of the Appalachian Mountains had a similar appeal to some of William Royall's neighbors and partially explains his own move to western Virginia.[19]

Debt was pervasive among the eighteenth-century Virginia gentry not just because it funded an extravagant lifestyle but because they were generally short of money. Moreover, many among the Virginia gentry expected that a gentleman would extend credit to other gentlemen should he be asked, either in the form of a personal loan or by putting his signature to a bond. To refuse reflected on a gentleman's honor and virtue.[20] Although such attitudes toward credit and debt began to change in the decades after the Revolution, particularly among the new commercial classes, these ideas remained entrenched among those like William Royall and his Tidewater relatives who were attached to older economic practices. In this environment it was difficult for an executor to call in debts owed to an estate too precipitously, especially when the money owed was tied up in land, slaves, and household goods. With little cash in the economy, auctions of land and slaves forced by the need to raise money to meet obligations rarely attracted the bidders or prices to cover the debt.[21] Consequently, although it was her duty as executor to collect the debts owed to her husband's estate, Anne needed to tread carefully in order not to disturb her neighbors' sensitivities.

Having dealt with those debtors and creditors she could, and made arrangements for the estate, Anne turned her attention to her own future. First, she completed her move to Charleston, uprooting her household including the four slaves belonging to the estate.[22] Shortly after doing so, she began to enter into various business transactions to exploit the economic opportunities available to her in Charleston.

She was quite adventurous, even rash, in her dealings, reflecting a willingness to invest in enterprises unconnected with agriculture or land speculation—William's main interests. The booming salt extraction business on the Kanawha River was an obvious opening, particularly as a steady demand for salt from the expanding interior made it seem a safe investment. Anne's arrival in Charleston coincided with an attempt to open up new brine wells along the Elk River, where William had earlier bought lands, and she quickly seized the opportunity this presented.[23] With Anna Malvina, she made an agreement with William Hensley to experiment for saltwater on the land Anna was to inherit at age eighteen. Although the experiment for saltwater was specifically at Hensley's own expense, and there were already a number of salt works around Charleston, this investment shows a degree of speculation that widows in more established parts of the country were not prepared to contemplate.[24] It was an enterprise from which few made much money, the Elk River drillings proving weak and short-lived. Anne's later comments reflected her own experience: "Immense quantities of salt are made here annually; upon an average about one million of bushels, which employ one thousand hands. This salt is sent down Kenawha river in boats to every part of the western country, and exchanged for articles of consumption. It appears, however, notwithstanding this great bounty of nature, that very few of the proprietors have realized any solid advantage from it."[25]

Whereas the agreement to experiment for saltwater probably cost Anne little in capital terms, a different partnership with John Reynolds and his wife to buy a plot of land in the commercial center of Charleston put her into considerable debt. She incurred further costs in building a house on the land and equipping it to run a tavern—an occupation more traditionally associated with widows than some of Anne's other enterprises, though not usually one undertaken by a gentleman's widow. Despite the apparent wealth she had inherited from her husband, a good deal of it was tied up in debt and not easy to gain an income from. The sale of part of the estate's lands rendered some cash, but in an economy that still relied on credit notes and resorted to the courts when debts became untenable, Anne sought ways to maximize her income. She made several attempts to exploit Charleston's booming economy but apparently without success.[26]

Anne's business enterprises and her plans for the estate were interrupted when in July 1814, William's niece, Elizabeth, and her husband, James Roane, filed a complaint in the Superior Court of Botetourt County challenging the Royall will. The Roanes claimed that William Royall had died intestate and that he had left no living relative but a widow who was entitled to her dower in the real estate and a portion of his personal estate. "But," they charged, "the said Ann fraudulently contriving to obtain what the law did not allow her, and to deprive your orator and oratrix of their just rights," had produced a paper purporting to be William Royall's will at the Monroe County Court.[27] They believed the will to be a forgery because Mary Butler was in Kentucky in November 1808, when the supposed will was drawn up, and James Wylie, the other witness, could not remember signing such a paper, nor was his name spelled correctly on it. Moreover, William Royall had never intended leaving his estate to his wife: "A woman, with whom he at first cohabited without marriage, but whom he afterwards was induced to marry. After their marriage she treated him in the most cruel and inhuman manner, so that towards the latter part of his life, and at the time when this paper purports to be dated, he had no affection for her." On the other hand, the Roanes asserted, William Royall had had a great affection for their son, William R. Roane, and had always promised to make him his heir. Not only was the will a forgery, they argued, but since Royall's death, Anne had taken all his estate into her hands "and is wasting and destroying it in a most reprehensible [?] manner selling and sacrificing both real and personal property." In particular, she had sold the property on which Royall had resided to James Wylie for $500 instead of the $5,000 the tract of land was worth—probably as a reward.[28]

The Roanes' motives in challenging the will Anne had presented for probate were not difficult to fathom—they felt cheated of their expectations and hoped that the courts would vindicate them—for that will destroyed their hopes of what they believed to be a considerable inheritance. Their claim that William Royall had frequently declared his intention to leave his estate to their son was only one part of the case they brought to wrest the estate from Anne. As William Royall's next of kin, Elizabeth Roane's hope of realizing this inheritance lay in having the will declared a forgery and overturned, and the complaint the Roanes drew up aimed to undermine Anne Royall's reputation and depict her as a likely forger.

Elizabeth Roane's claim to the estate was that she was the sole surviving child of William Royall's only brother, Joseph. Joseph Royall had received his portion of his father's estate at the time of his marriage to Rebecca Eppes, as was the usual practice in the eighteenth-century Chesapeake.[29] In 1774, Joseph died, leaving his portion of his father, Richard's, estate to his children. Thus, when Richard died shortly afterward, he left the rest of his land and residual estate to his surviving son, William, leaving nothing further to Joseph's children.[30] Joseph's wife, Rebecca, must have died shortly afterward for Elizabeth was placed under the guardianship first of her brother Joseph; then, on his death, she chose Benjamin Branch as her guardian. Elizabeth had no claim on William Royall's estate except if he died with no surviving children.[31] The will Anne had presented for probate, however, effectively excluded any of William Royall's immediate blood relatives from succeeding to the estate, for it was eventually to be inherited on her death by William Archer, a distant cousin.

The Roanes' concern about the alienation of the estate was based on hard economic facts. With at least seven children by 1804, they undoubtedly had financial worries. Like any other gentry family, they needed to provide marriage portions and an inheritance for each of the children, and this was a constant source of anxiety. William Royall had already supplied loans and gifts of money and property before his death, and the Roanes had expectations of more. Although James Roane owned several slaves and a certain amount of property, his investments were not very successful, and he had sold land to raise money on various occasions.[32]

James Roane's bill of complaint named all those who benefited from the will proved before the Monroe County Court, including James Wylie, but the attack centered on the widow, Anne Royall. As the immediate beneficiary of the will and the executor of the estate, she seemed to the Roanes to be at the heart of the attempt to defraud them of their "just rights."[33] The charge revealed considerable animosity toward Anne, which though partially a legal construction designed to strengthen the Roanes' case, also suggests the depth of hostility toward her. In their eyes, Anne was a lower-class woman, guilty of sexual impropriety, who had coerced William into marrying her because she wanted his estate. She had brought nothing to the union, and they could see no reason why she should profit at their expense. They resented the marriage, but the attempt to undermine her moral character and claim that she was cruel toward her husband suggests more. For ultimately the complaint sought to destroy Anne's character. In the Roanes' eyes, the woman who had married William Royall had only done so for his money; she had a questionable past and she would stop at nothing to grasp what was not rightfully hers. As a further indication of the widow's duplicity, the Roanes' bill of complaint hinted that Anne had been involved in a scandal of some kind even before she had attempted to defraud them of the estate. Their son, William, had written to Royall about it before his death.[34]

Exactly what these letters said about Anne can only be speculation, but they were sufficiently outrageous to cause William Royall's neighbors to remark on his anger, and for the matter to be taken to court. But William Roane had failed to appear to answer the summons against him, indicating that he was not prepared to defend his allegations.[35] The resort to the courts marked a clear breakdown in relations suggesting that even before Royall's death, there was considerable acrimony between the parties.

Disputes over property and inheritance were not uncommon in the early-nineteenth-century South. Charges such as those the Roanes leveled at Anne could sometimes be the result of family quarrels, especially when men disagreed with the ways in which a widow exercised her executorship. Occasionally where there were no direct male heirs, and widows seemed to be acting with too much independence, they became vulnerable to charges of self-interest. In these cases male relatives might resort to the equity courts to try to limit the widow's freedom of action in disposing of the estate.[36] The Roanes were clearly not alone in finding Anne Royall's position and behavior distasteful. The testimonies given by some of her neighbors in support of the Roanes' accusations reflect wider fears about women's independence and the anxieties associated with challenges to patriarchal authority and ideals, but they have a class dimension, too. Anne's social background affronted the sensibilities of those of her neighbors who regarded themselves as gentry. Although she had been married to William Royall for fifteen years, they still considered her to be little more than a servant girl, and they shared the Roanes' distaste for this social upstart.[37]

The Roanes' bill of complaint initiated equity proceedings and allowed procedures not necessarily available in the common law courts. It forced those named in the bill to answer the petition and ensured that the case would come to trial. For under the common law, once a will had received probate, there was no legal basis for overturning it. Equity proceedings gave greater powers to examine witnesses and required separate answers from each of those named in the bill. Consequently, Anne Royall, Anna Malvina Cowan, William Archer, and James Wylie responded individually to the bill of complaint under oath before a justice of the peace.[38] Each denied any wrongdoing, claiming that they had no suspicion of or involvement in fraud and confirming their belief in the integrity of the will presented for probate.[39]

Although the bill of complaint named the other beneficiaries alongside Anne, the material charges were focused on her. She gave her deposition in person before one of the Kanawha County justices of the peace, William

Morris. In providing her answer, Anne was determined to portray herself as an innocent woman, a dutiful wife in difficult circumstances, and someone with no cause to commit fraud. She therefore emphasized her detachment from the whole process of William Royall writing his will. To this end, she explained that her husband had always been very secretive about his will and had never discussed it with her. Despite his wariness, just before he set off on his last trip east in 1808, she had seen him writing something with unusual care. She recounted the circumstances in which Mary Butler and James Wylie had attested to the paper. She stressed that although she had paid little attention to such matters, she did recall that William had mentioned several times that "he had a will that she knew nothing of." Her main concern was to assert her innocence of the charges against her, concluding, "As to the foul calumny and base charges of fraud & forgery alleged against this respondent, in the bill, she denies it most positively, and declares it to be a groundless and base aspersion of her character. She denies that ever she used any improper means either by persuasion or duress to procure any disposition of the estate." Besides, she claimed, she had no motive to falsify such a will, for it gave her such a limited interest in the estate and its value was uncertain.[40]

Anne's answer was long and involved for she had to cover all the points in the complaint, and she had a great deal to lose should the Roanes' charges be upheld. Consequently, she was careful to ensure that she portrayed herself as incapable of committing fraud, and that the court be given no grounds for supposing that there was anything suspicious about the circumstances surrounding either the presentation or administration of the will. Still more important, she was determined to refute the charges that she had been cruel to her husband—an allegation she considered a "slanderous aspersion." She did not deny that occasionally "it was out of her power oftentimes, owing to the situation in which he placed himself, to treat him with the tenderness and manifestation of affection which it was her wish to have done." But, she explained, in his last years, William Royall was frequently drunk and became "outrageous and violent" in his conduct when under the influence of spirituous liquors. It was difficult to prevent him from "improper acts" when he was in his violent fits of intemperance, and she had had to resort to measures that might appear unkind, but "she conceives that she never used any harshness towards him, much less cruelty, but what was required by absolute necessity, and she feels conscious that she never performed an intentional act of cruelty towards him in her life." Thus she sought to deflect criticism of her own behavior and focus on her husband's drunkenness. She also attempted to incriminate the Roanes by claiming that William Roane had tried hard to alienate her husband's affections from her. Moreover, the scurrilous and defamatory letters he had written had caused her husband to suffer further violent fits.[41]

If Anne had hoped that her answers to the Roanes' bill of complaint would be sufficient to have the case dismissed, she did not understand the nature of equity proceedings. In initiating such measures, the Roanes ensured that the case would come to court. Even before they presented their complaint, they had begun to collect statements from the Royalls' neighbors in Monroe County that would support their accusations. Equity proceedings allowed greater latitude in questioning witnesses than was allowed in the common law courts, and not all those who testified were required to appear in court.[42] The parties, however, had to follow certain procedures, and both plaintiff and defendants had to be given an opportunity to submit questions to the witnesses. Otherwise the depositions would not be allowed or would be excepted as being taken without authority.[43] Even if they were later disallowed in court, such testimonies still permitted Anne's neighbors to repeat gossip and express opinions that she had little opportunity to gainsay. Her careful attempts to preserve her reputation in her own answer could be undermined by these depositions and add fuel to the Roanes' allegations.

While many of the depositions were concerned with the provenance of the document presented as William Royall's last will and the roles of Mary Butler and James Wylie as testators, others also addressed the issue of the relationship between William and his wife.[44] In their efforts to prove that Anne had treated her husband cruelly, and thus suggest that it would have been highly improbable that he would leave her even a life interest in his estate, the Roanes sought witnesses who shared their concerns about Anne's behavior.[45] During the summer of 1814 they collected several depositions that seemed to support their charges, though few of them were eyewitness accounts of Anne's supposed assaults on her husband.

Many of the witnesses were clearly responding to prompts from the Roanes, and their testimonies revealed little more than a predilection for scurrilous gossip, but in some cases they uncovered a deep unease about what they regarded as Anne's unacceptable conduct. Thus John Lewis, the proprietor of the Sweet Springs resort, condemned the Royalls because "previously to their marriage he lived with her for some years or kept her as a concubine, after which it was said he married her twice." Consequently, he had refused to visit Major Royall's house, but he still repeated the hearsay: "It was currently reported in the neighbourhood by people of respectability that his wife treated him with great cruelty."[46] Other neighbors described having been shown bruises that William claimed had been inflicted by his wife, and others recounted incidents where Anne had humiliated her husband, one having seen "Mrs. Royall catch her husband by the nose & squeeze it severely several times."[47] More damning still was the suggestion that she had encouraged the slaves to participate in the abuse of her husband. James Thompson alleged that he had "heard in his neighbourhood that Mrs Royall made the negroes hold sd Royall on the ground & that in that situation she through hot ashes into his face, & this deponent afterwards heard sd Royall say in a conversation with him that it was a fact."[48] Another neighbor reported seeing Anne standing in the yard shouting abuse at her husband, and when the witness reprimanded her, she went inside and "a negro girl came out immediately & abused her master in the same way her mistress had done she called him a damn quarrelsome old son of a bitch."[49]

The catalog of stories recounted by her neighbors portrayed Anne as a vicious and shameless woman who routinely treated her husband with contempt, if not cruelty. William Roane's testimony was even more damaging and might have ruined her if it had not been so obviously self-serving. He accused Anne of a still more heinous crime, claiming his uncle had informed him that his wife had tried to kill him several times, and had on one occasion "pushed him out of the door on his face when he could scarcely walk from extreme debility, the door is a considerable height from the ground."[50]

Anne's answer to the Roanes' complaint had aimed to counter such allegations, and several witnesses endorsed her explanations for what appeared to be callous treatment. A number of her neighbors gave evidence to suggest that William Royall did indeed have a problem with drink in his later years. Moreover, he became unsteady on his feet and probably violent when he was under the influence of alcohol.[51] The testimony of those from within the Royall household confirmed the trouble caused by Royall's drinking. Mary Butler claimed she had advised her daughter to restrain her husband when he had a fit of what she called "phrenzy," or drunkenness. She added that Royall was violent toward members of his household during these fits and "shewed a disposition to injure any person who was in reach of him," and on these occasions he had to be restrained or spoken to abruptly, otherwise he would cause harm to himself or others.[52] Several other observers testified to bruises he had sustained and a propensity to say anything that came into his head when he was intoxicated. Even the most hostile witnesses accepted that intemperance had impaired Royall's judgment.[53] From these accounts it emerged that, although Anne was not always patient with her husband when he was drunk, and that she tried to restrain him, this did not make her the cruel and cold-hearted wife the Roanes wished to portray her as.

Anne's explanation that her husband had needed to be restrained because of his habitual intemperance was unlikely to gain her much sympathy. Early-nineteenth-century southern society believed that male drinking was a sign of virility and drunkenness an aspect of masculinity that, before the founding of evangelical temperance societies in the 1820s, was not open to public criticism. Even when southern temperance societies were established, few of them utilized the kind of anti-male rhetoric characteristic of northern female temperance societies, and none of their constitutions instructed wives to defy their drunken husbands.[54] In the eyes of many of her neighbors, by seeking to control William, whether drunk or not, Anne disregarded accepted gender norms. For by the end of the eighteenth century, respectable southern society demanded an appearance of domestic tranquility that rested on the unchallenged authority of the white male householder and the subordination of white women and slaves. William Royall, it would seem, was no longer master in his own household, for apparently both his wife and, under her instructions, the slaves had gained mastery. Anne's reported behavior fed into the kind of anxieties about male authority over women and slaves that pervaded southern society at the time.[55] Both the charges of cruelty against her, and her own refutation of them, suggested that Anne was not always a dutiful wife who conformed to southern familial and gender norms. As such, although her position as a woman of property was likely to gain her respect in the courts, there were questions over her behavior. A more timid woman in the guise of a widow in need of protection might have been assured of judicial paternalism, but this was not a role Anne could play.[56]

Collecting depositions from witnesses, who in many cases gave highly partisan opinions of the relationship between Major Royall and his wife, was only the first stage in the court procedures. Recent reforms in the Virginia court system meant that although the will had been proved in the

Monroe County Court, the first court to hear the Roanes' complaint and the defendants' answers was the Staunton District Court of Chancery in Augusta County. But because of the allegations of fraud, the judge ordered that it should be heard by a jury. Disputes over which court should have jurisdiction and delays caused by each side as they sought to find more evidence to support their case meant that it was nearly three years before the parties eventually met in court for a full hearing. By that time costs had started to mount, and gossip was rife in the neighborhood.[57]

On Friday, April 11, 1817, the case of *Roane and Wife v. Royall et al.* finally came before the Superior Court of Law for Botetourt County. The superior courts had been created by the Virginia legislature in 1802 in an effort to avoid the necessity for all equity cases to be heard in Richmond, and were part of a wider attempt to reform the court system in the state.[58] During the Revolutionary Era, Americans had debated what the role of the courts and lawyers should be in a republican society—in Virginia such discussions emerged as a consequence of popular distrust of inefficient courts and mercenary lawyers. Nonetheless, lawyers were at the forefront of deliberations over the new state constitution and were instrumental in establishing a reformed system of courts and judicial review in the first decades of the new republic. Courts remained a central part of county life in early-nineteenth-century Virginia, the source of law, order, and authority at the local level. Judges also acted as the enforcers of community values: helping to establish and maintain the limits between admissible and inadmissible behavior, creating a sense of what constituted the social norm. The courts acted as "moral theaters" in which domestic relations and reputations could be weighed against the legal questions involved in a civil case, and in these disputes, judges frequently viewed the issues from a masculine stance.[59]

By the time the court met in April 1817, Anne was no stranger to court procedures, having attended a number of earlier hearings in the case. Nonetheless, with so much at stake, the carnival-like atmosphere and the crowds surrounding the courthouse with their noise, jostling, and confusion must have seemed daunting. Court days were an opportunity for the male inhabitants of the district to gather, exchange news, and discuss the cases before the court in the taverns built close to the courthouses. Business conducted in the court and the reputations of the parties involved therefore became public property. In the calmer environment of the courtroom, the ritual and the surroundings of the courthouse were designed to impress upon those who had business within its walls the dignity and solemnity of the law, so that the depositions of the witnesses and the arguments of their attorneys were heard in an atmosphere of order and decorum.[60]

On April 11, a jury having been elected and sworn "the truth to speak upon the issue joined," the court began to hear the evidence. Anne must have been nervous as she listened to the statements produced by the prosecution witnesses depicting her as a shameless and spiteful woman, and she tried to gauge the reaction of the court. It was not until the following day, after an overnight adjournment, that the parties finished reading the depositions, exhibiting samples of William Royall's writing, and hearing the arguments. After a short deliberation the jury presented the verdict that Anne had been hoping for: "The writing purporting to be the last Will & Testament of William Royall deceasd which is mentioned in the bill & answers in this cause . . . is the last Will & Testament of the said William Royall." Immediately the Roanes' attorney challenged the jury's verdict, demanding that it should be reported to the Court of Chancery that the verdict was contrary to the evidence in the case. The judge, dismissing the jury's judgment, endorsed the Roanes' request and certified to the Chancery Court that "in the opinion of this Court the weight of Evidence given to the jury is against the said Verdict, insomuch that if this Court had the power they would grant a new trial of the issue on the motion of the said Roane & wife." Counsel for both the plaintiffs and the defendants recorded bills of exceptions to the opinion of the court.[61]

Anne's relief at the jury's verdict was tempered by this new development. The jury's favorable judgment might well have suggested to those assembled in the courthouse that the accusations against her were not borne out by the evidence, but the judge's willingness to throw out the verdict did not help to clear her name. Judges had the right to overturn a jury's decision on a point of law, and Judge James Allen certainly did not believe that the jury had interpreted the evidence correctly. The defendants' counsel agreed that the evidence was contradictory in some respects and that the credibility of some of the witnesses on both sides was impeached, but his attempt to have all the evidence that had been presented to the jury incorporated in the bill of exceptions was unsuccessful.[62] Thus the report of the trial of issues returned to the Chancery Court at Staunton contained little of the evidence given in the court, with the judge's recommendation that there should be a new trial.

That the judge was so willing to dismiss the jury's verdict and recommend a new trial, while at the same time refusing the defendants' request that all the evidence should be presented to the Chancery Court, suggests that he may have had some sympathy with the Roanes. James Roane left little to chance in trying to secure a favorable verdict in any future trial of the issues. Believing that the jury had been biased against him, he sought to have the case moved to another court. As he explained to a magistrate in Richmond, "He does not think he can obtain a fair and impartial trial, by a Jury, in the Superior Court of law for Botetourt County," since the jury's verdict had been immediately set aside as "palpably contrary to the evidence exhibited before the said Jury." Moreover, he claimed, there was so much prejudice in the minds of the people of Botetourt County against him that "he fears a similar result of any future trial of the same issue in that County."[63]

Roane's request was not granted, but it caused further delay and he continued to work to secure a favorable verdict. This involved gathering more information about Anne designed to discredit her among those who had been her neighbors while at the same time attempting to use his influence among the judiciary in eastern Virginia to move the trial of issues to an environment where presumably neither William Royall nor his wife had been known.[64] Although Roane was denied his plea to have the case moved to a new court, the Superior Court of Chancery did order a new trial.

Anne, however, was absent from Virginia and not in a position to influence the outcome of the case. She had taken the opportunity afforded by Roane's attempts to have the case removed to another court to leave the state. From late 1817 until 1823, she lived in Alabama, returning to Virginia only when her presence was required for the court cases or to attend to other business. On more than one occasion her journeys back to Virginia were wasted: twice members of the jury withdrew, causing the whole jury to be discharged and requiring a new jury to be sworn in at the next term of the court. On another occasion the case was continued until the following court term because there was insufficient time to hear all the evidence.[65] After several further adjournments, on June 11, 1819, the jury elected for the new trial of the issues in the case finally returned a verdict.

It was not the outcome Anne had hoped for. The jury concluded that the paper before them dated November 4, 1808, and purporting to be the last will and testament of William Royall "is not the last will & Testament of the said William Royall, and that the said William Royall died intestate." Mrs. Royall's attorney immediately challenged the decision, objecting that the question of a subsequent will had been sprung on the court and that it formed no part of the controversy between the parties. The court differed, deciding that "such point was properly before the jury as involved in the issue whether the paper in question was really the last will and testament of William Royall." The defendants' counsel insisted that his objections should be included in the report to the Chancery Court.[66] Evidently, instead of deciding whether or not the will in question was a forgery, the jury had determined that William Royall had made a later will that superseded the one dated November 4, 1808.

Judge John Brown of the Staunton Superior Court of Chancery handed down the final decision in the case on July 7, 1819. The judge gave Royall's counsel the opportunity to elaborate further on his objections, suggesting that his clients had been put at a disadvantage by having the issue of a subsequent will sprung on the court. The judge was not to be persuaded and sustained the opinion of the Botetourt Court, dismissing the request for a new trial.[67] In accordance with the opinion of the lower court, Brown declared that the writing dated November 4, 1808, was not the last will and testament of William Royall, and he rendered the will under dispute cancelled and annulled. The judge then handed down a series of decrees that resulted from the decision: the defendants had to surrender all lands belonging to William Royall, commissioners were appointed to lay off Anne Royall's dower in the real estate, James Roane was appointed curator of the personal estate on condition he posted bond, and the costs of the plaintiff in prosecuting the case were apportioned among the defendants. The court appointed a commissioner to take account of the personal estate and Anne's administration of it.[68]

The Roanes had been unable to prove that Anne had forged the will she presented for probate, but they had placed sufficient doubt in the minds of the jury and the judges to cause the will to be annulled. Anne's attorney attempted to secure a further trial of the issues but he was unsuccessful, and the judge declared the decision of the Chancery Court final.[69] The surviving evidence suggests that Anne had been defrauded.[70] Unable to prove the will was a forgery, the Roanes' attorney claimed that there was another later will, but he was unable to produce it. Nor could the Roanes find any proof that Anne had deliberately destroyed a later will—a possibility that was surely implied by this line of argument. Their case rested on the assumption that there was sufficient uncertainty in the evidence to suggest that there may have been a subsequent will. Anne's own assertion that her husband had claimed several times during his lifetime that "he had a will that she knew nothing of," and her contention that she had "paid no further attention to it, nor did she know or enquire how many wills he might have had at that time," might well have encouraged the jury to accept the Roanes' insinuations.[71] The court was convinced there was sufficient evidence to indicate the document presented for probate did not reflect William Royall's intentions in disposing of his estate, with the consequence that his widow lost the case.

Anne Royall was poorly served by the Virginia courts and had been unable to defend her interests or reputation against the determination of the Roanes to acquire the estate. By exploiting neighborhood gossip and tarnishing Anne's character, they had succeeded in touching a nerve among the southern white men who served on the jury and the bench. While the charge of fraud was difficult to prove, by accusing her of cruelty toward her husband, the Roanes portrayed her as a woman who flagrantly disregarded widely held assumptions about female dependency. For although cases of domestic violence, especially of white women or slaves against white men, rarely reached the courts, when they did so the courts invariably upheld the patriarchal rights of individual white men. Wives, like slaves, in these cases often lost control of the situation and became the victims of the legal proceedings, since neighbors, kin, and legal officials were rarely sympathetic to the circumstances in which dependents physically attacked white men.[72] By raising the issue in their complaint, the Roanes invoked the specter of social disorder and a woman who threatened to upset the social hierarchy, in the form of subverting the "natural" line of inheritance.

In other respects, too, Anne was at a disadvantage in the court hearings. Certainly she had legal counsel for the trials, but by 1819 she was not in a strong bargaining position. The other defendants in the case proved unsupportive and offered her little protection against the Roanes' accusations. William Archer, who had been named as the residual legatee and was to have acted as an executor of the will, showed little interest in the case and renounced any claims to it once it became clear the will was to be overturned.[73] Had she been able to depend on him, his position as an established and respected member of the Tidewater gentry might well have added more authority to her case and acted as a counterweight to James Roane.[74]

In a situation where women rarely found courts friendly places, a widow needed the support and protection of influential relatives or other associates. Having married a man of a higher social status, Anne had no wealthy relatives of her own and did not naturally have such networks. Her failure to cultivate powerful allies among her neighbors and her husband's connections may therefore have been critical. Nor was her removal from Botetourt County shortly after William's death helpful. It meant that she was unable to create a base of support, and there was no one to contradict the slurs on her character that were spreading around the neighborhood.[75] In her absence, the deliberate attempt by the Roanes during the earlier court hearings to portray her as a woman of low moral character influenced the way the wider community, from which later juries were drawn, viewed her. The conclusion to the case meant that, to many unfamiliar with the nuances of the law and wishing to draw their own inferences from the verdict, the accusations against Anne Royall had been confirmed. Like one of the witnesses called upon by James Roane, they could assert, "I have very little personal acquaintance with Mrs. Royal but . . . I had frequent opportunities of hearing both of her character & conduct & have no hesitation in saying that from general report the world must have done her great injustice indeed or she must have been a very bad woman."[76]

Given the consequences of her absence, Anne's decision to leave Virginia in late 1817 and only return for the court hearings requires some explanation. The outcome of the April 1817 hearing seems to have raised concerns among some of her creditors. As a consequence, some of them decided to call in her debts—a common action in such circumstances.[77] Certainly Newton Gardner, her niece's husband, who had stood surety for a bond in respect of debts owed by the estate, began to press her. A series of complaints that Anne brought against Gardner at the November 1817 meeting of the Kanawha County Court signaled further quarrels between them. She was able to obtain an assurance and security for his good behavior toward her for a period of six months, giving her the opportunity to raise the money necessary to pay her debts.[78] The suit against Gardner can only have generated animosity between Mrs. Royall and her niece, and lost her an ally.

There were also several other lawsuits involving her neighbors and former business associates in Kanawha County, making it increasingly uncomfortable for her to remain in western Virginia. Most of the litigation was concerned with debts in which Anne featured both as creditor and debtor, but she also attempted to recover property belonging to the estate. These actions showed her readiness to use the courts to recover money owed to her, and her persistence in doing so. While no more litigious than her male neighbors, some observers considered her claims to be unreasonable, and they deeply resented her resorting to the law. Anne's increasingly aggressive lawsuits did little to improve her reputation among her neighbors.[79] But the uncertainty caused by the call for a new trial of the issues in *Roane v. Royall* in April 1817 meant that she was unable to resolve the outstanding business of the estate, putting her in a vulnerable position. Her debts were accumulating, and she had few resources to pay them. Attempts to sell one of the slaves on the open market had been unsuccessful, and it may well have been this failure that encouraged her to leave for Alabama.

The new territory of Alabama had become a subject of discussion in newspapers during 1816 and 1817 as the federal government began to open lands for sale. Andrew Jackson's defeat of the Creek Indians and the subsequent peace treaty with them in August 1814, as well as the end of the War of 1812, cleared the way for the settlement of these territories to the southwest of Virginia. Anne's curiosity was excited by the reports of Alabama, and it is possible that she saw the prospect of improving her fortunes by buying land there, though the greater likelihood was that she viewed it as a potential market for the slaves belonging to the estate. Her decision to travel to Alabama may well have been as much to investigate the prospects for selling the slaves as it was to explore the country.

Slaves were a valuable asset, and owners in western Virginia often regarded them less as laborers than as investments to be sold or hired out.[80] William Royall had hired out some of his slaves during his lifetime, and Anne continued to do so after his death. She also attempted to sell some of the adult slaves, with little success. In late November 1817, however, as she left Virginia, she stopped at Cabell County Courthouse to complete some legal business and to write letters apparently connected with the sale of a slave woman named Aggy to Newton Gardner. Anne had begun to negotiate the sale before she left Charleston, but disputes over the price and the amounts due to Gardner had caused delays.[81] Both the sale of Aggy to Gardner and other legal business at the Kanawha County Court that winter suggest the extent to which the uncertainties over the will case were affecting Anne's ability to continue conducting business in Virginia. In setting off for Alabama with a male slave named Davey, Anne may have been seeking a buyer for him, having exhausted the possibilities in Charleston. In the years following the end of the War of 1812, the market for slaves in the Appalachian region had become depressed, for there were more slaves than were required to grow agricultural goods for the market. The demand for slave labor was much greater in the developing cotton areas of Alabama, with the consequence that slaves could fetch a much greater price there. Although most of these interstate sales were carried out by traders, Anne likely felt that both discretion and her financial situation favored her traveling herself to Alabama. A sale at a distance from Virginia would save her the embarrassment of revealing her financial difficulties, and might produce a quick cash sale—factors which were important in ensuring that her creditors were not alerted to her situation.[82]

The court's decision in July 1819 put an end to Anne's attempts to sell the slaves, and to her control of the rest of the estate. The judge's declaration that William had died intestate meant that the estate was placed in the hands of an administrator, James Roane. As Royall's widow, Anne was still entitled to her dower rights in his estate—in Virginia, this amounted to a third of the real estate and, since there were no children, half of the personal estate including any slaves. She should still have been able to live comfortably on her dower, but as Anne was later to claim, "There was a great deal of smuggling between the whole of these Lawyers, judges and all, they got the whole of my estate between them, which was the rogue I cannot tell, it is said they made an equal division."[83]

Anne's claims to the contrary, the lawyers and judges were not wholly to blame for the loss of her estate, even though the judgment of the courts certainly played a large part in the downward spiral of her financial fortunes. The impact of the courts' decision was nonetheless serious. Having had the lifetime use of William's entire estate until his will was overturned by the courts, the depletion of her income was marked. Moreover, the remaining part of the estate was gradually whittled down by lawsuits, legal costs, and her failure to protect her own interests. For although the judge had apportioned the plaintiffs' costs between the defendants, Anne was summarily deserted by her co-defendants, who quickly came to arrangements with the Roanes, leaving her to bear almost the entire cost of the case.[84]

Acting in his capacity as curator of the estate, James Roane quickly demanded that Anne surrender all the slaves, papers, and books belonging to her husband's estate. This action was undoubtedly an attempt to prevent the widow from maintaining control of the slaves, thus forestalling any plans she might have had for selling them outside Virginia. The judge also ordered that all land belonging to the estate should be handed over to the court-appointed commissioners.[85] Each of these actions prompted further lawsuits, with the parties involved coming to agreements about the costs, often to Anne's detriment.[86] Absent in Alabama for many of these cases, she was not in a position to protect her interests, but equally she was slow to relinquish her control of items belonging to the estate.

Although it was to be several years before William Royall's estate was finally settled, the impact on Anne was much more immediate.[87] Besides the continuing costs of litigation, she quickly found that the income from the estate, which had allowed her to live in a certain amount of comfort, was taken from her. The most obvious effect of the court orders was a loss in the trappings of wealth, and she was particularly incensed at having the slave who had acted as her servant taken from her.[88] The court also required her to account for her use of the estate—a measure to ensure that half of the estate went to James Roane. The consequences of the court cases were therefore both humiliating and financially damaging for a woman who had believed herself to be entitled to the status and wealth of one of Monroe County's richer men. Moreover, when the judge made his final division of the estate, he allowed James Roane's claim for interest on her use of his portion of the personal estate while it had been in her possession. Included in this was interest on the notional income Roane assumed she had collected from hiring out the slaves—income she claimed not to have received.[89] In all, the judge calculated that Anne owed James Roane $3,835.71½ as well as her portion of the expenses. In order to satisfy the costs and with no one to object on her behalf, Judge Brown ordered that her dower rights in the slaves be sold off by the marshal of the court.[90] The sum gained from the sale was low because of her absence from the state and the fact it was a forced sale.

A good deal of Anne's share of the personal estate was consumed by costs and interest payments, but Roane was relentless in his determination to secure all his "just rights." He brought still further claims against her share of the real estate, and despite Anne's attempts to make counter-claims, he was generally successful. She was not in a strong position to plead her case. Her absence from Virginia had still other consequences, for it allowed Roane to portray her as recalcitrant for her failure to surrender the papers, books, and slaves to him as curator and to claim fines from her for noncompliance. By remaining in Alabama, Anne facilitated Roane's campaign to obtain the bulk of William Royall's estate and to damage his widow's reputation still further.[91]

By the end of 1823 when she left western Virginia to head for the eastern seaboard, Anne's circumstances were completely different from those she had enjoyed at her husband's death. Her reputation ruined and deprived of an income from her husband's estate, Anne was not only bitter about the outcome of the various court cases but also in urgent need of a new form of financial support. Although not as desperately poor as she was later to claim, she was reliant on little other than her own talents and resources. It was, moreover, no longer advisable for her to live in the western counties of Virginia. In Monroe and Botetourt Counties, where she had lived as a married woman, the case brought by James and Elizabeth Roane had succeeded in casting doubt on her morality and integrity. In Kanawha County, where she had lived for some years as a widow, she had alienated a number of influential men, to the extent that when she published her first book, the local newspaper editor could claim: "Such was the infamy of her character, and so notorious the prostitution of her person, that during her residence of Charleston, she was never admitted into the fashionable society of the place."[92] The claim was something of an exaggeration, but it suggests a few of the reasons why Anne Royall left western Virginia.

3 · Making Her Way Through Writing

The disastrous consequences of the lawsuit meant that by the early 1820s, Anne Royall was in desperate need of an alternative source of income. Her access to capital and credit had gone with the estate, so the kinds of activities she had participated in when she was first a widow were no longer viable. Moreover, the threat that she might be imprisoned for debt should she return to western Virginia meant she had to find somewhere else to live. Other widows in such a situation might have resorted to throwing themselves on the charity of relatives, but that option was closed, for she had alienated her most obvious source of support, her niece's husband, and her husband's relatives would never help her. She was therefore dependent on her own abilities, or public charity.

Opportunities for paid work were limited for a widow left without support by her husband's death. Unskilled work was poorly remunerated and often unstable, and the widespread assumption that women should be dependent on their husbands gave women few opportunities to make money. Consequently, in the absence of a male member of the family to provide for her, a woman found it a struggle to support herself.[1] Nevertheless, by utilizing the skills she had and exploiting the openings available to her, a widow could make a living for herself. For the widow from the elite or middling ranks of society whose husband had left her in impoverished circumstances, those talents might include a range of domestic skills enabling her to sew or cook, but increasingly such women had also been educated. As schooling became gradually more accessible to women in the early nineteenth century, a growing number were able to use their education to earn a livelihood from writing.[2]

In the 1820s, writing was still an unusual occupation for women. The cultural context in which they wrote was ambiguous, and the reactions to them in the literary marketplace were frequently contradictory, which meant that many women were deterred. Nor was it particularly lucrative.[3] Publishing remained difficult throughout the first decades of the nineteenth century, but for the persistent writer, determined to present her work to the public, there were opportunities. Anne Royall's writing career was certainly not typical of widows in the early republic, but her experiences illustrate some of the challenges and possibilities open to middle-class women in this period.

As Anne sought a way to earn a living in the aftermath of losing her widow's inheritance, her situation differed in crucial respects from her earlier period of self-support as a young woman. Most significantly, she had gained a more extensive education and had had the leisure to read widely.[4] Her experience of reading and, more importantly, of buying books enabled her to observe the traveling salesmen who distributed books in the backcountry—a method she later adopted as her own. She had also assumed the status of a gentleman's widow, a standing of some importance as she sought to make her living as a writer. It gave her the connections and confidence to believe that she had something to say to a wide audience, to have that work reviewed, and to approach printers in an attempt to get her books published. Significantly, it was Mathew Carey, one of the new republic's most successful publishers, to whom she turned when seeking to publish her works. He turned her down, but his advice on subscription lists and distribution methods was essential in enabling her to make her way through writing.[5]

Anne began writing while she was living and traveling in Alabama. Her first attempts to do so were a correspondence she kept up with a friend, Matthew, or Matt, Dunbar, who lived in Kanawha County.[6] Although she claimed later that the letters were not intended for publication but were "for the sole amusement of my friend," it is unlikely that he was the only audience she had in mind when she wrote them. Presenting a travel narrative in letter form was a common device for writers, and they frequently made similar claims about the projected audience for their work. In Royall's case, her inclusion of references to personal business would suggest that the initial audience she had in mind was not a group of strangers.[7] Travel diaries and letters often circulated among family and friends, and possibly a larger circle of acquaintances. Like newspapers, such letters brought news of the world outside the isolated community in which the recipient lived and as such were to be shared. Royall also showed the letters to acquaintances in Alabama.[8] Except for the first few letters, which suggest a more exclusive relationship, what later became the *Letters from Alabama* was not a private correspondence even if the letters had not been designed for publication.[9] Although constructed for what was probably a sympathetic audience, her observations, opinions, and persona were for public consumption, albeit at this stage a fairly small audience.

Dunbar and the others who read or listened to Anne's letters from Alabama acted as a sounding board as she developed her opinions and ideas. They were also a testing ground for her ability to engage an audience. Although none of Dunbar's responses to her letters survive, the continuation of the correspondence and her occasional responses to queries he had posed suggest he remained interested in what she wrote. A request from Dunbar in January 1818 elicited the response: "You want every-day things, common life, living-manners, evening-chat, and have I not done so? Not every thing to be sure, for I see and hear many things."[10] For the most part not greatly interested in the everyday, Royall related events and anecdotes she thought would entertain and interest. This was occasionally news of a mutual acquaintance, but there were stories of her childhood, accounts of conversations with local people and her fellow guests in the inns she stayed in, or the description of a recent tornado and its impact on the surrounding countryside.[11] She also provided Dunbar with information about the economic development of the area where she was staying, its products, and the transformation of its communities from little more than frontier settlements to prosperous towns.

In these letters Royall sought to amuse her audience, and she believed herself successful in doing so. She was particularly encouraged by Dunbar's response to anecdotes she related about a Mr. Burlison, a neighbor in Moulton. For the neighbor's life "is a complete novel," she exclaimed, and Burlison had led such an adventurous life that he "is equal to the best library; and, in fact, no library contains a greater variety of amusement. He can commence at the beginning of his life, and relate every incident, not only of himself, but of the times."[12] Dunbar's reaction to her stories may well have prompted her to branch out into other literary pursuits. Like many of her contemporaries, Royall had no high opinion of novels, so it is unlikely that when she made these remarks in 1819 she was thinking in terms of composing a novel herself. Apart from the works of Walter Scott, she considered most novels to be "insipid, frothy, nauseous, stuff." She judged most novel writers to be too willing to stuff their writing full of irrelevant words and philosophies that detracted from the subject. Like many other critics, she suggested that novels corrupted women's morals, in particular, and hardened their hearts to real distress.[13] It is, perhaps, surprising, that her first conscious literary endeavor should have been a novel. For by early 1824 she had not only written a novel but was attempting to find a publisher for it.[14]

Royall first made the decision to seek a wider audience for her writing while she was in Alabama. At this point she was still hopeful that the lawsuits would be resolved in her favor, so her initial resolution to become an author was not prompted specifically by her need to make money. She believed she could amuse and interest her readers, as she noted to Dunbar: "Am I not a good old lady to send you so much amusement. I *have* some notion of turning author some of these days. . . . Let me tell you I would not make the worst in the world . . . and if ever I do take up my pen, I mean to write a book."[15] She began by sounding out acquaintances in Huntsville, where she was living at the time, to comment on the literary merits of the letters. The response she received from these friends encouraged her to believe that she had the necessary qualities to write for a wider audience.[16] As the news from Virginia about the disposal of her husband's estate grew gradually worse, what had been a leisure pursuit for the amusement of her friends became a potential solution to her financial problems.

In mid-1823, Royall left Alabama to settle her affairs in western Virginia. Her decision to leave western Virginia in December of that year and head for the Atlantic seaboard was prompted by pressing debts and the draw of business in Richmond.[17] By this time she was seeking a publisher for the letters she had written in Alabama and her novel. She had made a few enquiries while she was still in Huntsville, but these had come to nothing.[18] Although her journey east took her first to Alexandria, for "all travellers going from north to south, or from south to north, and so of the east and west, have necessarily to pass through Alexandria," her intention was to go to Philadelphia, New York, and Boston. These were the centers for the publishing trade in the early decades of the nineteenth century, and thus more likely sources of both patronage and printers.[19]

Royall embarked on her career as an author at a time when American publishing was experiencing a period of transition. The rise in literacy rates driven by the spread of elementary school education in the early nineteenth century narrowed the literacy gap between men and women. As a consequence, the market for books of all kinds began to develop. Much of this reading matter was of a religious nature—Bibles, sermons, and religious tracts—but it also included secular materials such as political pamphlets and almanacs, as well as novels, geographies, and histories. The vast majority of these works were by foreign, and more particularly British, authors, often reprints or even pirated versions, among them works by British and European women such as Maria Edgeworth, Frances Burney, and Madame de Staël. By the end of the eighteenth century, some of the bestselling books in America were by these female authors, most notably Susanna Rowson's *Charlotte Temple.*[20]

Publishing was a highly localized and risky business until at least the 1830s. Few publishers gained much of a return from their businesses, and authors rarely did. Until well into the century, printing, publishing, and marketing were part of the same business. An author would contract with a printer to have his book printed—what he received in return depended on what the printer finally decided to pay him. Frequently the author had to pay the printer the costs of production, with the publisher or bookseller acting as distributor on a commission basis.[21] Such transactions were as risky for the printer as for the author, and the market had to be carefully assessed. A printer might test the market for a particular book by advertising a title before it was printed to see if it elicited any interest, or opt for an edition of a work by a known author, which did not carry the risks of an untried product. In practice this meant that many American printers relied for their steady trade on reprints of British books, with the consequence that American writers often found it difficult to find someone willing to accept the risk entailed in publishing their works. American writers were further put at a disadvantage by the U.S. copyright law, passed in 1790. While it protected their works, it did not cover foreign authors, with the result that the pirated works of foreign authors were more profitable to American publishers than the works of native writers.[22] Consequently, American authors were seldom seen on booksellers' shelves, a fact Royall was later to comment on. As she noted, all booksellers were "a vile set of swindlers, who look American books out of countenance, and then have the impudence to ask, 'Who reads American works?'"[23]

American authors in the early decades of the nineteenth century rarely profited from their writing, and still more rarely reached a national audience. Printers usually supplied a local market, and until the advent of the railroad, distribution of books beyond the locality or at least the hinterlands of the larger cities was extremely difficult. Some of the larger Philadelphia and New York publishers aimed to establish distribution networks by using traveling clergymen and salesmen to supply the backcountry. Others set up exchange networks among booksellers. Inefficient transportation and poor roads hampered these endeavors, however, as did the costs of employing traveling salesmen even though they worked on commission. While canal building and the establishment of regular stagecoach routes gradually made transportation more efficient, these improvements were generally confined to the Northeast.[24]

Although by the early 1820s the publishing trade was beginning to change as technological advances and improvements in transport transformed the market for literature, few of these innovations had much impact on Anne Royall's career.[25] She entered a publishing world still dominated by eighteenth-century practices and by two kinds of reading matter—works by English authors and cheaply produced religious tracts and pamphlets.[26] It was also a world where writing as a profession was only just beginning to emerge from eighteenth-century assumptions that equated authorship with the ideal of the scholarly gentleman who wrote as a leisurely pursuit. As literary scholar William Charvat has written, such a gentleman did not write for pecuniary purposes, "he never wrote for money, never put his name on what he wrote, and rarely even condescended to put what he wrote in print. He addressed his work to a small group of equals."[27] These gentlemen wrote in order to demonstrate their gentility and learning, and they considered writing for a large audience for money to be vulgar. Such assumptions clearly excluded women from the world of publication. As the ideal of the leisured, amateur author persisted into the nineteenth century, however, authorship became increasingly compatible with notions of respectable middle-class womanhood.

In the decades following the Revolution, both the literary marketplace and women's relationship to print culture began to change dramatically. A new understanding of women's intellectual capacities, together with a recognition of the essential role they might play in the new republic, hastened the development of women's educational opportunities. The female academies established during these years put a new emphasis on writing and composition as well as reading, with the result that more women began to acquire the skills necessary to become writers.[28] The expansion of print culture encouraged some of these women to become the producers as well as consumers of books and other print media, with the effect that an increasing number of women began to write for a broader public than the small private audience for whom earlier female authors had written. Their education also taught them that they could be actively involved, through their writing, in influencing public opinion.[29]

Writing was an attractive occupation for those women who had the education, leisure time, and opportunity to do so, for it could be done in the privacy of their homes. As such it could be characterized as an activity compatible with their domestic obligations. In the period following the Revolution, Americans increasingly urged women to put their education at the service of others, encouraging them to believe they could have a positive influence on their husbands, children, and even the nation. For some women writing became a means to fulfill this responsibility.[30] It continued to be regarded as a pastime, however, to be pursued in a woman's spare time rather than to provide a livelihood. Consequently, while a significant number of women may well have written for themselves or for an audience that was known to them, few of them sought commercial publication. By the mid-nineteenth century, this had begun to change, and some women were making a living—sometimes an extremely lucrative one—through their writing, though few were prepared to admit that they did it for purely pecuniary reasons. Many were also unwilling to acknowledge their authorship, frequently publishing under a pseudonym or appellation such as "An American Lady." For under the protection of such anonymity, the woman writer was able to enter the public sphere represented by commercial publication while maintaining the social proprieties.[31]

Although some early-nineteenth-century female writers concentrated on writing novels aimed at a female audience, this was not true of all women authors. Women produced a much greater variety of writing than scholars initially recognized. In the decades following the American Revolution, female authors wrote in many different genres, both fiction and nonfiction, for a variety of audiences, and they did so for diverse purposes. Some experimented with different forms of writing, which included novels, histories, travel narratives, and biographies, as well as poetry and articles for magazines and newspapers. Nor were they timid in expressing themselves, for they also asserted their right to know and comment on the world outside the home, and to publish their opinions and knowledge for a wide audience.[32] This comparatively flexible situation continued until about the 1830s, when female writers became progressively more cautious in their claims to authorship and the types of writing they undertook. Increasingly publishers and audiences expected women to be associated exclusively with domesticity, with the result that the range of writing by female authors gradually narrowed.[33]

Anne Royall entered the literary marketplace at a point when distinctions between male and female writers were still relatively fluid, and when both sexes had to display considerable adaptability and entrepreneurial skills in order to make a living. In seeking publication, she was joining a significant number of other women who wrote with the specific intention of getting their work published. While some of these female authors may have been reticent about openly making money from their work, Royall had no compunction in doing so. She made it clear to her readers that her intention was to raise sufficient funds to support herself. Aware, perhaps, that she might be criticized if she appeared to be motivated only by profit, she laid considerable stress on her poverty and her dependence on the benevolence of others. Although this was less true of her first published work, *Sketches of History, Life and Manners in the United States,* which she wrote under a pseudonym, it became increasingly apparent in her later works. Her decision in these books to emphasize the extent of her indigence when she first arrived on the East Coast was as much a ploy to gain sympathy, and thus subscribers for her books, as it was a description of her situation.[34]

Royall was undoubtedly in real financial difficulties when she arrived on the East Coast. As she later recalled, "It is well known that I came to the Atlantic Country in a state of unequalled distress, a total stranger, without one cent in my pocket, or one change of raiment, badly drest, in the dreary month of December."[35] But her poverty was relative, particularly to the standard of comfort she had known during her marriage and early widowhood. Although her finances were much depleted, she did still have some resources and was not as destitute as she later wished her readers to believe. She had sufficient money to arrive in a stagecoach and put up at an inn in Alexandria. She was also well enough dressed to have the appearance of a respectable woman. Nonetheless, if her later claims are to be believed, she quickly ran out of money and was fortunate to come under the benevolent notice of a Mr. Claggett, who ran the City Hotel. He took her in from December 1823 until April of the following year, apparently expecting no payment.[36] Although dependent on Claggett's charity, she was comfortably housed and able to spend her time writing and seeking a means to get her work published.

Royall was not successful in persuading a publisher to adopt her work. It is unlikely that her sex presented an obstacle, for an increasing number of American women were being published as authors by the late eighteenth and early nineteenth centuries. A much more plausible explanation was the commercial risk involved in publishing the work of an unknown author, although Royall hinted at another reason. In a letter to a potential publisher, she claimed that Cohen and Company of Baltimore were "fearful of publishing" the *Letters from Alabama.* The only rationalization she could give for this was "perhaps from political reasons which the laps of time since those letters were written, might [?] render them particularly with those who are great politicians—for my own part I am none. Nor did sense a thing with my head at the time."[37] Her lack of success with the Baltimore publishers prompted her to look elsewhere, and to seek information and support from patrons with a view to having her works printed privately.

In trying to bring her work before the public, Royall took advice from several people. She sent drafts of two books to the Philadelphia bookseller and publisher Mathew Carey to ask his opinion on their merits. Carey was one of the most successful publishers in America at this time and probably the most innovative in his distribution methods.[38] His use of traveling salesmen to solicit subscriptions for his books in the backcountry to the south and west of Philadelphia may well have brought him to Anne's attention. She was clearly acquainted with these backwoods salesmen and peddlers who supplied the countryside with books and other merchandise, and may well have bought books from them herself.[39] Her most pressing purpose in writing to Carey was, as she noted, "to solicit your patronage & through you the service of some literary, some generous friend to humanity, to overlook the works or a part of them & to announce them to the public. Poor & friendless as I am, I can not succeed without the patronage of the liberal & humane."[40] In a series of letters, she asked Carey and his associates for advice regarding the size of the edition she should have printed, the price she should charge, and what form her subscription list should take. Aware that Carey was the most experienced publisher in the field of subscription lists, she persisted with her enquiries: "You know, what the nature of the information much better than I can dictate, briefly what sum will be necessary for each of these works you have. Dear Sir send me a form of the preamble to the subscription as you may well suppose stranger as I am in this place I can not affect my purpose without your aid."[41] Royall's later gratitude suggests that Carey replied with the advice requested. She used his model of subscription lists to fund the printing of her first and subsequent works.[42]

Another Carey method, traveling salesmen, inspired her to travel the country to sell her books. But he was unwilling to take on the printing of her work himself, and it was a New York bookseller, Charles Wiley, whom she finally engaged to publish her work. His death in early 1826, just as she was ready to go to press with her first work, was a serious setback. As she noted, "None, however, with the exception of his family, had more cause to lament his death than myself, as it was a death blow to all my hopes."[43] Wiley had no immediate successor, and she was forced to find another publisher. This was not an easy matter, for although she had a list of subscribers for her books, several booksellers in New York refused to publish. Given the risks involved, the paucity of capital in the publishing business at this time, and the fact that any serious reverse could wipe out their small profit margins, Anne was fortunate that she eventually found a publisher in New Haven, Connecticut. Wiley had been prepared to take a risk with her books, as he had done with James Fenimore Cooper's work, but it is doubtful that he expected to profit much by it. Few publishers were willing to finance the publications of native authors, and Anne Royall was no exception.[44]

Royall's first book, the *Sketches,* was "Printed for the Author" later in 1826 by a Mr. G. F. Woodward, proprietor of the *Connecticut Herald* of New Haven, but she was highly dependent on the generosity of several men in New Haven for the final appearance of this book of travels. As was a common practice at this time, she had to advance the money to the printer in order to finance the publication of the book, and the subscriptions she had already gathered were not sufficient. As she later gratefully (and extravagantly) acknowledged, "I was indebted to several distinguished men in New Haven; but more particularly to the amiable G. F. Woodward and his partner, and even Yale College itself nobly stept forward in my behalf. May Heaven shower its choicest blessings on New Haven, the very spring and fountain of benevolence. Those dear men, who aided me in the hour of distress, will recognize themselves in this very poor tribute of applause." On the front page was an apology for the book's unavoidable delay and for variations from the prospectus.[45] Fortunately it sold well, but she continued to have difficulty raising the money to pay for the printing of her second book, her novel *The Tennessean.* Each of her subsequent books—in total she published ten volumes of travel writing and a novel—was "Printed for the Author" meaning that she had paid a publisher to print them.[46]

The generosity of her subscribers and patrons in New Haven supplied Royall with the capital to have her books printed, but she still had to market and distribute them. Borrowing techniques from more established distributors like Matthew Carey, and possibly also the agents of the American Bible Society, she developed means to sell her books.[47] She proved adept at persuading people to buy her work, sometimes modifying her methods and the contents of her books to increase her market. She utilized a number of different approaches, most of which relied on personal contact with potential customers. In this she differed from most other contemporary female authors who relied on the services of booksellers. Working on commission, the bookseller might advertise in local newspapers and display books in their shops, occasionally enlisting the services of book agents to sell beyond the locality. Such methods enabled female authors to maintain their private character, but it also meant sales were often limited to a local readership. Unconcerned with maintaining her privacy and determined to make money, Royall thrust herself into the marketplace and eventually created a national circulation for her work.

As she became more confident in selling her books, Royall adopted more aggressive sales techniques, but initially, as an impoverished widow, she wished to maintain a sense of propriety in her dealings with potential readers. Thus, she emphasized her sensitivity to the demands of polite society by distancing herself from her authorship. Even though she had already collected some subscriptions for her first book before it was published, she had it printed under a pseudonym—"A Traveller." As she explained in a letter to Thomas Jefferson, "From motives of delicacy I suppress my name in those works but have no objection to be known as the author in any other way."[48] In following the practice of many other female authors, Royall's decision to embrace anonymity reflected a desire to retain the impression of gentility. It was not an artifice she adopted for long. The need to gather subscriptions, as well as her travels around the country, meant that the authorship of the book was soon well known—something she seemed to take pride in, as she noted to a correspondent: "The title page is 'Sketches of history, life & manners in the United States' by a traveller. My name is not known in the book but through the oversight & kindness of my friends has got out." All her subsequent books were written under her own name and even had the byline "By the author of Sketches of History, Life and Manners in the

United States." Royall had no desire to hide her identity; indeed, increasingly, her name sold her books.[49]

With little experience in the bookselling business but with a clear sense of purpose, Royall's initial attempts at selling her work drew on traditional methods of petitioning for help. Thus it was not the merits of her books she sought to sell but her need for help as the distressed widow of a Revolutionary War officer. As she wrote to Jefferson, "A poor and friendless female asks of you to patronise her work. . . . I have not the vanity to believe that these works the prosecution of my very poor tallents will be of interest to you or to the public further than from the consideration of having contributed to the relief of human distress."[50] It was a theme she referred to repeatedly in her writings, though it hardly reflected her situation. Clearly it was significant in attracting patronage. Not only was she a widow, and thus a traditional beneficiary of charitable aid, but she was the widow of a Revolutionary War veteran. This was particularly important in the 1820s as Americans celebrated the fiftieth anniversary of the Revolution and its heroes. The enthusiasm engendered in the country on the occasion of the Marquis de Lafayette's return tour in 1824 also prompted her to emphasize her connection with this passing generation of patriots who had won Americans their liberty. Her identity as the widow of a Revolutionary War officer was still more salient at a time when Congress was beginning to debate the issue of pensions for Revolutionary War soldiers and their widows. As she made clear to one correspondent, members of Congress were key targets of her campaigns to gain subscriptions.[51]

Royall's portrayal of herself as the impoverished widow of a war veteran certainly gained her patronage in some quarters, but it was a claim she had to use with caution, for it connected her to a less respectable side of the expansion in print culture. She had to ensure she distanced herself from the charge of begging and its association with fraud. The spread of literacy in the early decades of the nineteenth century meant that the publication of books was no longer the preserve of polite society. Certain texts circulated beneath the kind of impersonal literature, newspapers, and pamphlets that made up the bulk of print matter in the early republic. Paupers with a personal narrative or tale of suffering and access to a sympathetic publisher could use print to turn their tales of misadventure into cash. By hawking their books door to door, they would appear in person before their potential readers and thus give a kind of authenticity to their narratives.[52] The increasingly commercial society of the early nineteenth century, which made it possible for these beggars to find a market for their books, also created a society in which people no longer knew each other. Poor men and women were forced to move around the country in search of work, which meant that if they fell on hard times, they were not known to those from whom they begged alms. In the growing towns and cities, the poor were no longer neighbors but strangers and as such viewed with suspicion. Consequently, the storytelling beggar who sold his books as a means of receiving alms was widely distrusted by those wary of fraud and skeptical that the stories being sold were true.[53]

Although the majority of those who wrote, published, and sold the stories of their experiences were male, some of Royall's methods were not very different. She sold her books in person and traveled around the country to do so. Initially she also emphasized her status as the impoverished widow of a Revolutionary War officer. But she quickly discovered that she needed to negotiate a place for her works that distinguished them from those of the beggars. When she first started to sell her books, people occasionally accused her of mendicancy, and she was even thrown out of houses and charged with fraud. Consequently, she took great pains to ensure she could prove her authenticity as a decent and upright woman who had fallen on hard times.[54] She did so by identifying her markets carefully, making certain that she had letters of introduction where she was not known, and ensuring that the books she sold were not in themselves open to question. Her concentration on selling travel writing rather than a personal narrative generally lifted her above the suspicion of fraud.

Despite the possible pitfalls, Royall was remarkably successful in gaining patronage, both from those she identified as "friends" and from a broader group who bought her books but who were not called upon to do anything further to help her. Royall was not always clear who these friends were, and she seems to have used the term loosely to refer to anyone who supported her. She was fortunate, however, in winning some influential benefactors whose names she could add to her subscription lists in the early stages of her career. As she claimed in a letter to an acquaintance from west Virginia written after the publication of her first book, "I have been patronised by Presidents Governors Generals Philosophers & statesmen to a degree beyond any thing ever witnessed in the US. This was in great measure owing to the heaven-sent Genl Lafayette under whom my Husband served in the revolution who honoured me with his purse and his name."[55] She did not elaborate, but Lafayette's patronage appears to have been vital at a critical time. His letter of introduction provided an entrée to the homes and offices of politicians and other "notables" who had entertained the general on his tour of the United States.[56] By exploiting her husband's connection with Lafayette, Royall began to build a network of benefactors, though they almost certainly would not have recognized themselves as her "friends" in the way she described them.

One of her major sources of support, particularly in the early years, was the Freemasons. William Royall had been a Mason, and as a consequence, his widow was able to call on Masons all over the United States for help. The Masonic obligation of giving charity to fellow Masons, and particularly to their widows and children, provided her with a ready source of support in towns where she was a stranger. Thus, in each town she visited, she invariably called first on the Masons to solicit patronage. Their many lodges across the United States also gave her an immediate market for her books. The most spectacular example of their charity was a theatrical benefit in her honor organized by the Masons of New York City, which raised $180. Individual Masons helped in less ambitious ways, by paying her stagecoach fares and, on more than one occasion, providing her with clothing and hospitality. Although a total stranger in many of the towns she visited, as the distressed widow of a Mason she had ready access to charity that might otherwise have been unavailable to her.[57] Her books provided her with frequent opportunities to express her gratitude to them, both individually and as a group. Moreover, as the Masons came under attack in the late 1820s, Royall continued to commend their charity.[58]

The Masons could not remain her only source of support. Before she had established a reputation for her books, Royall had to work hard to gain subscribers. Her appeal as the widow of a Revolutionary War officer clearly worked with some people and had proved invaluable in gaining Lafayette's patronage.[59] Once her books were published, the charitable element became less important, and Royall began to sell her books based on her reputation and their own merits. She also began to develop techniques to ensure that when she arrived in a town, people subscribed to her books.

The method she developed was to establish herself at a tavern or inn in the center of a town and then call on the most prominent inhabitants. They would include judges, merchants, and professional men, as well as ministers and local politicians. These social calls allowed her to solicit subscriptions from a town's leading citizens and to personalize the business of selling her books. Perhaps borrowing from the practices of Mathew Carey's traveling salesmen and even the agents of the American Bible Society, these personal contacts often secured subscriptions.[60] As Royall published new books, she would sometimes leave a volume at a house as a kind of calling card, coming back the following day to collect payment. Her calls had a dual purpose: to sell books and to gather materials for her next works. Such social visits continued to be part of her sales strategy, although by the time she took her final tour in the southern states, she had herself become the focus of attention. She began to hold court at the taverns where she stayed, and receive her admirers and the curious as they came to visit her. These occasions became opportunities for people to donate money to her—a development that she increasingly regarded as a kind of tribute rather than charity.[61]

While Royall continued to see personal visits and contacts as an essential part of her marketing, they were often resented by the recipients of the calls and were unproductive. She soon realized that there were quicker and perhaps better ways of reaching a wider audience. Whereas the agents of the American Bible Society might use the pulpit, Royall found that by calling on the editor of the local newspaper, she could speedily spread the news that her books were available. Not all newspaper editors were responsive, but they were as a group the men she most frequently referred to as "friends."[62]

The notice of newspaper editors could be of great help, even if they did not always have a positive attitude toward her. Some of the newspaper editors were quite effusive in their descriptions of Royall's visits in their columns, while others merely noted her presence in the town. Others agreed to place advertisements for her books in their papers. Some of these advertisements were little more than an announcement of a book's publication, though occasionally a newspaper columnist took the trouble of reviewing it. Historian John Tebbel has argued that reviews rarely helped to sell books, though Royall's experience would seem to suggest otherwise. For if the reviews were not always favorable, they did at least pique the curiosity of potential readers.[63] Her choice of subject matter was also designed to create a market. So for instance, she declared in an advertisement for *Mrs. Royall's Pennsylvania:* "Proposals by Mrs. Royall, to publish a book under the above title, which she promises shall be a faithful mirror, to reflect the virtues and vices of the heroes of the work. Having taken much pains to collect materials for this book, she will spare neither exertion nor expense to render it a valuable acquisition to a Pennsylvania library. She trusts that the justice and generosity of the citizens of this wealthy, intelligent and patriotic state, will be called into requisition in her favor."[64]

Subscription lists, notices in newspapers, and visits to Masons and other prominent citizens were all very personal ways of selling books. They relied heavily on individual contact with an audience and were an important part of Royall's purpose in journeying around the United States. As she traveled the country to collect material for her next book, she also gathered names of subscribers for the work she was researching, and delivered to earlier subscribers those already published. By so doing, she could gauge her audience and exercise her persuasive powers in selling her books. While such sales techniques echoed those of Carey's backcountry salesmen like Mason Locke Weems, they were not the usual methods of women writers and occasionally excited derogatory comments. For it was not until the advent of railroads made travel easier and safer that a significant number of women became book agents.[65]

The editor of *Niles' Register* was certainly disparaging of Royall's techniques: "This female having obtained considerable notoriety in the United States, as a travelling merchant*ess,* for the sale of her own 'home made books.'"[66] To this editor such practices suggested the female peddlers and hawkers on the streets of America's cities. This behavior was clearly not what he expected of a woman who was due the respect, kind attention, and protection of a middle-class man. To the experienced printer and bookseller Isaiah Thomas of Worcester, Massachusetts, such sales methods were extraordinary, as he noted in his diary: "A woman, who has travelled, as she says, from Alabama to Boston in the Stages, called to see me—has published a book, intitled 'Sketches of the History, Life and Manners of the United States, by a Traveller,' of which she said she was the authoress. She came with her Books for sale." Nonetheless, Thomas did recognize that such visits could be regarded as social calls. Certainly Royall looked on the calls she made on prominent people both in terms of the patronage she could solicit and as engaging in the social ritual of calling. As such, she regarded them as a legitimate exercise for a respectable woman.[67]

Personal solicitations for patronage were not the only means by which Royall sought to sell her books. She also placed copies with booksellers in some towns in the hope that they would sell the books. This initiative met with varying degrees of success. Some booksellers refused, while others took the books but made no effort to sell them. In all likelihood, the booksellers simply did not believe that her books would sell, but Royall accused them of treachery, charging them with being in league with the British book trade in their refusal to sell American books.[68] Still others took the books willingly and sold them quickly.

Royall came to realize that she needed to keep a close eye on her sales and ensure that books were available where demand was strong. As she passed through towns, she visited booksellers where she had deposited books and chastised those who did not have her works displayed prominently. She noted that on a visit to Baltimore, she called unexpectedly on one bookseller: "I stepped on to the store and found the clerks greatly dismayed at my sudden appearance. My first volume they said was gone, excepting one copy, and the second was not yet bound! I had sent several copies of the latter, in sheets, to Mr. Coale, and found they were not in the store—'they were just finished, and would soon be brought in.'"[69] As she became more experienced, she wrote to booksellers to inquire how her works were selling and to check that books were in the right place to achieve maximum sales. She also used booksellers to deliver books that had been subscribed to and sent them unsolicited to be sold on commission where she thought they would be popular. For instance, she instructed one bookseller in Albany: "Having forgotten the name of your Firm I take the liberty of sending 20 copies of the Black Book to you—Will you have the goodness Sir to pack & direct 10 copies with 2 Sketches you will find enveloped to 'Mr Mills Bookseller Burlington Vert' & the remaining 10 please to sell at $1.25 on commissions advertise if you please as the small towns near Albany through which I travelled will be anxious to get the book, & the work is going so fast that I will not I fear have enough."[70]

Occasionally such long-distance attempts to sell books would end disastrously as they fell into the hands of unsympathetic booksellers or she simply did not receive her payments. Royall attempted to prevent or recover such losses by asking acquaintances in the locality to intervene, but sporadic misfortunes of this nature were an occupational hazard, especially when her demands were perceived as rude and presumptuous. So too were thefts and customers who took the books but refused to pay. As Royall complained to one acquaintance in Huntingdon, Pennsylvania, "I beg of you to inform me how many of my books were received at your town & send me the amount of sales should any have been made & let me know how many 2d vol to direct to Huntingdon as it is useless to send unless I hear from you. I have been basely used by a blueskin Bookseller Mrs Dickson of Lancaster who continues to detain the books in her hands 3 months & I lost the sale of

400 & those who did receive have not paid except Lewistown so that I have sunk about $1000."[71] There were still other hazards in the loss or theft of her subscription lists, which made it difficult to deliver books. Here too she would resort to writing to acquaintances in a town to try to trace subscribers.[72] Selling and delivering books while traveling the country was only a small part of her distribution network. Unable to retrace her steps every time a book was completed, Royall was highly dependent on the goodwill of booksellers, "friends"—very frequently merely people she had met on her travels—and the postmasters of towns to ensure that her books were sold.

There were problems as well in supplying books to subscribers and booksellers and in maintaining a tally of how many she had received from the printer. Her relationship with her printers in New Haven, Messrs. Durrie and Peck, was fraught with misunderstandings and an anxiety on their part that they would not receive payment for the books they supplied. Royall, often writing from some distance, alternated between irascibility and obsequiousness, sometimes in the same sentence: "The work was so badly done that it would not sell in N. York & many copies destroyed & rendered unsaleable by being eaten with the rats—when you do send me more do dear gentlemen put none of these rat-eaten ones up it is cruel to treat me in this manner. Meantime rest assured that I would not knowingly defraud you out of one cent for worlds & I expect the same honest & gentlemanly conduct from you." Aware of the need to satisfy demand for her books and anxious that she not miss a sale, she was often demanding and impatient with those on whose goodwill she depended: "Pleas inform me & also whether you sent any books to Alexandria. I shall be truly distressed if you have not & was just setting off to that place where I expected a great sale as the Backwoods merchants to whom I am known was to call there for them. I would not for double the am[oun]t disappoint them & as you did not apprize me of the fact or sent me any information on the subject I am much distressed."[73]

Nonetheless, through a combination of personal contacts and friendly booksellers, Royall's books did reach a wide audience—testimony to her books' appeal and her aggressive business methods. Not persuaded that either her sex or age should place any limitations on her activities, she operated successfully in the commercial world. Moreover, she was able to create what was almost a national distribution network when most booksellers and publishers were still local and decentralized. She quickly became adept at working out the best ways of getting books to the places where demand was high, utilizing the same forms of transport that she used herself. Thus, instead of relying on the vagaries of the weather, on one occasion she asked her printer to employ other, quicker means: "You say you are waiting for fair wind dear gentlemen why not ship them aboard the steam boat to New York to be reshiped in the Boston packet or a part of them by the Providence steamboat to Providence to be forwarded from thence by the stage."[74] Her methods were informal and often fraught with difficulties, but she found them a more secure way of selling books and gaining profits from them than reliance on her printer's own selling methods.[75]

Royall was successful in selling her books and was eventually able to support herself adequately from the returns she made, but she was careful to assure her readers that she did not earn sufficient sums to be able to retire or even live in comfort. While it was certainly to her advantage to maintain a plea of poverty, there was some justice in her claims. Initially she had a considerable number of expenses that cut into her profits, and the volume of her sales was never as high as later authors, who had the benefits of new technology, realized.[76] Her greatest expense was paying her printer and repaying money advanced to her for printing costs. She had to pay commission to booksellers, and intermittently she employed a collector to deliver books to subscribers and collect their payments. Besides these items, she had the expense of travel and accommodations while she researched her books and distributed those she had already completed. While she had considerable success in selling her works, particularly in Boston, as she explained to her printer, "I am sincerely afflicted at my inability to benefit both you & myself as well as Mr Woodward by the eagerness of the people of Boston to render me independent & happy. . . . I have to allow the booksellers 20 per cent so that after deducting my expenses 9$ in coming here & $4 per week board with freight & I have nothing worth sending out of 100 books if it were in hand."[77] She was, or so she professed, unable even to buy herself a new dress.[78] Nonetheless, the sales of her books relieved Royall from her immediate poverty and meant that she was no longer dependent on the benevolence of others. Shortly after the publication of the *Sketches,* she wrote to a number of her benefactors informing them of her success in overcoming her distress and her relief at being financially independent again.[79] But few authors made much money out of their writing in the 1820s, and Royall was no exception to this general rule.

Gradually she improved her situation still further, but she forcefully denied any suggestion that she was making large profits from the sale of her books. Such accusations were absurd, she declared: "The booby, every book

I ever had printed, exclusive of expenses, would not amount to the *fourth* part of $10,000. Every one acquainted with publishing, however, knows this. It must be a popular work, indeed, that pays for itself; and I owe, at this moment, for the first work I ever had printed."[80] Lest anyone think that she wrote books and traveled for the purpose of providing herself with luxuries, she continued, "Every one of common sense might know that, if I had half the sum, I would not, at my advanced age, encounter the fatigue, dangers, and difficulties of travelling over mountains, and through storms of winter snows, to say nothing of the insults of unprincipled men."[81]

Royall was careful not to reveal how successful she was, for any suggestion that she was making significant profits from her books would have provoked criticism and lost her sales. Consequently, it is not easy to judge what sort of a living she made from her books, especially as she persisted in pleading poverty even after she began to have some success. There are some clues. A number of observers continued to note the poor state of her wardrobe as she journeyed around the country. Certainly, in the early days of her travels, she was in an extremely precarious financial situation, as her exaggerated gratitude for the charity she received at this time testifies.[82] As she sold her books, that situation improved, and she reached a sufficient level of financial security to be able to employ a servant girl while living in Washington, and to maintain her own household in a house she appears to have inhabited rent-free. By then she could also afford to renew her wardrobe occasionally, but her income was not great enough to indulge in the material goods necessary to a middle-class lifestyle.[83]

It was not until the mid-nineteenth century that many authors or newspaper editors began to make substantial profits from their undertakings. Among those who benefited were a number of female authors whose books, especially novels, reached bestseller status. Few of these women admitted to writing for any pecuniary reason, claiming instead a moral or cultural purpose. Like Royall, many of these later female authors launched their writing careers from financial necessity, the result of the sickness or death of their male economic providers.[84] But whereas Royall had had to navigate the economic realities of the publishing trade of the 1820s for herself, these later women could rely on their male publishers to undertake the business side of publication. Not many of these female authors had the kind of personal financial contact with their audience that Anne Royall had possessed.[85]

Royall's decision to make her way through writing launched her on a career that in the 1820s was risky and unlikely to prove very profitable. Her ability to exploit her status as the widow of a Freemason and a Revolutionary War veteran allowed her to utilize networks and tap sources that would not usually be available either to men or to the widows of non-Masons, helping her to create a market for her books. Although her methods may have been unusual for a woman at the time, neither her decision to become an author nor to be involved in the commercial world of the 1820s was particularly remarkable. Other women became female merchants and entrepreneurs, and while the law of coverture made it difficult for married women to benefit from their entrepreneurial activities, this was not true for widows. As a number of historians have suggested, although emerging cultural constructions of dependent womanhood might seem to preclude women from the public and economic sphere, the reality was often different.[86] The notoriety Royall gained was not due to her choice of career or because she entered into the supposedly male world of business. Rather, her sales methods, and the subject and contents of her books, provoked certain elements within Jacksonian society to criticize and eventually attempt to silence her.

4 · Mrs. Royall's Travels

While touring New York State in the late 1820s, Anne Royall remarked on the beauty of the scenery: "Every person of taste who has made the tour of New York, will say, that no description that ever has or ever will be given of it can possibly convey an accurate idea of its beauty, either singly or combined. Floods of ink would not do it, all works of art or science has a name, but for the scenery of New York there is no name; it being the work of an *Almighty hand.*"[1] She professed to be overwhelmed by the magnificence of the natural scenery and rhapsodized on its wonders, imitating the language of the sublime. She used such artifices in order to display her own sophistication as well as to associate herself with others who took the "fashionable tour"—people of taste who could appreciate the landscape. Self-consciously situating herself in the realm of the literary and constructed, she sought to provide herself with the credentials necessary to give her credibility as a writer of elegant travel narratives.[2]

On other occasions, too, she embellished her writings with similar literary devices, deliberately echoing the travel narratives she had read herself. Thus, in the opening remarks of her first published book, she imitated the comments of these authors in outlining the purpose of her writing: "With a view to divert my mind from melancholy reflections, to which it was disposed from ill health, I resolved to note every thing during my journey, worthy of remark, and commit it to writing, and to draw amusement and instruction from every source." Acknowledging contemporary travel literature and linking her own work with that of other, more established travel writers, she added, "In doing this, I shall not imitate most journalists, in such remarks as 'cloudy, or fair morning' and where we stop, dates, etc. This is all the preface I deem necessary."[3] But although she might initially have sought to emulate the work of the leisured amateur authors who wrote many of these earlier travel journals, she also aimed at a wider audience. While she persisted in incorporating allusions to high literary style in her publications, there was much that was prosaic both in her subject matter and the way in which she described it.[4]

Her works afforded other perspectives too. On one level her books were traditional travel narratives replete with descriptions of scenery and people, but on another they provided a forum in which she presented her ideas and opinions. Often taking the form of criticism, and frequently voiced in strident and forthright tones, she declared her own views on the issues of the day. Although occasionally somewhat fragmentary, her stance on such aspects of national life as the proper behavior of women and women's education, slavery, and the place of Native Americans was often at variance with the positions of other women who articulated opinions on these subjects. Her ideas constituted a particular vision of America, and she paid little heed to the sensitivities of those who might not share her views. Asserting the righteousness of her way of thinking, she forced her prejudices on her readers. Despite their idiosyncrasies, their frequent repetition, their sometimes limited scope, and their highly opinionated nature, Royall's travel narratives sold well, and they provided her with a living. Indeed, the popularity of her work suggests that she offered a viewpoint that was attractive to her readers.

Royall had traveled quite extensively even before she started to do so in order to earn a living. Her straitened financial circumstances meant that neither travel nor travel writing was an obvious choice of career. She had lost her horses and slaves when her husband's relatives seized her inheritance, so her explorations of the United States were dependent on commercial transportation, such as the stagecoach and various forms of water transport. Whereas her sojourn in Alabama had been unhurried and leisured, giving her the freedom to explore with few time constraints, she had a quite different prospect before her in July 1823 when she left the state.[5] Between 1823 and 1830, she traversed the length and breadth of the settled United States and some parts not yet open to settlement. She visited every part of the country accessible by stagecoach, steamboat, sleigh, canal, and occasionally on horseback or foot. She did so alone, and as she traveled, she took notes for her books. In the pauses between her tours she wrote and had her books printed, and on her subsequent journeys she sold these books while researching for her next volume. In all she published nine travel narratives covering this period together with the *Letters from Alabama.* Nonetheless her choice to combine her need to earn a living with a desire to see more of the United States was, in a number of respects, a risky undertaking.

Royall's decision to concentrate on writing travel narratives was influenced by her own reading and by her experience in penning letters to Matthew Dunbar from Alabama. She had found the process of writing a novel much less gratifying than that of describing new places and people, and after completing one novel, she did not attempt another.[6] Her own reading was dictated by the limited availability of books in western Virginia and Alabama, but she still managed to read widely, and having no household of her own to run in Alabama, she had the leisure to do so. Only occasionally did she mention particular authors or literary works. At the Sweet Springs plantation, she had had access to her husband's books. These included Hugh Blair's *Sermons* and Tobias Smollett's *History of England,* although his library may also have encompassed works of philosophy, science, and history by Enlightenment scholars, for she indicated that she had read Buffon and Voltaire. She discussed what she had read in the letters she sent to Dunbar, revealing the pleasure she took in a variety of types of literature. Among these were more modern works, including some by American authors such as *Salmagundi* by Washington Irving and James Kirke Paulding, and English works like Lady Morgan's *France* and the novels of Walter Scott.[7] Her disparaging remarks about other novels suggest that she had read some of them. Certainly she was knowledgeable about the plot twists, romantic venues, narratives of seduction and betrayal, and heroic action that constituted the standard fare of these novels, for she modeled her own on the same devices.[8]

Despite the limited availability of books, Anne consumed a surprising variety of reading matter, but her own writing was particularly influenced by travel narratives. From her reading she learned to experiment with various forms of travel writing, trying out the structures other authors had used, such as letter and journal forms, as well as engaging with discussions about landscape and Native peoples. She put to use the understanding she had acquired from her reading of contemporary travel writers such as La Rochefoucauld-Liancourt, Isaac Weld, and John Ledyard as she began to produce compositions of her own.[9]

Royall joined a growing number of women who journeyed in the United

States in the early nineteenth century and wrote about, and even published, their observations and experiences during their trips.[10] Until the nineteenth century, travel writing had been a predominantly masculine genre. During the eighteenth century, it had been based on rigid conventions, widely recognized by contemporaries, with the aim to instruct and please. In keeping with these conventions, the travel writer would not talk of himself, nor would he include anecdotes or trivial information, since these would detract from the main purpose of the literature—to be improving.[11] By the end of the century, these conventions had become more flexible, to the extent that travel writing grew to be an elastic genre both in form and content. Thus it was an inviting vehicle for many women. As Royall acknowledged in the opening words of the *Sketches*, for many women the travel book equated itself with a journal—a form that was both informal and commodious, and with which women had long been familiar. The letter form appealed to women as well, for it was a mode with which they were comfortable and well-acquainted. Both styles allowed them to include a wide variety of material and note everything that caught their attention while also informing and amusing their audience.[12]

There were practical reasons why travel writing had previously been a predominantly male genre. Prior to the nineteenth century, conditions for traveling around the United States were difficult. The roads were poor, settlements scattered, public transport unpredictable, and accommodations on the road uncertain. Only those with the necessary financial resources could afford to own or rent a horse or carriage and hire a guide. Consequently, women rarely traveled for leisure, and when they did so, it was usually to visit family.[13] In the early nineteenth century, with improvements in roads and the establishment of regular stagecoach and steamship lines, as well as more regulated lodgings, travel became easier and more predictable, although it remained arduous and uncomfortable.[14] The greater availability and reliability of transport made travel possible for many more people, including women, with the result that they could make trips for pleasure apart from those they had previously made to visit family. Women joined other family members in traveling to such newly developing tourist spots as Niagara Falls and the springs in Virginia and New York, but such activities were still the preserve of those with leisure and wealth. Men and women of lesser means might take the occasional short trip on a stagecoach or steamboat, but few had the time or money to travel widely. Even with improvements in commercial transport and the development of new routes, which stretched into areas previously comparatively inaccessible, extensive travel remained unusual, especially for women.[15]

Thus, although her travels and decision to produce narratives about them were not common activities for women of Royall's time, neither were they a particular source of comment or criticism. Generally married middle-class women were too tied to their families and domestic duties to leave their households for any length of time, except to visit family or for the sake of their health. When they did travel they were usually accompanied by a male relative or servant, and wealthier women would use a private conveyance—a carriage or horses—as Royall had done on her trips to Alabama. Wealthy white women usually traveled with relative security even in remote areas, with or without a chaperone, for their social status, as displayed by horses and servants, provided protection against molestation. As Royall's own observations demonstrated, a poor woman traveling alone was not treated with the courtesies that a woman who appeared to be wealthy commanded.[16]

As public transport improved it made travel more accessible to women of more modest social status with sufficient funds to afford it. Although those who took advantage of this greater availability still tended to be escorted by a male relative or acquaintance, women did negotiate the stagecoaches and steamships alone or accompanied only by a female companion. Female evangelical preachers and Quaker women traveled between religious meetings, sometimes alone, restricted only by the relative expense of the stagecoaches and the fact that, despite improvements, trips were still slow and exhausting. Other women made journeys alone when they needed to for family or business reasons, but many were fearful of doing so because of the dangers of robbery or even sexual assault.[17] Occasionally such women were the subject of comment, usually because their dress or demeanor excited disapproval rather than because their fellow passengers considered lone women to be out of place on commercial transport. Not until the 1830s and 1840s did organizations such as the moral reform societies raise an outcry about the sexual vulnerability of unaccompanied women on stagecoaches and steamboats. Increasingly the concerns these societies raised placed the onus on lone women travelers to prove that they were respectable through their modest and retiring behavior, for, they were warned, the consequences of not doing so put their safety at risk.[18] In the 1820s, however, while individual women might be fearful of traveling alone, they could still travel on commercial stagecoaches and steamboats with few restrictions on their conduct. Journeys alone and on public transport remained a relatively unusual activity for women, but it was not the fact that Royall toured the United States alone or without a male chaperone that elicited criticism. Rather, people censured her for what she wrote and how she behaved in the places she visited.

In the 1820s, touring the United States as a leisure activity was still limited to the relatively wealthy, but many other Americans, unable or unwilling to travel themselves, were keen to experience the pleasures of travel vicariously. By reading about their country, Americans could learn about its landscape, people, and history, and they could also share in the experiences of adventure and new places through the printed word. Consequently, there was a ready market for travel books written by foreign visitors but also increasingly by Americans writing about their own country. European travelers had been visiting the new United States since the late eighteenth century, many with a specific purpose in mind, styling their expeditions on the Grand Tour of Europe. Such tourists often set themselves solemn questions—a model European commentators such as Alexis de Tocqueville, Harriet Martineau, and even Frances Trollope followed when they traveled to the United States.[19] Others came out of simple curiosity, but among both groups, the travel journal, whether intended for publication or not, became a popular means by which to record their experiences. A significant number of the European travelers' accounts of their journeys in the United States were published, some with extensive social and political commentary.[20] Such works were available to an American audience as reprints and pirated copies, but by the early nineteenth century, Americans were beginning to seek a uniquely American culture, and they looked to American writers to explain that culture to them. Authors such as Mercy Otis Warren, Royall Tyler, and Susanna Rowson supplied this need through histories, dramas, and novels, and journalists also sought to identify a national literature based on American experience and traditions. American travel writers too began to contribute to this sense of patriotism, as they revealed to Americans the value of their native land as a source of amusement, observation, and culture.[21] In writing about her travels, Royall exploited a growing market of Americans seeking to learn about their country.

Few American travel writers in the 1820s had either the time or money to visit more than a small part of their country, nor did many of them have the energy to endure the long and often difficult journeys that Royall undertook. Some embarked on shorter trips, often following in the footsteps of foreign visitors, taking the "fashionable tour" of New York and New England.[22] Royall was exceptional for her time in the extent of her travels, for she did not confine herself only to the Northeast. While on her expeditions she took notes of her experiences, which she later copied, improved, and then published, to be sold on her subsequent tours—a method that few other travel writers employed. Unlike most of these writers, her journeys were rarely solely for pleasure. Over the course of seven years, from the time she left Alabama in 1823, Royall traveled throughout the United States on a number of distinct tours, returning at the end of each expedition to Washington. The nine volumes of travel writing that she produced in this period each covered a different section of the country.

Initially it was not evident that Royall intended to explore the United States as extensively or for as long as proved to be the case. She may well have expected to return to western Virginia after she had found a publisher and conducted her business in Richmond and Washington. The continuing cases against her for debt, and her consequent fear of being imprisoned, together with the unpredictable reception she might receive in western Virginia, soon closed that option to her.[23] Nor did she have a very clear idea as to how much of interest there was to see and report on. Her enthusiasm for including everything was curbed by the need to produce publishable volumes and to attract a sufficient number of subscribers to make the volumes viable. As she noted, "When the proposals for this, as well as two other works, were published, the author was unapprised of the extensive matter embraced in the work, and found it impossible to comprise any thing like a satisfactory description of the atlantic and western country, in a book of this size."[24] She quickly became adept at tailoring her books to her market, and learned that her route and subject matter should be dictated by the necessity to sell her works.[25] Consequently, she planned her journeys to include the larger population centers and areas where she believed she would receive a good reception, shunning those where she did not expect any sales. Except for the large East Coast cities, where possible she avoided visiting the same area twice so that she could package a particular volume to maximize her audience.

As she traveled, Royall was constantly preoccupied with the need to earn a living—a concern she frequently voiced to those she met on her expeditions. Her journeys served the dual purpose of research for her new books and a search for patrons to buy those she had already written.[26] Unlike her earlier trips to Alabama, Royall's later journeys were rarely pleasure trips alone; she always had business of some kind to transact. On the very rare occasion when she admitted to taking a "jaunt" for pleasure, as she did to Saratoga Springs for the July 4th holiday in 1827, she was still on the lookout for subscribers and materials for her books.[27]

To begin with, Royall's intention in writing about her travels was to describe and explain the United States to its people, and this remained at the forefront of her writing. This was evident in her prefatory remarks to the *Sketches:* "The work herewith presented to the public, contains a description of the public institutions, manners and appearance of the inhabitants, and the history of the principal places visited by the author, with sketches of principal characters, physical remarks on the country, &c."[28] Her books were travel and guidebooks rather than accounts of voyages of discovery or exploration.

Royall was soon distracted from her initial purpose of merely portraying the United States to its inhabitants without comment. Nonetheless her travel books do describe, in some detail, her journeys through the settled areas of the country, and even to some of the more remote areas not accessible by stagecoach or steamboat. As had been the case in her letters to Dunbar, she sought to provide physical descriptions of the countryside, towns, and villages, and of developing manufacturing and commercial areas. More so than her subsequent books, *Sketches* was a guidebook to the United States. Not yet entirely certain who her readers were, it included information of use to other travelers as well as her own impressions of people and places.[29] Her later books, sometimes deliberately, sometimes subconsciously, have a more obviously autobiographical element to them, and clearly had a particular audience in mind. But they remained descriptions of her travels in the United States, the difficulties caused by transport and terrain, and anecdotes about the incidents along the way.

Each of Royall's books detailed her tour of a particular region, for new parts of the country provided fresh opportunities to find markets for her books. She maintained that her routes were dictated by a demanding public—for so many of her "friends" wanted her to describe their towns that she had invitations from all over the country. While this assertion cannot be verified, she was certainly able to attract well-wishers and patrons in many of the places she visited—a testimony to her growing celebrity.[30]

Besides her self-important assertions that she was merely serving her public, Royall planned each of her tours to cover a certain region and encompass places she believed would be of interest to her readers. Factors such as the availability of stagecoaches, canals, and steamships helped to determine her itineraries, but occasionally she visited less accessible spots, chosen because she had become acquainted with them through her reading. On her first tour, beginning in the spring of 1825, like many other travelers in the United States at this period, Royall visited the towns and cities of the eastern seaboard states—Richmond, Washington, Baltimore, Philadelphia, New York, Albany, and Boston. She also called at the military academy at West Point and some of the smaller places in New York State and southern New England, and spent some time in New Haven.[31] After the publication of her first book, she took what she called her "fashionable tour," imitating the route taken by popular travel writers and growing numbers of wealthy tourists. This included the Hudson Valley, Niagara Falls, and a trip along the newly completed Erie Canal—an experience she found particularly pleasing: "This manner of travelling is extremely pleasant, much preferable either to the stage or the steamboat, being alike safe from the accidents of both; nor are you liable to be covered with dust as you are in the stages, or crowded to suffocation."[32]

Occasionally Royall would pass through the same towns in order to deliver the books for which she had previously gathered subscriptions. Thus after her "fashionable tour," she passed through New York, New Jersey, and Pennsylvania on her way south to Baltimore, Washington, and Virginia, before returning to Philadelphia. This gave her the occasion to note the changes in these places, but her key aim was to cover a different part of the United States in each volume. So volumes 2 and 3 of the *Black Book* took her to northern New England, having first passed through Albany, western Massachusetts, and Boston. She traveled along the coast of Maine and then inland right up into the mountains of New Hampshire and Vermont in the snow, where the settlements were isolated and remote. Retracing her steps, she took the stage and steamboat down the Hudson to New York and thence to Washington.

Her decision to take a four-month trip devoted to one state was, Royall claimed, the result of a persistent invitation from supporters in Pennsylvania. She was certainly fêted by admirers in some towns, and at the height of her celebrity, their encouragement may well have prompted her to visit their state.[33] The result, the two volumes of *Mrs. Royall's Pennsylvania,* documented a tour that conveyed the author from Philadelphia through the economically developing areas around Mauch Chunk and Pittsburgh to the western edges of Pennsylvania, still sparsely populated and not greatly

Anne Royall's Travels

changed from her childhood. There she visited her sister, who still lived in the area where they had spent their childhood years, before returning through Harrisburg where, Anne boasted, she viewed the state legislature, received many plaudits from its members, and attended a dinner held in her honor.[34]

Her final tour, detailed in the three volumes of *Mrs. Royall's Southern Tour,* saw her traveling down through the Blue Ridge Mountains and then visiting the states of North and South Carolina and Georgia, of which her knowledge was limited: "So little is the Geography of our country known, that I only knew, there was such a place as Macon; but as to laying out my accounts to halt at it, or even that it lay in my way, never entered my head: and now I find another considerable town, *Columbus,* ahead of me! It would take six months, at least, to visit Georgia alone."[35] Here she reached the edges of American settlement as she passed through the Creek Nation on the road to Montgomery, from where she took the steamboat downriver to Mobile and thence to New Orleans. Her journey up the Mississippi on a steamboat took her past some of the new settlements on its banks—providing an opportunity for nostalgia as she described Helena, one such settlement: "But the dear little new log cabins on the shores, were my delight. The still independence and rural simplicity they brought to my mind from having spent my early days in them overpowered my feelings."[36] St. Louis, however, proved unfriendly, and unable to get a passage to the mouth of the Ohio River, her friends spirited her quickly across Illinois to pick up the steamboat farther upriver. The final pages of the *Southern Tour* describe her trip to visit her mother and brother in new settlements in Indiana and Illinois, before returning to Washington via Cincinnati.

Following the standards of the travel writers she had read, Royall took her reporting obligations seriously, describing the countryside in some detail, as well as enumerating the manufactures and buildings of the towns she visited. Like these earlier writers, she emphasized the diversity of the country and its economic growth, as well as the importance of educational and social institutions in maintaining American prosperity and liberty. Her "fashionable tour" encompassed many of the natural phenomena that were beginning to attract tourists in the 1820s—some of which were still in the early stages of commercial development. After taking in the popular resort of Saratoga Springs, she visited Niagara Falls, which was on the itinerary of many other writers. Her description of that visit emphasized both her practical approach to her subject and her desire to show off her knowledge of literary forms. But occasionally, as if to accentuate the hardships she endured for her readers, she made it clear that she anticipated no pleasure from many of her excursions. Thus in participating in a guided tour of the falls, which took her between the column of water and the rock, she commented tartly:

> This is a fool-hardy undertaking; dangerous and difficult; and yields neither pleasure nor information. The danger is in the falling in of the rock, occasioned by the great weight of water; 2d. the want of air to breathe; and 3d, from the danger of missing your step, by which you would soon be ingulphed in the abyss; and, besides the water pours on you more profusely than the most copious shower-bath. . . . The rock on which you pass under the fall is shelving and slippery from the number of eels which cover it; . . . But the greatest difficulty I found was in breathing, and on my first entrance would have suffocated, if my guide had not led me out.[37]

If she was not enthusiastic about this aspect of her visit to the falls, she still found the experience impressive, and seeking to show off her knowledge of the refined and sophisticated, she pronounced her fear "that the subject of describing the falls was not only above the power of language, but one so hackneyed, that nothing was left for me to say." Words might fail her, but she managed to suggest some sense of the grandeur of the scene: "But no language can convey an idea, or express the sensations of the human mind upon viewing the falls; a nameless majesty rests upon them which to understand must be seen."[38]

There were other occasions too when she sought to associate herself with the "people of taste" who took the "fashionable tour" by showing off her ability to appreciate the landscape. In commenting on Bellows Falls on the Connecticut River, she claimed a sense of refinement for herself: "Who ever is fond of rich scenery, may gratify their wishes to the full, at Bellows fall. Terrific rocks, hills, towns, cataracts, boats, canals, with mills and saws, and continual thunder. It attracts the attention of all travellers of taste."[39] In her enthusiasm for scenes of natural beauty, she self-consciously made reference to the works of other writers, echoing the descriptions she had read. Thus she described the White Mountains of New Hampshire: "Whippled cream may give some idea of its appearance, at this distance. The figure of each of these vast domes, is perfect symmetry and proportion. Thus, lonely, tranquil, firmly, gracefully and majestically, the White Mountains for the first time met my eye through the window of the stage house at Middleton.

The effect was delight and astonishment, of which no words can give an adequate idea." She even took issue with those who had compared the silence and sublime beauty of the White Mountains in New Hampshire with the grandeur and thunderous noise of Niagara Falls: "It lacks nothing but noise and motion to equal the Falls of Niagara, in sublimity; the effect is of a much more pleasing nature. It has none of that shrinking awe, which a view of the falls create. Some have gone so far as to say, the White Mountains are more sublime than the falls, but this is mere fancy, and contrary to established rules of taste, as great sound, is always more sublime than silence."[40]

If for the most part Royall sought to imitate the elegant style and rhapsodies on the sublime that many travel writers utilized, just occasionally she aimed to appeal to a less sophisticated audience. Toward the end of her tour of the southern states, possibly recognizing that her audience for this work was not as well-read as her northern patrons, she adopted a more homely approach. Denying her earlier desire to be associated with "people of taste," she asserted in a moment of ostensible self-deprecation outside New Orleans: "It is understood I never have, nor am I capable, of dressing out my subject in learned phrazes or bold images or any of the elegances of style." In a direct appeal to her audience, she continued, "Judging of others by myself, I seek only to give such a description of things as may bring them as near as possible before the eyes of those who have not an opportunity of seeing them, and that in my own homespun way without regard to style or rules of composition, which I know nothing of, and care as little as I know."[41] More concerned to attract patrons than be consistent, Royall may also have been reacting to critics who lambasted her for her unsophisticated style. Despite occasional moments of apparent doubt, she continued to rhapsodize about the splendors of the American landscape.

Royall was not only interested in commenting on the beauty of the countryside or in showing off her mastery of literary style; she was fascinated by some of the new industries in places like Pittsburgh. Her curiosity occasionally took her to places her friends considered inappropriate for a woman due to the dirt or danger they posed. Undeterred, Royall boasted to her readers of her willingness to explore such places. For instance, her observations about the Pittsburgh foundries were framed to highlight her daring: "A female, was doubtless, the last thing these men were thinking of, and such was my curiosity to see these far-famed founderies and workshops, that without consulting a friend, I popped into one the next day of my visit."[42] Thus she tried to persuade her readers that she would overcome all obstacles put in her way in her determination to inform them about their country.

Like many other travel writers, Royall commented on the mundane practicalities of her journeys—the difficulties of getting to places not served by regular stagecoaches, variations in the standards of accommodations, and sometimes the necessity of hastening her trips to avoid the worst of the hot or cold weather. She noted her disappointment that she missed the scenery because the stagecoach schedules obliged her to travel at night.[43] Invariably seeing all aspects of her travel from her own viewpoint, she judged stagecoach companies, stage drivers, and innkeepers by the way they treated her. Expecting to be cared for with the courtesy she believed befitted her status, she would pass judgment on the merits of one stagecoach or steamship line above another based only on their behavior toward her. Where they failed to meet her expectations, she would condemn them vehemently.[44] The same was true of the places she stayed. Less interested than many other female travelers in the domestic arrangements of the taverns she encountered along her routes, she nonetheless documented their virtues or shortcomings in vigorous terms. She described one tavern in Lebanon Springs as the best in New York, another in Connecticut received praise all round: "The chamber-maids and waiting-maids, are perfect ladies; the charges low; the tables good; the rooms neat, and the most assiduous attention."[45] By contrast, southern taverns were not as well managed, and she took the opportunity to suggest this was due to the laziness of many southern women: "The women here are too proud or too lazy, or too something to attend to public houses. In the North, woman is the life and soul of a tavern."[46] Only when the proprietor treated Royall with sufficient respect and admiration did she express her enthusiasm for a tavern, as she did for one in Columbia, South Carolina: "Left me in the largest and most splendidly furnished parlor I was ever in in any part of the Union. It wanted little, if any, of being equal to the east room in size or beauty! More costly or more highly finished furniture I never at any time saw in a public house, and it is the first time I ever found the owner and house equally matched."[47]

Besides the practicalities of travel, Royall echoed other travel writers in reporting details such as the number of churches and public buildings in the towns she passed through, their commerce, and the development of manufacturing in some areas of the country. But such materials could be gleaned from newspapers and other guidebooks, and it is unlikely they were what encouraged people to buy her books. Rather, as one newspaper editor made clear, people were fascinated by her combative opinions: "We have dipped into the last Black Book, and have been highly entertained; she shews in her writings as in her manner, that perfect off-hand independence which so strongly marks every thing she does. There is no circumlocution, no palavering, but straight to the point she goes."[48]

Since she began penning letters to Dunbar, Royall used her writing as a vehicle through which to express her views and ideas on many subjects. Forceful and opinionated, she considered few areas of American life to be outside her purview. Although occasionally she acknowledged that her discussion of certain issues might be thought inappropriate by critics, she was rarely limited by what others viewed as the social proprieties. Undeterred by and even courting disapproval, Royall expressed her opinions on a wide range of topics as incidents on her journeys prompted her reaction. Many of the issues on which she made pronouncements reflected wider contemporary debates, but she also had personal prejudices that she did not hesitate to share with her readers.

The behavior of other women often infuriated her. She had no patience with those she considered to be silly, and she criticized them with some venom, suggesting she had little in common with her own sex either young or old. In talking about other women her tone was frequently one of superiority laced with contempt, for she believed herself to be better educated and better informed than the majority of women. Thus she mocked women's fashions in Baltimore, seeing them as a reflection of their wearers' characters: "What man of sense wishes to marry a bundle of silk and lace? If they would expend a tenth part of their dress in improving their minds, they would enjoy life, and receive the applause of the world. . . . Pride and affectation is a certain consequence which all the silk and lace in the world cannot conceal. I blush for my countrywomen."[49] She was still more scornful of those women she referred to as "old maids." Two unmarried women who ran a Poughkeepsie tavern attracted her particular disdain: "Alas for my sex, how ridiculous they make themselves, in their partiality for the other sex; and this partiality defeats their purpose. Had these ladies been sweet tempered, affable and modest, they would not have been old maids at this late day."[50]

Despite her derision for the vacuous minds of the Baltimore and Poughkeepsie ladies, she could still admire the grace and elegance of some women in the eastern cities. The ladies of New York do not read, she observed, but "this is perhaps owing to their numerous sources of amusement. Such as the theatres, gardens, etc. The ladies of New-York have one excellence, however, peculiar to them; that is their elegant and graceful walk. This excellence is attributed to their smooth paved Broadway, upon which they practice walking to a degree which has been crowned with success." To her taste, the ladies of Boston were far superior: "But the excellence of the Boston ladies is found in the improvement of their minds, which gives ease to their manners, and an intelligence of countenance, which forms a striking contrast to the vacant stare of the ladies of New-York. The pleasure of the former is intellectual, that of the latter is sensual." There was an element of self-interest in her observations, for she was able to sell her books more easily in Boston than in New York, especially to the women.[51]

Royall's vituperative comments were frequently retaliation for the treatment she had received from these women, but they were not entirely self-seeking. She had a more serious point to make. She believed passionately in the importance of education. Early in her travels she set out her thoughts on the centrality of education to the welfare of the nation and its people: "Hence arises all our mistakes in religion, morals, and politics. When our reason is cultivated and our minds are enlightened by education, we are enabled to strip off that disguise which knavery, bigotry, and superstition wears. It rectifies our judgments, holds the reins of our passions, in short, enables us to discover whatever tends to promote our present and eternal welfare."[52] Derived from her own reading, she claimed reason as the key benefit of education and believed this applied to both sexes and all classes of people. Appalled by the ignorance of the "great mass of the people" and their prejudice against learning, she believed that only through education would the country prosper and its institutions survive. For the ignorant would soon have the administration of public affairs in their hands, and, she argued, this could only damage American liberties. Thus, she contended, "One would think that it would be the first and only object with men of letters, to set on foot some method to enlighten the great mass of the people, as they must, inevitably, and that before long, have the management of matters in their own hands!"[53] She warned of the dangers of ignoring the problem, but she did not offer any specific solutions beyond advocating the establishment of schools and colleges.

The subject came up quite naturally in her writing for Royall regularly visited schools and colleges of all kinds on her tours. Educational institutions were often on the itineraries of tourists as they were seen as reflections of the new republic's cultural development, and visitors came to enjoy the spectacle of the students' exercises. If tourists had letters of introduction, they might be conducted around the schools and colleges by the headmasters or college presidents; should they not have the proper credentials, they were likely to be rebuffed.[54] Royall was occasionally refused entry, and the rejection would prompt an angry riposte in her books, but sometimes she also voiced a more measured response to the institutions she visited. Certainly there were some colleges that received her plaudits, but there were equally those that failed to live up to her expectations. She was especially displeased at ones run by clergymen, such as Western University in Pittsburgh, which she believed taught its students nothing: "I am astonished that legislatures do not see these priests have become too abandoned to church and state principles, to have any thing to do with the education of youth; and the money had better be thrown into the fire, than wasted in this manner. Learning is entirely extinct."[55]

In some parts of the country she censured the absence of schools. She concluded that this was the result of disputes between the enlightened and ignorant over the provision of schools for both sexes.[56] Even in Washington there was little encouragement for learning: "From all accounts, education is in its infancy. There are no academies, no grammar schools, and but two free schools, for the exclusive benefit of the poor; these are supported by the corporation." She considered the teaching in the Washington schools to be indifferent: "The dissemination of knowledge does not appear to have received the encouragement which we would expect in the first city of the nation."[57] She was fearful of the influence of "priests" on the future direction of education, and advocated that state governments should take measures to ensure the distribution of knowledge among all young people, free from clerical control.[58] While she was frequently disheartened by the pervasiveness of what she perceived as ignorance in the country, she also found many examples of excellent schools and dedicated teachers, notably in the backwoods of Pennsylvania. She was cheered by the promise of new methods and ideas for teaching children, and described at length and with considerable enthusiasm the experimental school run by William Neef in Pennsylvania, based on Pestalozzian methods. She expressed a hope that schools of this description would be established all over the United States, for they seemed to offer the best chance of overcoming ignorance and encouraging independence.[59]

Royall might admire or disparage the educational institutions she visited, but she was particularly mindful of the failures in women's education, and

she used her books to make her readers aware of the importance of educating women as well as men. While not alone in promoting education for women in the 1820s, her approach was different from that of many other educational reformers. Expressing her uneasiness about the ignorance of many of her countrywomen, she emphasized the dangers to the public good of leaving women uneducated. Some of her arguments echoed those of reformers like Benjamin Rush, who in the 1780s had begun to encourage education for women. She suggested that educating a woman was to the benefit of society. Their influence on their husbands and children made it essential to the future of the American republic that women were educated, for an unschooled woman could, in Royall's opinion, cause untold damage.[60] On the other hand, an educated woman could be a positive benefit to her family, for "there is one advantage in having an education above all others, which is, that in the event of misfortune it leads those who have children to give them an education if nothing else."[61]

While occasionally Royall hinted that learning in a woman was in itself a desirable end, like many of her contemporaries she tended to see education for women in terms of making them more attractive marriage partners. A woman who was properly educated and interested in improving her mind was, she believed, much more likely to capture a husband than one who was interested only in fashion. This was a theme she frequently declaimed upon, voicing her impatience even with the women who sat in the galleries at the Virginia constitutional convention: "These silly women, whose minds were empty, thought to captivate by outside show, and when the Convention was about to meet, fabricated these large umbrella bonnets, which they named *Convention*-bonnets. These were made of white silk, with feathers stuck in them one yard in length—all this was to draw attention, and if the *bonnet* failed, the feather could not; this lack of learning and want of sense defeated their object."[62] She continued to denounce frivolous women and admired female academies when she came across them, but she did not offer a careful analysis of what women should be taught or if their education should differ from men's.[63]

While Royall visited schools and colleges wherever she traveled, condemning some and praising others, she steadfastly emphasized the importance of education for the protection of American liberties and the future health of the republic. Her views on education were presented in uncompromising terms, but on some of the other subjects of debate on which other women offered forceful opinions, she was much less forthright. Her

childhood on the frontier and her reading in the literature of the sublime meant that her attitudes toward Native Americans were often ambiguous and frequently contradictory, tendering none of the moral certainties found among many evangelical northern women. Similarly, her identification as the wife of a slave-owner and the owner of slaves herself meant that her views on slavery were in direct opposition to the developing anti-slavery movements in the North. Believing in the superiority of her own racial attitudes, she had little time for those who challenged them or who represented other races or ethnicities.

The question of Indian removal to the west of the Mississippi had become a topic of heated discussion by the late 1820s, but Royall's encounters with Native Americans predated this debate. She had lived through Indian raids on the Pennsylvania frontier as a child but made no explicit connections between these early experiences and the various different nations of Indians she encountered on her travels. The situation of the eastern Indian tribes had changed dramatically by the time she first wrote about them from Alabama, and they were no longer the threatening presence she had once known. She arrived in Alabama territory shortly after Andrew Jackson's defeat of the Creeks, which had destroyed their power in the region. Jackson's treaty negotiations over the next few years extracted vast tracts of land from the Cherokee, Choctaw, and Chickasaw tribes by means of bribery and threats, so that by 1820, Indian lands from the middle of Georgia to the Mississippi and from Kentucky to West Tennessee had been opened to white settlement, and the Indians themselves pushed into the least fertile lands.[64] It was in this very different context that Royall wrote about Native Americans. She continued to regard them as obstacles to be removed, not because of the threat they posed but because they stood in the way of white settlement. The attitudes she conveyed in her writing, however, could be contradictory.

Royall's musings on the Alabama Indians in her *Letters from Alabama* reflected the romantic literature of the time, rather than a real encounter with Native Americans who had been forced off their lands. Thus on crossing the Tennessee River at the Muscle Shoals, she noted, "I was pensive and melancholy; for, being told by my guide I was to pass by several Indian farms, it struck a damp on my spirits, of which he was unconscious. He speaks of the Indians and their departure with perfect indifference."[65] The tragedy of the dying or disappearing Indian had become a staple of American literature since the 1780s. Rather than the bloodthirsty demon

of colonial writing, the Indian had been transformed into a Noble Savage, and became as such a fit subject for artists, writers, and poets. For Royall Indians became figures in a sublime landscape in the same way they did for other writers, one whose passing evoked sentimental feelings.[66]

Her rhapsodies on an abandoned Indian farm in Alabama reflected this romantic vision. Representing the landscape as comparable to the Elysian Fields, she depicted the farm itself in domestic terms: "About ten o'clock we came in sight of the first Indian farm—but Indian farm no longer! The smoke was issuing slowly through the chimney. Why, these Indians have been like us!—could not be savage—cornfields—apple trees, and peach-trees. Fences like ours, but not so high—trusted to their neighbor's honesty. . . . The house looked tight and comfortable."[67] Continuing with her wistful theme, her portrayal of the Native, a man named Gourd who had lived there, was very clearly modeled on the sentiment common in the romantic literature of the time.[68] As she had done in her descriptions of scenery, Royall emulated the language of other writers, making a claim to elegance and taste. But whereas the Indian in the abstract might be a noble and tragic figure, her observations of real Indians were rarely framed in such romantic terms.

When she did meet Indians in person, Royall depicted them as an inferior people who had no place in the United States. She was disappointed in the appearance of those she encountered in Alabama: "I have heard much of the elegant figures of the Indians; true, some nations of Indians are elegantly formed, but such is not the case with the Cherokees. They are low in stature, and there is nothing majestic or dignified about them."[69] Although she recognized that there were differences between the tribes, she frequently generalized about their characteristics. She described the Indians she came across in other parts of the United States as brutish, silly, or drunkards, and was unconvinced by claims that the Oneida were civilized: "It is a burlesque on the word to say these Indians are civilized. Their clothes, their farms, and their houses, too evidently show sloth and indolence; their small patches of corn and potatoes; their ragged fences, evince any thing but civilization; and their land, the finest in the State, is no advantage to them." Although she conceded that the Cherokee were "far advanced in civilized arts and manners," she was not impressed by their ability to adopt white ways.[70]

Abandoning her sentimental view of Indians, by the late 1820s Royall had a very different attitude toward the Native American tribes she encountered on her travels. She refused to believe that any Indians could ever be "civilized" because they refused to embrace the English language. The efforts of those like Gideon Blackburn to assimilate the Cherokees had been, in her view, a total failure, and the only solution was for the Indians to be removed from proximity to white people, at rifle-point if necessary.[71] While she reflected the attitude of many in the South at this time, her view was more antagonistic than that of many politicians who were still advocating voluntary rather than forced removal. In 1830, as she passed through Creek Territory on the way to Montgomery, her suggestion of what should be done was couched in rather more conciliatory language, but she did not accept that the Indians had a right to live on lands white settlers wished to occupy: "Indeed it is absurd, to let these Indians lie about here and do nothing—since all the land we own came by the Indians, and through us has been reclaimed from a wilderness! Why not give them back some of our lands on our eastern coast, since they will not work—barren land will do them as well as any." Insisting on their laziness and inability to provide their own food, she suggested that it would be easier to supply them with provisions on these exhausted lands than if the Indians were removed to the West.[72]

Royall's comments were timely, for in 1830 the issue of Indian removal was at the forefront of public consciousness. In December 1829, Andrew Jackson had asked Congress for federal money to remove the southeastern Indians to west of the Mississippi. His request generated a massive petition drive by those opposed to removal and a national debate. Among those who entered the dispute were many evangelical northern women who in the 1820s had begun to take an interest in the welfare of Native Americans. Through their charitable organizations these women were at the heart of attempts to Christianize the Indians, raising funds for missions and Indian schools in the Northeast and South, seeing it as part of their moral and benevolent duty. The debate over Indian removal mobilized many of these women to organize anti-removal petitions, which asserted the right of Native Americans to their land and their own "right to speak" on the subject.[73] Royall viewed such efforts with scorn, echoing instead some of the arguments of southern legislators who depicted the Indians as unable or unwilling to make their land productive. She remained contemptuous of attempts to "civilize" the Indians, and she concluded that it was white attempts to "convert" them to Christianity that were at the bottom of many of the Indians' problems. Like the evangelical women, she believed she had a right to speak on the subject, but she took a very different stance. Prejudiced against many Native Americans and only able to see them as an obstacle in the way of white settlement, if she acknowledged the petition campaigns of these women at all, it was only to point out the erroneousness of their cause.[74]

Indian removal was not the only subject of public interest that mobilized women during the late 1820s. The future of slavery in the United States had long been a matter for public discussion, although it was not until the 1830s that large numbers of women became involved in campaigns to organize anti-slavery petitions.[75] Interestingly, since she was so vocal about many other subjects, Royall did not have a great deal to say about slavery, despite the fact that she traveled widely in the slaveholding states, especially during her final tour. When she did voice her opinions on the subject, they were generally at odds with those of many northern evangelical women. Her views were shaped by the fact that as a married woman she had owned slaves, and she had only reluctantly relinquished them as a consequence of the disastrous legal battle over her inheritance. Assuming her own superiority as a white woman, she saw no reason to challenge slavery. She reflected the attitude of many others from the slave states before the early 1830s, one of unquestioning acceptance of the "peculiar institution." For these people, slavery was an integral part of southern life, occasionally regarded as a necessary evil but also an institution that benefited all involved with it. As was true of her observations of Native Americans, however, Royall would sometimes romanticize what she considered to be picturesque aspects of her travels, particularly in her correspondence with Matt Dunbar. Her very occasional emotional outcries against slavery need to be seen in this context, against her much more usual acceptance of it: "As I lingered behind the party, thinking of my own negro children, the little things flocked around me, and as they were looking up in my face, eager to be caressed, I discovered the traces of tears on some of their cheeks. The sight pierced me to the heart. Oh, slavery, slavery! nothing can soften thee! thou art slavery still! Is there no hope high heaven?"[76]

While for the most part Royall accepted slavery, there were aspects of it that she did not care for and occasionally she remarked on them. She claimed to loath the effects of slavery on both whites and blacks because of the impact it had on the sensibility of their feelings, and the failure of slave-owners to enlighten the minds of their slaves. Thus she could remark, "Not that the slaves are treated bad. If we except the total neglect, on the part of their owners, to enlighten their minds, they live as well as their masters; and are by no means hard tasked. But they are the most immoral and cruel brutes in the world." Slavery as an institution did little to civilize either the slaves themselves or, frequently, their owners, she concluded.[77] In Alexandria she remarked on the varying colors of the black people, some of them almost white, and was appalled that a freeborn American could impose slavery on his offspring.[78] But if she was repelled by certain facets of slavery, she showed no inclination to condemn the institution for that reason. In her eyes, slavery was neither immoral nor cruel, for the slaves were well-treated and benefited from the paternal attitude of their masters: "Many of our northern people who cry out against the south, for slavery, I fancy would be glad to swap situations with these slaves. I have been told it is the pride of those southern people to treat their slaves with kindness and lenity, it is their interest to do so, and the looks of the slaves prove it."[79] She evinced no interest in the morality of slavery itself, despite her concerns to protect American liberties—for white people.

Royall's racial attitudes were not very different from those of her contemporaries. She was convinced of the superiority of the white race and was paternalistic in her attitude toward African Americans, seeing them as childlike and in need of guidance. She expected her authority to be recognized, however, and was quick to condemn any behavior she construed as insolence. Her sense of superiority was not confined only to the slave population, for she displayed similar attitudes toward other groups. In her reaction to free blacks, it is evident that she did not believe they were equal to white Americans. She was particularly incensed by the demeanor of free blacks in Washington where many were employed as doormen to boardinghouses. Affronted by their refusal to allow her entry or their "insolence" when they did, Royall condemned free blacks as a class for carrying out the orders of their employers. She admitted that there was little to distinguish the doormen's manners from those of the boardinghouse proprietors, but her ire was concentrated on the doormen.[80]

Rarely moderate when expressing her views, she displayed a similar dislike of other groups she regarded as "inferior." She described Irish immigrants as the "most unpolished, uncouth looking people." The women especially were "the most disgusting in their appearance and manners, of any females I have seen."[81] Moreover, although she did not address the subject of slavery as an institution in great detail, she was zealous in her arguments in defense of it in the District of Columbia. When Benjamin Lundy launched a petition campaign to abolish slavery in the district, she denounced the initiative in the pages of her *Black Books*. She was adamant that the slaves in the District of Columbia should not be emancipated, and that both they and Washington society would suffer if they were. By liberating the slaves, she argued, the city would be flooded with free blacks who would pose a danger to the public: "But what relief to the evil complained of is to be effected by liberating the slaves? are they to be sent off? or are they to flock here? We are now devoured with them. Their number is dangerous and a serious evil, inasmuch as the bread and clothes they devour would go to the relief and comfort of the suffering poor."[82] Besides, she declaimed, the number of free blacks in Washington already contributed to the indigence of whites—since they took most of the available work and money away from more deserving white widows and their children, leaving them without the means of support.[83] With little interest in the welfare of the slaves, she dismissed the activities of the colonization societies and any attempts to free the slaves.

Throughout her tours Royall espoused opinions on subjects that revealed her sense of the values of the American republic, but also reflected a class and regional perspective. Her viewpoint was the product of her own experience and was often self-serving—she was, for instance, much more concerned about poverty and the causes of it than many of her contemporaries.[84] She frequently echoed the themes of male travel writers, but she did not generally display the same kind of boastfulness about America and its institutions that many foreign travel writers declared was the general attitude of the Americans they met.[85] On the contrary, she was fearful for the future of America's ideals, and as a consequence was more judgmental of her fellow Americans than were later American writers. These writers were often defensive in reaction to the stinging criticisms of British writers such as Basil Hall and Frances Trollope. Royall, writing slightly earlier, was largely unconcerned with these foreign travel writers. Her main interest was in her fellow Americans, and she was not afraid of being critical, even if this meant effectively endorsing the views of foreigners.[86] Nonetheless, she was not unpatriotic. She took great personal pride in the United States and the traditions of American liberty, and believed that many of the faults she found among her fellow Americans were due to ignorance and a want of republican principles.[87] Often impatient and critical, she was quick to condemn when confronted by aspects of American life that did not seem to her to uphold the cause for which Americans had fought the Revolutionary War.

Like many other travel writers, Royall aimed to entertain her audience as much as to expound her views on the social and political state of the country. Her books were full of anecdotes, descriptions of curiosities, and tales of her experiences. She depicted herself as an indefatigable traveler who sought out the most beautiful vistas, most up-to-date facts and figures, and the "best" people to describe to her readers, alongside the less pleasing aspects of American society. She also maintained a sense of adventure throughout her travels, and was rarely deterred either by fear for her own safety or by a sense of propriety. As she grew older, however, her willingness to endure discomfort or danger diminished, and she increasingly emphasized the trials she underwent to bring her works to the public. In describing her adventures on the road, she highlighted the sacrifices she made on behalf of her readers and the stoicism with which she overcame the obstacles in her way.[88]

Despite the improvements in transportation, travel in the 1820s could be dangerous and unpredictable, especially where the terrain was difficult and the area remote. During her early tours she accepted natural hazards as part of the adventure of travel and eagerly embraced them. Mountains and valleys inspired her with a sense of awe, and she described her perilous progress through them in language borrowed from her reading. Thus in western Virginia on a journey on horseback, she enthused, "At length, from the summit of a frightful chasm, formed by the passage of New river through this mountain, you behold that foaming river rolling far beneath your feet, while with shivering fear and dizzy head, you wind your way down to it."[89] Her stagecoach rides through the mountains of Pennsylvania and her river trip up the Mississippi could elicit a similar response, but as her initial enthusiasm for travel waned, she became increasingly unwilling to put herself at risk voluntarily.

The difficulties occasioned by the poor roads were unavoidable, and though she sometimes reacted with impatience, she generally took them in her stride, or so she asserted in recalling the incidents. She frequently used these occasions to portray herself as the savior of the situation and the only person with the presence of mind to solve the problem. Her account of a road blocked by a fallen tree outside Charleston, South Carolina, was typical. She, rather than the stage-driver, organized her fellow travelers to unload the stagecoach, lift the body off the wheels, lead the horses around the tree, and carry the wheels over it. This was done with the help of a "Negro" to whom she gave 25 cents—an act of benevolence, she boasted, which was not copied by the other passengers who gave him nothing. Even under her direction, she maintained, it took a full hour.[90] Sometimes the hazards were more serious, but in her version of the stories, she never lost her nerve and was always to the forefront in rescuing the situation. Thus, in the late autumn of 1828, as the stagecoach in which she was traveling drew near to Middletown, Pennsylvania, it became clear that the Swatara River was flooded. The only means to cross the river was to place the coach in the ferryboat, but the river was high, and the boat with the stagecoach aboard quickly became lodged on a tree stump. Since no other boat was available, no assistance was possible from the shore. As Royall observed,

> The ferrymen, however, were doing all they could, by running the stage to the stern, and working hard with their poles to set the boat either back or forward. I persuaded the young man to put his shoulder, not to the wheel, but to the pole, and push for his life. He did so. I encouraged them all—told them "No danger—only keep her steady—we will soon be free—push hard my boys—that is right—a little more—it is coming.["] Their faces were red from exertion, and by persevering and the aid of the wind, we succeeded. A miraculous escape, indeed! Had our horses been wild we would doubtless have to sink or swim, like the witches of old.[91]

Royall's near escape from drowning in the swollen rivers of Pennsylvania, and the delays caused by fallen trees in South Carolina, were just some of the many hazards she and other travelers of this period experienced during their travels in the United States. But if such crises resulting from poor weather conditions, bad roads, and difficult terrain were common at this time to all travelers, there were other dangers peculiar to Royall. For, while she attracted an audience for her books and claimed to have friends willing to help her all over the United States, there were also those who did not find her opinions acceptable. Moreover, her behavior as she traveled attracted attention, much of it unfavorable. Certainly she was not the only woman who journeyed alone on public transport during the 1820s, but Royall's demeanor, her insistence on her right to express forthright opinions, and her increasing focus on religious and political issues meant that she made many enemies.

5 · A Virago Errant in Enchanted Armor

In mid-1830, Anne Royall arrived by steamboat at Vicksburg, a new settlement on the Mississippi River, and as she did so, she remarked on the beauty of the spot: "The site is one of the richest, as to the soil and scenery, I would suppose on the river. A richer soil or more romantic scenery, nature never formed."[1] But her reception there did not match the wealth of the scenery. She had expected to be greeted by supporters, but the man she had summoned walked past her remarking, "I want nothing to do with you madam, I dislike your character."[2] When she attempted to claim the room in a tavern her friends had secured for her, the landlord ordered her out of the house. More was in store for her. Having failed to find a room in the tavern, she called on the master of the Masonic lodge, expecting that her status as a Masonic widow would afford her an introduction as it had on her earlier travels. He refused to aid her, even when she offered him money to find her a room. A young man eventually helped her to obtain lodgings in a different tavern, but she was shaken and affronted by the reception she had received. Unwilling to concede that her own behavior or reputation might have been the cause of the insults and poor treatment, she asserted haughtily that the first tavern keeper was a man of bad character and had lost all his possessions to debt. All the others, she supposed, were influenced by the presence in town of "missionaries" who "preach all day and murder all night."[3] Still worse, though the newspaper editors were friendly, she concluded that neither of them was independent enough to afford her the treatment to which she believed she was entitled. She employed the episode to decry the dangers of a corrupt press, perverted by the missionaries and the Bank of the United States: "I fear our American press is done. We can no longer say we have a free press; and, I take it, a corrupt press is the *greatest* enemy of the people. A corrupt press is worse than an invasion—it is the true war pestilence and famine."[4] As she left the town two days later, she commented again on the beauty of the place, as if nature could atone for the rough treatment she had received: "The magnolia was in full bloom, and would seem to compensate one for the rudeness of the place."[5]

If Royall was insulted by the reception she received in Vicksburg, there were those who were equally offended by her behavior. Convinced that she was in the right, she conceived of herself as the injured party and condemned the people of Vicksburg for their hostility toward her. But she failed to acknowledge the effect her writing could have on others. The account of a witness to the events suggests that the incident in Vicksburg was likely the result of her own provocative conduct, and his remarks were echoed by the reactions of others to similar episodes elsewhere. For by 1830 Royall had gained an unenviable reputation as an intrusive and abusive woman, and they did not wish to be associated with her. The account by William Bodley, a visitor who encountered Royall in Vicksburg, sheds a quite different light on her reception there:

> We have also had within a few days past, a union of those moral pests & more—Mrs. Royall & the Methodists. These latter had their 3 days meeting while at the same time & within the very verge of the sanctuary, that modern xantippe held her heathenish court & abused Gods people & his "saints" without measure or mercy. She is the very she devil—I had the courage to pay her a visit & that at a most alarming season—when she had just driven out of her room a gentleman who had gone to make humble acknowledgments for a supposed offence, a very trivial one too.[6]

While Bodley may well have embellished his story in trying to amuse his female correspondent, his reaction to Royall reflected some of the concerns other observers had about her. Many people found her treatment of "respectable citizens" and her ill-mannered anti-clericalism repugnant—Bodley's disgust was not unusual. As he continued his story, he confessed that he had approached the authoress with some trepidation because of her reputation: "My first view of her ladyship was when she was driving this gentleman out, & her face seemed full of the furies. On my entrance however she received me graciously. My apprehensions kept me in the background & I only *listened* to her conversation with myself & others who were present. Prudence chained my tongue. She has ordered no less than 5 gentlemen out of her presence in the 2 days she has been here. I was completely disgusted with the old hag."[7] His prudence paid off. Despite her habit of caricaturing those she met, he was overlooked in Royall's description of Vicksburg.

The incident in Vicksburg was not the first time Royall encountered a hostile reception when she arrived in a town. Neither was her claim she had been attacked by pernicious forces for exposing their designs anything new. Nor was it the first time that observers had expressed their distaste at Royall's behavior or opinions. As she journeyed around the United States people welcomed her, but just as frequently they greeted her with insults or injury. Royall divided public opinion. Most obviously this was because of the flattering or abusive descriptions of individuals she published in her books. Her readers understood these to be dependent on how she was treated by those she portrayed. More significantly, as William Bodley hinted, she used her books as a forum from which to express an impassioned anti-evangelicalism and to wage a campaign against the developing evangelical influence in the new republic, particularly their efforts to convert women to the cause. Moreover, she attacked their efforts to impose Sabbath observance, especially their attempts to repeal the federal law allowing for the delivery of the mail on Sunday. As the evangelicals sought to gain ascendancy, Royall frequently clashed with them. Occasionally they reacted violently, but more usually they branded her as an enemy of religion. Thus the furious reactions to Royall were not simply the resentment of those she portrayed unsympathetically in print, but a reflection of the depth of support for the evangelical cause in the late 1820s.

After the publication of her first book, there were few places, even in the most remote parts of the republic, where Royall was not known by reputation. The more she traveled, the more likely she was to encounter various hazards, which were largely the consequence of the notoriety she quickly acquired on her tours. In the course of her trips around the country she was physically assaulted more than once, mobbed by students, almost ejected from a stagecoach by the driver and her fellow passengers, and feared for her life on more than one occasion. According to her own account, stagecoach drivers, passengers, innkeepers, and others she met on her tours insulted and slandered her in letters. Many newspaper editors published comments about her, some of them contemptuous and others little short of abusive.

Royall often deliberately provoked such episodes. Her abrasive personality and lack of respect for others' reputations did much to irritate people, and they often reacted badly when she attempted to call on them. They took further offense when she included unflattering descriptions of them in her books. For while Royall focused initially on depicting the places she visited on her travels, she quickly realized that one of the most popular features of her books was what she called "pen portraits" of prominent citizens in these towns and villages. The often-colorful descriptions of people soon gained a name for their author, and she believed that the pen portraits, even the uncomplimentary ones, encouraged people to buy her works. As she argued, "I wish to write books that people will read, and I find that there is nothing like throwing in plenty of spice, and possibly many gentlemen may not like his portrait (for which he can give no reason) yet twenty other gentlemen may, and may buy the book for the sake of the portrait."[8] The novelty of such descriptions attracted a readership, for there was nothing of this nature published in the newspapers of the time, and they enabled her readers to picture what eminent citizens looked like. Royall's belief proved accurate; people often bought her books to discover what she had written about them, as well as their friends and acquaintances. Others clearly avoided her to ensure they did not appear in the pages of her works, but even prominent men awaited the publication of the books with a mixture of anxiety and eagerness. John Tyler of Virginia, for instance, noted in a letter to his daughter: "Mrs. Royall's book is here at last. . . . She speaks highly of all of us, particularly of yourself." Still, he added, "But mark now, Mrs. Royall's praise is of very little value; and, therefore, you are not to be rendered vain by it."[9]

Most of the pen portraits were benign in character, and they were often formulaic and repetitive. The element of excitement came from their novelty and her colorful portrayals of prominent and lesser citizens, which she made readily available for all to read in print. Royall attributed to her subjects physical traits that were designed to reflect their characters, and she became adept at using the portraits to convey her opinions of people. Thus she described President John Thornton Kirkland of Harvard College as a gracious and upright man: "President Kirtland is of middling age and stature, portly figure, and fair complexion, his face round and comely, with a blue eye, his mouth small, his teeth regular and beautiful, his countenance noble, frank, and intelligent."[10] But other portraits were more acerbic and occasionally biting, such as the sketch of a Mr. D. of New Haven who had refused her aid: "His face resembles a full moon, in shape, and as red as a fiery furnace; the effects of drinking pure *water*, no doubt. His red face, contrasted with his white head (which, being grey, he covers with powder, being ashamed of his grey hairs, as well he may) gives him an odd appearance. His countenance, arrogant, haughty, and imperious."[11]

Although many people bought Royall's books because of the pen portraits, others were irritated by the imposition. Her descriptions of the receptions she experienced as she traveled provoked angry reactions, for she was fulsome in her praise of those who welcomed her, bought her books, and supported her in other ways, but vitriolic in her comments on those who rebuffed her. Refusing to acknowledge that her invasion of people's homes and demands that they should buy her books might be at the root of the hostile treatment she received, she would portray herself as the innocent victim of these encounters. Moreover, she insinuated that those who repudiated her were uncharitable and unpatriotic, for they had refused aid to the poor widow of a Revolutionary War officer, a woman who deserved the support of her countrymen because her husband had fought bravely for their liberties. Thus she besmirched the characters of people who crossed her without regard for their social status or reputation, concerned only with the way they treated her.[12] But the rude descriptions of individuals and stinging comments about the demeanor of those she encountered led her victims to retaliate. These people were affronted by Royall's behavior, they found her manners uncouth, and she violated their understanding of refined womanhood. She exhibited none of the modesty and retiring nature that they had come to regard as the traits of a woman from the respectable middle class, and for this reason they felt no compunction in expressing their distaste for her.[13]

Among those who criticized Royall's behavior was John Quincy Adams. He made telling remarks in his diary about what he thought of the pen portraits and her conduct: "Mrs. Royall came from Boston in the same stage with my son Charles. She is going to Plymouth, and travelling about the country to make another book. She continues to make herself noxious to many persons; tolerated by some and feared by others, by her deportment and her books; treating all with a familiarity which often passes for impudence, insulting those who treat her with incivility, and then lampooning them in her books."[14]

Others besides Adams objected in private, noting their feelings in their personal correspondence. Her methods were evidently widely disliked. A Mr. J. G. Meem of Lynchburg, Virginia, reported Royall's visit in terms that were not untypical: "The celebrated Mrs. Royall of slanderous renown is on a visit to this place at present—she has thrown our town into confusion, the old and the young, the pious and impious, male & female are all smarting under the lash of her impious and uncontrollable tongue, or fearing a rencontre with her from which no one feels secure as she boldly stalks into home & counting house shop & tavern and assails without rhyme or reason—I didn't buy her book—and therefore I am to have a place in her black book."[15]

Others were more open and public in their dislike of Royall's manners and books. Newspaper editors quickly began to comment on her bookselling methods, which became so infamous that, it was said, some public figures hid when a visit from Royall was expected. One editor tried to treat her practices as a joke: "She cleared one day all the cabinet of Washington out of the city. Would she not be a useful auxiliary to his majesty's ministry?"[16] Many tried hard to avoid her in order to escape her unfavorable reports, but this did not always protect them from her comments.

Royall's public lambasting of prominent members of the community amused some people, but others were exasperated by her behavior and the popularity she gained through her biting comments on public figures. Newspaper editors reflected a range of views, copying editorials from other papers to add force to their own opinions. The impassioned reactions and extreme language used by these editors in condemning Royall's demands for attention, and their irritation at her forwardness, reflected the unsettling effect she had on many of the people she came across in her travels. She provoked anxiety in them because she claimed to be a respectable woman with honorable connections, and yet her behavior was, in their opinion, that of an unruly, lower-class woman who forced herself into their consciousness and private spaces, without regard to the niceties of polite society. Their discomfort suggests that Royall reinforced their more general fears about uncontrollable women, for she contravened their understanding of submissive femininity and affronted their sensibilities at a time when such notions were being debated and reframed in the context of social and economic changes. As one New York publisher revealed before even seeing Royall's first volume in print, "A more contemptible work was never palmed upon any community. The author possesses no one quality of a book maker, unless it be confidence, of which she has a competent share." His objections to her method of collecting subscriptions suggest that she violated many of the conventions of polite society: "She goes into families without the least ceremony, and if her reception is not such as suits her, she will threaten the master or mistress of it, with *exposure in her book*. . . . Many very respectable persons are grossly abused in her first volume, apparently for the sole reason that they did not treat her with as much attention as she thought proper to demand; and it is probable many others will meet with the same fate in her second."[17] Some of her critics believed that Royall had to be silenced for she made a mockery of attempts by an emerging middle class to create private havens of their homes and impose their own notions of what constituted "proper behavior" on the wider society.

The attitude of these newspaper editors echoed a more general alienation from Royall's methods, and these men's opinions were important in influencing the reception she received as she traveled around the United States.[18] Certainly some editors supported her, but even those who were sympathetic might ridicule her in the columns of their newspapers, emphasizing the absence of delicacy in her person and writing. One editor quoted extensively from her latest publication but then commented, "If Mrs. Royall has talent (and she certainly has a *tact* at writing,) for making books—and if they are either to be forced upon the public, or the people who refuse to be abused for refusing, let it at least be composed of language, which would not disgrace those 'Syrens' who promenade our streets at certain seasons, 'chanting the eulogy of deceased mackerel.'"[19] Most editors were much more concerned about her behavior, however, than her language. The editor of the *New England Galaxy* mocked what he saw as her unfeminine conduct and her expectation that gentlemen would protect her from the consequences of her behavior:

> Mrs. Royall, the celebrated traveler, who lately challenged, a gentleman at Johnstown, New-York, to fight her with pistols, has arrived in the city of New-York, from the fashionable tour to Saratoga, Niagara, Arrarat, etc. The editor of the *Advocate* states that she called on him and asked why he had been so ungallant as to suffer the widow of a revolutionary officer to be assailed by two or three of his neighboring editors, without raising a hand in her defence. In this dilemma he says, he made the best reply he could, by telling her that she herself was so competent to the task that he was unwilling to spoil a good defence by forestalling her own talents.[20]

Although neither Royall nor even her books might have been seen in a particular part of the country before, she would be known by reputation. The spread of literacy following the Revolution led to a rapid expansion in the number of newspaper titles published daily and weekly, and these attracted a new and diverse audience. Newspapers distributed information rapidly, and news items began to travel quickly across regions as people subscribed to newspapers from distant towns and editors reprinted stories gleaned from other titles.[21] As editors gathered stories from across the country, snippets of gossip and items that poked fun at public figures were spread around the nation—a Boston editor might copy from a New York paper, and in turn a piece might be reprinted in a southern newspaper. In this way Royall began to enjoy a certain celebrity, but it might also mean that the enmity of an editor in one part of the country could have unexpected consequences.[22]

Celebrity came in different guises in the early republic, but it became national when "heroes," and even "heroines," traveled around the country and their tours were reported in the press. Thus a revolutionary hero like the Marquis de Lafayette was fêted when he traveled the country in 1824, presidents were greeted with pageants and civic dinners as they toured, and those who won acclaim on the stage might be equally lionized. On a lesser scale, Deborah Sampson, the Revolutionary War soldier, could attract considerable crowds to her lectures because of the novelty of her story.[23] Royall's fame, however, rested largely on her reputation for intruding on "respectable" members of society and abusing those who refused to buy her books. To the newspaper editors who contributed to the publicity surrounding her, it was a celebrity based on bad, but more particularly unwomanly, behavior. But it also sold her books.

Royall frequently emphasized that her books were popular, and she boasted of the crowds of well-wishers she attracted in the towns where she stopped. She declared too that "friends" invited her to visit their towns specifically to write about them, because her books were so much in demand. Occasionally, prominent local citizens such as those in Harrisburg treated her as a person of importance, held dinners in her honor, and escorted her around town.[24] The inclusion of such details in her books boosted her sense of self-importance, but this was not just idle boasting for her visits did generate considerable interest. The publicity generated by newspaper commentaries, whether favorable or not, had made her well-known, and as a consequence, she drew crowds curious to see her in person.

For many people Royall's status as an author made her an attraction, for if she included them in her future books, they too could gain a share of publicity—if some avoided her for this reason, others sought her out for the same object. Even as they were affronted by her rough manners, newspaper editors recognized that Royall's books offered her readers what they wanted—aspects of their country's history associated with particular places, portraits of the leading citizens in each town, and descriptions of landscapes that most of them could not enjoy personally. Despite the irritation they provoked among many, the pen portraits contributed toward creating a market for her books.[25] In some of the towns she visited Royall was celebrated as a popular author. These more positive aspects of her celebrity were often lost on those editors who believed she should not be encouraged. The receptions she encountered were frequently influenced by the accounts that appeared in newspapers, and as a result, could not be predicted.

Given her reputation it is not surprising that on hearing who she was, Royall's fellow stagecoach passengers responded either by trying to avoid her attention or by insulting her. Occasionally this went beyond verbal abuse. Although she was prone to exaggerate the gravity of incidents, her accounts of the treatment she occasionally received suggest that her celebrity had its drawbacks. For instance, in February 1830, she visited Charlottesville, Virginia, where she announced her presence in town. On arrival, she reported, she was mobbed by students from the University of Virginia who surrounded her carriage, shouting and yelling. Outraged, she declared that this could only have been done with the intention of frightening her horses. Moreover, they did not leave her in peace in the tavern where she was staying. That evening a large party of students invaded her sitting room, and it took some time to push them out. The next day, on returning from a day's trip to view Monticello, they again mobbed her parlor. While the landlord stood guard, the students thundered at the door. Her escape was effected eventually, but only with the help of the landlord and a number of "fine gentlemen."[26]

The reaction from the faculty of the university was quite different. They simply laid low—an attitude she found equally insulting. As she commented, "Thus it has happened to the celebrated University (of vagabonds I was going to say) of Virginia! And the faculty have had the effrontery to apply to the legislature for more money. I understood they were a parcel of low dissipated Englishmen, who, like so many gluttons, spend their time gormandizing—eating and drinking up the funds, and suffering the students to run wild. How true the first part of this is, I cannot say, as the faculty took care not to show their faces, but the conduct of the students goes far to confirm it."[27] The incident frightened Royall, and she was grateful for the protection she received, but in her usual style, she attacked the faculty for their failure to control the youthful exuberance of the students. She expected that they, rather than the unruly students, should have greeted her in a manner more appropriate to her status.[28]

By the time she visited Charlottesville, Royall was a well-known public figure, and she had gained many enemies. But the intensity of the reaction to her cannot be explained only by the irritation of those she lampooned in her pen portraits or the disruption caused by her social calls. Their criticisms were just one aspect of the response, for she divided opinion and incited mixed reactions, as she remarked: "Since the appearance of my sketches, I have observed one thing in my travels, which I did not when writing the Sketches, viz. the moment I make my appearance in any town or village, one part of the community avoid me as they would a pestilence, while another part advance to meet me with demonstrations of anything but fear." She did not offer a reason why, as she continued, "The cause of this difference is not my business: my business is simply the facts."[29]

As an author Royall's subject matter and her writings were highly controversial, and when coupled with her willingness to confront those who did not share her views, the outcome was both divisive and potentially hazardous. But reactions to Royall also exposed some of the tensions in American society during the 1820s, especially those related to the growing impact of the evangelical revivalists and their influence on women. For Royall entered fully into the controversies surrounding the role of the churches in the public life of the new nation, and she deliberately goaded and aggravated the agents of the evangelical revivals, whom she called variously "missionaries," "Presbyterians," "priests," and "blackcoats." They did not accept her constant attacks passively, as her strident opposition offered a challenge from a quarter they were not prepared to ignore—a woman with a public voice and an audience.

From the outset Royall expressed her disdain for what she regarded as false piety and religious bigotry, and throughout her travels she took a particular interest in the behavior of clergymen of various sects. She was especially troubled by the progress of the evangelical revivals that gripped different parts of the country, and her books became a vehicle to chart the developing authority of the "missionaries." Unlike many other women of the time, she did not regard these "priests" as a benign agency; rather, she depicted them as a pernicious and treacherous force. Condemnation of the revivals and their instigators began to dominate her books as she sought to warn her countrymen of the dangers they posed to American liberties. Her concerns reflected the religious turmoil of the 1820s, with the evangelicals seeking to assert their influence and convince Americans to embrace revived Protestantism while attempting to overthrow Enlightenment and freethinking rationalism. Although the evangelicals did eventually win ascendancy, this was not a foregone conclusion.[30] Following disestablishment in the decades after the Revolution, religious affiliation became a matter of individual choice, as allegiance to a state religion ceased to be a requirement. Consequently, the clergy of the established churches, especially the Congregationalists in New England, had to compete in an open market for converts as one of a growing number of diverse Protestant sects. They were remarkably successful, but the revitalization in religion did not happen spontaneously—evangelicals consciously fostered revivals, and they also sought to crush opposition to their goal of creating a Christian society.[31]

The evangelical movement avowedly and deliberately sought to permeate all aspects of American society. Its leaders set about doing so in a highly organized manner. The evangelical movement was methodical, vocal, and nationwide at a time when there were few other national institutions, and the federal government was comparatively weak. The leaders of the evangelical movement self-consciously sought to democratize Christianity through revivals and by means of voluntary societies. Many of their efforts were aimed at augmenting clerical influence by expanding church membership but also through initiatives to train more clergy and encourage the laity to support training schools for missionaries. The leaders sought to arrest the increasing secularization of American life, and aimed to shape society and opinion to reflect evangelical values. During the 1820s especially, as they attempted to establish their hegemony, the evangelicals were sensitive to any opposition to their aims. In this context, Royall's activities and her harassment of the evangelicals in print and person seemed to many of them to be a danger to their goals.[32]

Royall's writings exposed her deep-seated animosity toward the evangelicals. While it is unclear where this originated, it seems to have grown out of the rationalist ideas she absorbed as part of her education. Drawing on the Enlightenment authors she had read and the conversations she had had, both with her husband and with Matthew Dunbar, she cultivated strong views about the practitioners of Christianity and the role of the church in American life. Her anti-clericalism and attacks on the "priests" echo those of the rationalists and Deists of the Revolutionary Era and later Freethinkers.[33] Although she rarely explored her own religious beliefs in print, she retained her belief in God, as she revealed in one of her few observations on the subject to Dunbar in 1817: "In the firm belief, that the worship of God is paramount to all other duties, I spurn the narrow mind, which is attached to a sect or party, to the exclusion of the rest of mankind. Can *I* not implore the Divine mercy? . . . I am far from being among the number of those, who set at nought the worship of the Deity, however I may deplore the abominable prostitution of that religion which is pure and undefiled."[34]

Her comments suggest that her anti-clericalism was well developed by the time she moved to Alabama, and it was drawn from her reading and experience. Her early remarks about the revivals she witnessed in Alabama foreshadowed some of her later attacks on the more orthodox clergy, for she suggested that the priests were power-hungry: "But the Priests, I perceive, are precisely the same they were centuries passed—they all aim at power. Their drift, I see, is to gain as many proselytes as possible, without regard to the *conduct* of their flock—they will not suffer them to possess any will of their own—perfect despots." They were uninterested in whether their followers adhered to the precepts of the scriptures or acted in an appropriate manner. As long as they were submissive to the "priests," they could behave however they liked and not one of them was interested in relieving the poor.[35] Condemning both these priests and their converts for ignorance and hypocrisy, she asserted that the clergy had no interest in teaching their adherents the true meaning of Christianity.[36]

If Royall had been scornful of the ignorance and duplicity of the frontier preachers and revivalists in Alabama, the extent of her prejudice became still more obvious as she moved east. She made only a few remarks about the evangelicals in her first printed work, but as she traveled around the country, they seemed ubiquitous and her animosity toward them developed quickly. Initially she denounced them only for their lack of charity when they failed to help her. "It is a burlesque on religion to say they are Christians, or even civilized; the heathen whom they pretend to convert, could not have behaved more savage," she declared, "those Calvinists, a furnace seven times hot, would not melt *them* to pity."[37] While she continued to excoriate the "missionaries" for their hardheartedness, her condemnation of them became much more pointed.

Some of her attacks were very personal, poking fun at their appearance and their concentration on converting women rather than men: "They are uniformly dressed in black, an emblem of their business. Their visage is long, their complexion a dirty wan; they are generally tall, gaunt, and supple! distant and vulgar in their manners, the gloom in their countenance is never interrupted with a smile. They usually have a train of women after them with the same lowering looks."[38] She would also accuse the missionaries of ignorance, hypocrisy, and greed. Her attitude was more than just a personal matter—having developed a deep skepticism about certain forms of religious practice, she shared with others a dislike of the bigotry of evangelical religion. Increasingly she also charged them with malicious designs. She aimed to persuade her readers that the evangelicals should be stopped. Unconcerned that her views would alienate a section of the national community and affect the sale of her books, she vented her spleen against the evangelicals and focused on the damage she believed they were doing to the country and its principles. As a consequence, her books began to polarize opinion: both on the issues surrounding the evangelical revivals and on the way people perceived her.

Her attacks on these ministers became more and more strident, as she moved beyond the personal to lambast their motives and actions. In her eyes they were the source of all the country's problems, and she took a highly simplistic view. Thus, in an attempt to persuade her readers of the dangers posed by these "priests," she attributed the poverty and crime in some towns and states to the hypocrisy of what she called "pious preaching" and their emphasis on "conversion" rather than moral behavior. In Vermont, she noted there were twice as many occupants of the state prison as in either New Hampshire or Maine, while the population of the state was smaller. The difference, she suggested, was that Vermont was overrun with missionaries. As she commented, this should be a lesson to everyone: "This ought to open the eyes of the people to priestcraft: the whole State, I am told, or at least a great majority, are your godly orthodox. Whence then comes all this wickedness. The abominable hypocrites—why do they not employ their missionaries at home."[39]

Hypocrisy and false piety were not the only transgressions with which Royall accused these ministers. She also quickly began to focus on their money-making activities and the wide range of organizations they established. Because she traveled so widely, she was able to observe the extent of evangelical influence, and she used her books as a platform from which to inform her readers of her concerns. Aiming to alarm, she initially concentrated on the breadth of their activities and the way that these enabled the "priests" to enter into every area of American life. Thus, she wrote from Petersburg, Virginia:

> And here, even here, in this garden spot of taste and refinement, the missionaries have crept in! Can no part of our fair country escape the griping fangs of those ferocious marauders? From Maine to Georgia—from the Atlantic to Missouri, they swarm like locusts; and under the name of *foreign* missions, *home* missions, *Bible* societies, *tract* societies, societies for educating *pious* young men, to spread the gospel, *pincushion* societies, *cent* societies, *mite* societies, *widows'* societies, *children's* societies, *rag-bag* societies, and Sunday school societies, they have laid the whole country under contribution![40]

It was not just the ubiquity of the evangelicals or the range of their activities that worried Royall, but the sums of money they collected for these societies. For, she continued, "figures cannot calculate the amount collected by those public and private robbers; it is more than would liberate every slave in the United States; it would pay the British debt!"[41]

Royall framed her criticisms in terms of a plot to overrun the country, and she saw their money-making activities as the preparation of a war chest to overturn American liberties and establish a religious tyranny.[42] She also maintained that there was evidence the missionaries were building their forces to impose their rule, and women were crucial to their aims. Hence she broadened the focus of her attacks to embrace the women they sought to convert. For, she feared, the evangelicals were gaining an excessive and destructive influence over these women, causing them to lose their natural charitable impulses and spend their time and money supporting missionaries. Consequently, men were beginning to lose their respect for women, and she warned her sex that until the missionaries were defeated, men would look down on them:

> I am determined those blackcoats shall not hold my sex any longer in subjection. I will never have done until I banish priestcraft, religious tyranny, superstition and bigotry from amongst my sex—to be sure it is some-

> thing like overturning a mountain, but this does not deter me, if I cannot turn the mountain over, I will cut through it. The impious frauds of those priests have too long disgraced the fairest part of creation. Dress woman up in the fair face of *true* religion, dealing charity and blessings around her, she is the most enviable of nature's works—she would no longer be slighted by the other sex.[43]

As she traveled around the country, Royall made it clear to her readers that the priests' sway over women was mounting quickly, and that they must be stopped: "The blue-skins are increasing fast in Augusta; if these southern gentlemen, do not look sharp to their wives and daughters, the Missionaries will have the whole of them,—I was told they had got on the right side of about two thirds."[44] Once converted, she admonished, these women would become uncharitable and spend all their time chasing around after the missionaries, running Sunday schools, raising money, distributing tracts, and neglecting their duties to the destitute and afflicted.[45] Still more disturbing was that once the priests had converted the women, "it is easy to gull the men." She could not understand why women could be so foolish, and she began to despair of her sex: "I would ask my sex, if they can be so blind to those wicked priests? it is impossible they can, but I have no hopes of reclaiming my sex, after what I have seen and heard myself."[46]

The consequence of her warnings, she asserted, was that the missionaries encouraged these "godly" women to turn against her when she arrived in certain towns. In Carlisle, Pennsylvania, where her supporters had invited her to give the "blueskins" a "dressing," one of these women was overheard to say that Mrs. Royall's guide was gallanting a harlot. She was still more incensed to receive a letter sent from Carlisle, which "was the most obscene piece ever penned," and in her view could only be the work of a woman.[47] For while these women were the dupes of the Presbyterians, they fueled the priests' activities and neglected their true duties as Christian women: "It is the popularity of those priests with our women, that has ruined the country; our females will go all lengths to oblige them; they stint themselves, starve their children and servants, live on half allowance, work day and night, lay all schemes, and even steal from their husbands to give to these priests; the duties of a christian, the duties of a mother, the duties of wife, friend, and neighbor, are all sacrificed to those money-glutted monsters."[48]

Royall's remarks about the evangelicals' insidious influence on women highlight the developing acceptance among some women of evangelical ideas about female behavior and duties. But such ideas were not embraced without a contest, as her warnings and recognition of the many women who were not the "dupes" of the "priests" suggest. She saw the change in very negative terms, decrying the loss of compassion she perceived among evangelical women and the undermining of older female values. In her portrayal of the women she met, she emphasized the worth she put on those women who were charitable and treated her with kindness—characteristics she also claimed for herself. In contrast, she accused the evangelical women of false piety and disparaged those who made a great show of attending church. She was especially critical of those involved in missionary societies, for in her view, they did not display true Christian behavior.[49]

Royall observed on her travels what historians have subsequently argued, that numerically women often represented the greatest number of converts during revivals and made up the great majority of churchgoers. As she noted, many of the evangelical clergy sought women as their allies against the increasingly secular society of the early nineteenth century.[50] By the end of the 1820s, through religious revivals and church organizations, evangelical ministers had encouraged many women to join their churches and assume a major role in the Christianization of America. They convinced these women to become involved in sponsoring missionaries, establishing benevolent societies, and creating associations to reform society. They did so in large numbers, and as a result, ministers and social commentators began to portray women as by nature pious.[51] But there was no inevitability to the correlation between women and evangelical religion; women had to be persuaded of the advantages of piety and, possibly of more importance, the dangers of irreligion. For the intimate relationship between women and evangelical religion was neither as logical nor as predictable as some historians have suggested. During the 1820s, this notion was still contested, and the evangelical clergy worked hard to convince women, particularly women of the emerging middle class, of their attachment to religion. They worked equally hard to suppress any opposition to their objectives.[52]

For this reason, the evangelical clergy reacted strongly to any threats to their authority or their attempts to Christianize women, especially if those challenges came from women. As Royall discovered, in areas where the evangelicals were active, they did not welcome her intrusions. The attacks on her may therefore be explained as attempts by these evangelicals to protect their position and to prevent her from being taken seriously. They aimed to diminish her, and sometimes they did so by questioning her morality, as they had done in Carlisle when an evangelical woman accused her of being a harlot.[53] Like Frances Wright, whose lecture tour of the United States coincided with Royall's own tours, Royall's anti-clericalism was deeply disturbing to the evangelicals because she had an audience. While she did not go as far as Wright in her religious skepticism, Royall noted her approval of some of Wright's ideas and her admiration for Wright's writings. Royall praised Wright for her attacks on the evangelicals and expressed her appreciation of Wright's willingness to stand out against them: "It is certainly honorable to the sex that one of them, at least, has had the spirit to resist the daring impudence of these gospel spreaders, and to oppose their imposition on the sex."[54]

While she recognized that Frances Wright might be an ally in her own confrontations with the evangelical clergy, Royall remained wary of some of Wright's more radical ideas and maintained a distance from her. Royall's interest in Wright was only fleeting as she concentrated on her campaign against the evangelicals. Nonetheless, the comparison with Wright was not missed by the evangelicals themselves, nor some of the editors. Royall's anti-clericalism may not have been accompanied by social radicalism, and as a consequence she did not represent the same kind of threat as Wright, but Royall was sufficiently vocal and commanded a large enough audience to be a source of irritation and even alarm. Her name was occasionally coupled with Wright's and, like Wright, her behavior was deprecated as a warning against irreligion: "This is the age for popular ladies. Miss Wright and Madame Royall go about like roaring lions—the first to devour men, the second to vilify them—and it is hard to tell which of the two is most notorious. . . . Truly, these are perilous times; a couple of women-kind are bouncing about the country to gain proselytes, or to gain money; and it is as much as a man's reputation is worth, to attempt to stop their tongues."[55]

The attacks came in a number of different forms, some more menacing than others, but occasionally they took physical shape. When she encountered violence, Royall was quick to report it to her readers as evidence of the despicable methods of the "Presbyterians." Thus she described a visit to Burlington, Vermont, in 1827 in which she was forcibly ejected from a house by a man she called a "missionary," who refused to buy one of her books. She maintained that he had taken her by the shoulders and pushed her with such force as to send her down the steps into the street. If it had not been for the snow, she claimed, she would have been smashed to pieces. She was incensed by the attack and noted, "He must have been 'ribbed with iron' and his heart barred with 'bolts of brass.' Thus, to attack a female, an aged female, who was procuring an honorable subsistance. Now this monster was a missionary, that is a black Presbyterian, a contributor and supporter of the whole missionary scheme."[56] The incident left her with a dislocated ankle and several other injuries rendering her unable to walk for at least six months. She insisted the Burlington incident was evidence of the missionaries' malevolent practices, and claimed they intended to put an end to her and her writings. The missionaries had ignored her injuries, she alleged, and refused to help her as she recovered, further evidence of their unchristian behavior.[57]

Others saw the incident differently and used the occasion to suggest that Royall had got the treatment she deserved. For, as one newspaper editor argued, she had been trying the patience of the public for too long: "We learn from the papers that 'Mrs. Anne Royal is confined at Burlington with a broken ancle. The accident occurred in too unceremoniously leaving a store where she had been disappointed in disposing of her literary wares.' Thus it is, she that never was known to give up a disputed point in argument, must have her *blue stocking* raised by the doctor's orders. From the manner in which it is hinted the accident occurred, we infer that this literary virago has at last received what she has so long merited,—'a brief ejectment.'"[58] Most were more sympathetic, but few editors acknowledged that her pronouncements against the missionaries had any justification, preferring instead to put the incident down to her own overzealous attempts to sell her books to unwilling customers: "It appears that the old lady, had presented her Book to a gentleman, and requested him to purchase it, which he refused to do. Indignant, at this apparent want of gallantry, and entire absence of every sense of justice, the old lady like Xenophon, made a hasty retreat from the enemy's country—not *a la mode* Col. Jarvis, and in her haste, stumbled, fell, and broke her leg! In the midst of this her season of sorrow and misfortune, we offer her our sincere testimonials of condolence."[59] Although few editors openly attributed the episode in Burlington to Royall's campaign against the Presbyterians, she herself made much of the confrontation, claiming that her life was in danger at the hands of ruffians and missionaries. But she refused to be deterred by the incident, seeing it as evidence of the despicable lengths to which the blackcoats were prepared to go. Such episodes were unusual, however, the evangelicals preferring to undermine Royall's influence by more insidious means.

The evangelicals tended to favor associating her with many of the same charges of irreligion and immorality with which they vilified Frances Wright, but they found her difficult to contain because she addressed herself to a wide audience. Royall reacted to the charges of irreligion with outbursts against the threat the missionaries posed. She peppered her writings with warnings about their influence on women, their money-making ventures, and their conversion campaigns, but the aspect of their activities that worried her the most was the perceived evangelical assault on American liberties. As she traveled around the country, Royall was insistent in the alarms she sounded about the power of the evangelicals, and she employed her writings to alert Americans to the danger they were in: "The missionary scheme is a wicked conspiracy against our lives, liberties, and laws; the principle is hostile to our happiness and safety, and every man, woman, and child, in the missionary ranks, are alike guilty of treachery, robbery and treason."[60] The country ignored her at their peril, she asserted, for these "priests" would attempt to undermine the freedoms of the republic and establish a tyranny and theocracy: "These wicked priests who always thirst for blood and power—who never were friends to liberty or virtue, finding the ease with which they could gull the ignorant, by telling a plausible tale about the heathen, and getting upon the right side of the women, have laid a plan that Beezlebub himself would never have thought of."[61] To hammer her point home, she added later, "Glutted with women and money [the missionaries] have become not only beastly wicked, but are in every part of the U.S. aiming to overturn our government and establish the reign of terror."[62]

Insisting that the priests were involved in a conspiracy, she identified it in the attempts by missionary and Sunday school societies to preach for the keeping of the Sabbath and then to lobby for laws to prevent its violation. In a long aside in one of her books, she presented evidence to her readers, outlining the plans she believed these missionaries had hatched to impose a national religion and sweep aside the people's liberties. As she argued, Americans were finally beginning to recognize the dangers posed by the evangelicals: "The friends of virtue and religious liberty are divided in opinion on this business; some say it has the union of church and state for its object; others say the idea is chimerical; while all unite in denouncing it a serious and alarming evil; but the truth has at length burst upon the people. Their late attempts to establish their power by law, in the Pennsylvania legislature, has at length resolved the doubting, and left no room with the most credulous to question their designs."[63]

She pointed to further evidence in the sermons of a number of leading evangelicals, whom she accused of preaching for the creation of a national religion and the imposition of "blue laws." A sermon preached by a Reverend Black in Pittsburgh seemed to her particularly dangerous: "This sermon is treason against our liberties from beginning to end," she asserted. "And so lulled are the people into security, and so blind to the conduct of this dangerous sect, that I have never heard it mentioned by a single individual."[64] But it was Reverend Ezra Stiles Ely's sermon on July 4, 1827, on "The Duty of Christian Freemen to Elect Christian Rulers" that sent her into paroxysms of rage. For in her eyes the sermon was a call for a Christian party in politics and an attempt by the "priests" to enter politics.[65] She made it very clear where she stood on the issue: "The whole of this fourth of July sermon is treason from beginning to end, and the time was when any man who would utter such treason in our country would be strung up."[66] The Sabbatarians' campaigns to petition Congress to prevent mails on Sunday were to her the culmination of a much more longstanding attempt by the evangelicals to use the powers of the federal government to establish their own rule—a plot she had warned her readers of at every opportunity.[67]

Royall's criticisms were strident and alarmist, but they were not merely the ravings of a paranoid woman. The reactions to her suggest that her allegations were the source of some nervousness to her opponents, but also that she had "friends." Her concerns were shared with others who were worried by the onslaught of the evangelical enterprise, and it is likely that some of these were the friends who invited her to visit their parts of the country in order to expose the missionaries.[68] Many men shared her anxieties about the aims of the evangelical movement, and expressed disquiet about the means by which the evangelicals sought to achieve their goals. Among these were Freethinkers, who were possibly the most vocal in their condemnation of clerical dominance, but others who came from a rationalist tradition voiced their dislike of the ascendance the evangelicals were gaining in some parts of the country.[69] Their numbers were relatively small, but there were others who resented the growing influence of evangelical culture and the imposition of their values for more secular reasons. For although efforts to enforce Sabbath observance and to encourage the reform of morals were logical extensions of the desire to promote a Christian nation, many people viewed these aims with suspicion.[70] In the eyes of critics like Royall, evangelical initiatives to promote reforms such as temperance, the reformation of manners, and various benevolent projects were possibly the most pernicious aspect of the blackcoats' grandiose schemes, for they seemed to undermine fundamental American liberties.

Opposition to the evangelicals' objectives came also from populist Christian sects who sometimes expressed themselves in violent, anti-clerical terms. For despite efforts to keep itself free from sectarian bias in order to attract as wide a constituency as possible, the evangelical reform movement remained mostly Presbyterian and Congregational in its membership. Its schemes were viewed by other groups, such as the Methodists and Baptists, as tyrannical and preoccupied with predestinarian theology and clerical control.[71] An array of groups opposed the purposes of the evangelical movement, and often all they had in common was a determination to preserve their independence against the onslaught of the revivalists.[72] The attempts by the evangelicals to enforce Sabbath observance and to reform society brought many of these groups together, and forced what had been a purely religious movement into politics.

As Royall was at pains to tell her readers, the evangelicals were not content only to convert individuals but aimed to Christianize the whole nation. In order to do so, they sought to enforce Sabbath observance, for to them the violation of the Sabbath represented an attack on the very foundation of their religion. Consequently, they began to press their cause by political means as well as by preaching and publications, arguing that it was the duty of the civil power to enforce existing laws to protect Sabbath observance. They had some success in persuading various state legislatures to pass and enforce new Sabbath observance laws, but they encountered stiff opposition in others. Royall remained at the forefront of this counter-offensive, and she was not slow to declare that her books and visits played a vital part in rallying the opposition, claiming a direct influence on a measure to defeat the evangelicals in Pennsylvania: "They are precisely pursuing the measures I have for sometime suggested to the public, that of holding meetings, and entering into resolutions to discountenance and discard those wolves in sheep's clothing from society."[73]

Local setbacks did not deter the evangelicals from pursuing their goals, and in 1827 they launched a massive attack on the federal statute that provided for post offices to be open and the mail to be carried on Sundays. The General Union for Promoting the Observance of the Christian Sabbath provided the means for the evangelicals to organize a nationwide petition drive aimed at forcing Congress to repeal the offending statute. Their actions stirred up widespread opposition against such an overt attempt to undermine the separation between church and state, marking a popular protest in favor of keeping the federal government free from religious interference. The leaders of the counter-campaign to uphold the Sunday mails ranged in social background from merchants in the expanding commercial areas of the "Burned Over" district of New York State to the artisans of Philadelphia. Those who signed the anti-Sabbatarian petitions were of still more diverse origins.[74] While they were generally less organized than the evangelicals, they were remarkably effective. The Sabbatarians were defeated by Congress in January 1829, when the Senate Committee on Post Offices advised the rejection of their petitions. The committee's report, authored by its chair, Colonel Richard M. Johnson of Kentucky, robustly asserted the federal government's commitment to the separation of church and state. A second wave of Sabbatarian petitions in 1830 was greeted by an equally forceful response from Johnson backed by the anti-Sabbatarian campaign.[75] Royall, in her only direct participation in the petitioning campaign, proudly printed Johnson's first report in her *Black Book*.[76]

The extent of Royall's involvement in the anti-Sabbatarian petition drive is not clear, but she used her books as a forum from which to denounce the evangelicals and their plots at every opportunity. She alerted her readers to their petitioning activities in strident tones: "Through the aid of these Presbyterian Post Offices, this treacherous sect are carrying on their treasonable plots . . . loading the mails with papers, for the purpose of wresting from us our dearest rights. If they have one spark of love or desire for Liberty left, they will unite for the common safety, and put a stop to this outrage."[77] Drawing on the legacy of the Revolution, she emphasized its heritage of liberty and freedom of religion in an effort to alert Americans to the dangers they faced if the Sabbatarians continued their campaigns unchecked. Her apocalyptic rhetoric and warnings of a conspiracy to overthrow the government and establish a religious tyranny were rooted in the Revolutionary Era, but her arguments converged with contemporary fears. For while she may not have been at the center of the male petition campaigns, she was certainly vociferous in her calls to action, and she seems to have had some impact. The anti-Sabbatarians used the same language as she did in the petitions they presented to Congress.[78]

Royall's attacks on the "blackcoats" and Presbyterians were part of a wider challenge to the attempts by the evangelicals to enter politics and influence the federal government's involvement in religious issues. This opposition eventually found its political home among the Jacksonian Democrats, who developed a broad policy of protecting people from religious tyranny and promoting the separation of church and state against any suggestion of an evangelical "Christian Party in Politics." Thus, by the late 1820s, the Sabbatarianism of the Presbyterians, Congregationalists, and other radical revivalists had begun to define the divisions of an emergent second political party system. The evangelical revival proved extremely divisive, to the extent that, as historian Daniel Walker Howe argues, "evangelical religion interacted with economic development to polarize the population, creating the basis for two broad alliances." These alliances saw political form in the Democratic and Whig Parties of the second party system, but the divisive political culture from which they emerged permeated all aspects of American life.[79] Although often more strident in tone, Royall's arguments were similar to those of the Jacksonians in the elections of 1828. Anxious not to appear too overtly partisan, as a number of her contemporaries recognized, she was effectively working for the Jacksonian cause.[80]

The evangelicals stirred resistance in many quarters in their efforts to Christianize the American people, but wherever it came from, they were not prepared to ignore opposition nor to take it lightly. In the contest for Americans' allegiances, they used various tactics to crush their critics. The reactions of the evangelicals suggest that they took Royall's activities seriously. Her bitter attacks on clergymen, her persistence, and the fact that she had a significant audience for her books meant that her comments did not pass without notice. As she noted herself, in many areas where the evangelicals had been particularly active, she discovered she had acquired a reputation as an enemy of religion and was unable to sell her books. She was indignant at such methods, claiming that some people shunned her because her name had been besmirched by missionaries: "I guessed in a moment who had defamed me, and told him it could be no other than the missionaries—he did not either acknowledge or deny it, but expressed much pleasure at our interview. Is it not astonishing, that those abominable defamers of mankind should be so countenanced as they are, to the complete prostration of common sense, and that their slanders does not rouse the indignation of the people."[81]

In a period of religious turmoil, when the evangelical movement was trying to establish itself and gain converts, Royall's vocal attacks on their persons and purposes hit a nerve and represented a possible threat. As she was at pains to tell her readers, the evangelicals used a variety of methods to tarnish her reputation in the eyes of her potential audience. If Royall emphasized the physical attacks on her, the evangelicals and their allies more frequently used other methods in an attempt to diminish respect for her and reduce the threat that she posed. They tried to dismiss her as uncouth, mad, or a "Bedlamite," citing her public outbursts. More insidious were their attempts to label her as unfeminine and to restrict her activities.[82]

Royall's righteous anger at being branded irreligious by the missionaries should not obscure the fact that she consciously goaded them and sought to undermine their cause. She had deliberately developed a public presence that was rare among contemporary women by openly courting public attention through announcements of her presence in towns and her contacts with newspaper editors.[83] Increasingly, she held levees in the places she visited, encouraging her "admirers" to come and meet her, and no doubt also to hear her views. Although she did not make public speeches or appear on the public stage, she used her books and the interest they aroused as a means of promoting herself and her opinions. She wrote to newspapers for similar purposes. Thus she used her celebrity to pursue her campaign against the growing power of the evangelicals, denouncing the missionaries and insulting them at every opportunity. As a consequence, she was not easy to ignore for she had an audience and her persistent attacks posed a challenge to the evangelicals' project.

Despite such aggressive behavior, Royall professed to be offended when the missionaries retaliated—she expected that her gender, her age, and even her reputation as an author would protect her from indignity. Clearly they did not.[84] It was, however, in Washington where she had made her home, that the most sustained attack on her by the agents of the evangelical revivals occurred. On this occasion, the design was to humiliate her and trap her within the developing ideology of middle-class femininity by questioning the propriety of her behavior. The aim was to diminish her in the eyes of her audience and thus undermine her influence and the threat she might pose.

6 · A Political Woman and Common Scold

In mid-July 1829, the editor of the *New York Observer* offered his readers a piece of gossip from Washington: "Mrs. Royal has been presented to the Grand Jury as a nuisance, and a bill has been found against her." Assuming his readers' acquaintance with Mrs. Royall, the editor reported that she had come into the court to obtain a list of the grand jury. Such was her temper, he continued, even the respect and honor due to the grand jurors' office would be little protection "against the vituperative powers of this giantess of literature. She menaces them with a fearful visitation of her displeasure, and her menaces seldom evaporate in thin air."[1] The power of Anne Royall's threats existed only in the overblown rhetoric of the editor and were no deterrent to the grand jury. A few days later, Royall went on trial in Washington, accused of being a "common scold." Royall's existing reputation, together with the nature of the indictment, caught the imagination of editors across the country.

The employment of this ancient but largely obsolete charge highlighted the way in which Royall's controversial behavior was perceived by her enemies. Her tireless and abusive opposition to the evangelicals had engendered hostility. The attacks on them in her books, and her ability to attract an audience, meant that the evangelicals used a variety of means to marginalize her in order to curtail her influence. The nature of the charge against her also denotes what some scholars have seen as a more general concern—the disquiet many evangelicals felt about some of the public activities in which women became involved, and the evangelicals' attempts to limit and control female behavior.[2] More particularly it shows just how central the evangelical project to equate femininity with religiosity was to developing notions of respectability. But as both the trial itself and the reaction to it by some newspaper editors suggest, these ideas were not universally accepted.

Royall's prosecution as a common scold was an attempt to humiliate and control her by labeling her an unruly woman. By 1829, however, she was more than a mere scold who disrupted the peace of her immediate neighbors. She was a well-known public figure and a woman who exercised some influence through the national audience she had gained for her writings. She was, moreover, an active participant in the partisan politics of the time, and many of her contemporaries believed that she was being put on trial because of her political activities. By 1829 she was associated with Andrew Jackson's new administration, and John Eaton, Jackson's secretary of war, was to be a witness on her behalf at the trial. Her prosecution should be understood in the light of her career before 1829, her role in the political culture of the 1820s, and the implications that can be drawn from the gendered nature of the charge.

By the late 1820s, echoes of Royall's fears about the growing power of the evangelicals were finding a political home among the followers of Andrew Jackson.[3] But although Royall was clearly a supporter of the Jacksonian cause, like many contemporary Americans she asserted her indifference to partisan politics. In her case, she professed that her gender precluded such an interest: "As to politics, I have never made it my study, and if I were as learned as Cicero, I think no woman has any business with politics." To press home her point, she continued, "There is something so masculine, and opposed to female delicacy, in meddling with the affairs of state, that I view it with sovereign abhorrence. Nature has designed woman another sphere."[4]

Royall had expressed her admiration for Andrew Jackson from her earliest writings. Passing through Tennessee in 1817, she made a point of praising him to her correspondent Matthew Dunbar, exclaiming, "As I rode to the Inn, where I now am, I was informed, that I was in *Tennessee,* and I immediately fell into a train of pleasant musing. The victory of New Orleans, the battles of Tallushatches, Talladega, and Emuckfau, all passed, in retrospection before me—the brave, the intrepid, the invincible JACKSON, and his brilliant achievements engrossed every faculty of my mind."[5] Her admiration reflected that of many other Americans in the years following General Jackson's victory over the British at New Orleans, for many regarded him as a hero. The stories she related to Dunbar portrayed Jackson in epic terms, as a military genius, and as a man who was magnanimous to those he defeated and who recognized the nobility of the Indian leaders. There were many others in the western country at this time who worshipped Jackson in the same way that she did, so much so, she observed, that some people even put his military prowess on a level with that of General George Washington.[6]

Jackson's celebration as a military hero, the savior of the nation and the vanquisher of the Creek Indians, was widespread in the years after the end of the War of 1812. His popularity may be credited in large part to his military successes, but he also appealed to a popular republican culture concerned with preserving the rights of free Americans in the face of tyrants and oppressive forces.[7] As yet only vaguely articulated, Royall's concepts of liberty as well as her admiration for Jackson echoed this popular republicanism. Building on the political enthusiasms she had learned from her husband, she began to write of the general as the personification of American values and the defender of American freedoms. Even after his Florida campaigns gained him many enemies, Royall's respect and veneration for Jackson remained constant, for she defended him against all criticism in her correspondence.[8]

Almost ten years later, as she traveled around America, Royall's sympathies had become still more pronounced.[9] At a period when Jacksonian democracy was not itself clearly defined, her prejudices and enthusiasms reflected the broad nature of the Jacksonian alliance in the 1820s. Her attacks on the agents of the evangelical revivals, her anti-Sabbatarianism, and her pro-Masonic stance convinced contemporary commentators that she was a Jacksonian.[10] In other respects, too, she revealed her political leanings, particularly in her later attacks on the Second Bank of the United States. But she was no believer in mass involvement in politics, and in this respect, she sided with Jackson's critics. She especially detested the crowds at Jackson's inauguration and despised those she saw as the "lower sort." Such elitism, however, did not detract from the fact that her political instincts made her a Jacksonian, and reflected rather the wider contradictions among Jackson's supporters at this time.[11]

Notwithstanding all the indications that she was a Jacksonian, Royall persisted in claiming a disinterest in politics, and she denied having an affiliation to any party. In the months before the election of 1828, this was a hard position to maintain. The atmosphere was bitterly partisan, and few newspaper editors believed that any public figure could remain above the fray. In these circumstances, her claims that, as a woman, she was remote from the partisan struggle were quickly dismissed by the editors. They assumed she would shortly declare for one party or the other: "[She] indignantly denied the assertion that she had *come out* for Gen. Jackson. On this last subject, she remains, like the great Van Buren, 'uncommitted and unpledged,' and has not yet determined into which scale she will throw the weight of her great talents and commanding influence."[12] She kept to her position, however, insisting that she was indifferent to partisanship of any kind, as she assured her readers: "It is well known that I am of no party in politics, or sect in religion. I am neither (as the phrase has it now) an Adams-man nor a Jackson-man—I am my country's man, or woman, which you please, and the people will always find me on their side, no matter who rules: I never was, nor ever will be, a tool for any party."[13]

Royall's insistence that she was of no party in politics reflected a more general discourse about parties. Many Americans in the first decades of the new nation regarded political partisanship as contrary to the public good and a danger to the republic. Parties were equated with factions and as such were seen as divisive, corrupt, and self-seeking. Even those who, like Jackson himself, acted in a highly partisan manner felt obliged to declare themselves opposed to party spirit and its association with political immorality.[14] Royall's reluctance to declare herself for one party or another was, moreover, a recognition of the ambiguity of women's role in party politics during the 1820s.

In recent years, historians have acknowledged that women were not as absent from politics, even party politics, as had previously been assumed. Women were frequently seen in political public spaces—historian Susan Branson notes their presence and participation in political salons in Philadelphia when it was the nation's capital in the 1790s, and their attendance at debates in Congress; likewise, Catherine Allgor suggests that during the first decades of the nineteenth century, ladies often visited the public galleries to listen to the congressional debates in Washington, while life in Washington was in itself politicizing for women because social events and even living arrangements centered around politics. Nor was it just national politics that attracted women, for Elizabeth Varon has remarked on the presence of women in the public galleries during the debates over the Virginia constitution in 1829–30. Royall too commented on the number of women attending both federal and state congressional debates, although she dismissed their presence as frivolous—a desire to be seen rather than to hear the debates.[15]

Nor have historians commented only on the passive presence of women in political institutions. Women were also involved more actively: in seeking and obtaining patronage for their male relatives, in expressing their political views in their diaries and letters, and in shaping the debates about women's participation in the politics of the early republic. On occasion political parties also deliberately sought female supporters, hoping that they would add luster to their cause. Thus, in the 1790s, the Federalists encouraged women's support and participation in party events, and honored their contributions to the polity because of their supposed role in shaping the manners and morals of the nation. Such women tended to be drawn from the propertied and wealthy classes, and were unlikely to be the instruments of radicalism or social upheaval.[16] Similarly, in the early 1840s, the Whigs articulated a new ideal of feminine civic duty, that of "Whig Womanhood," embodying the notion that women could and should make a vital contribution to party politics, or at least to the Whig Party. Women's presence at Whig rallies would testify to their party's moral rectitude and add to the dignity of the proceedings. The Whig Party's support for the evangelical movement and the "benevolent empire" meant that it was attractive to many women from the developing middle classes, and they wrote pamphlets, conducted meetings, and even made speeches for the party. The Democrats, however, were less willing to embrace female involvement, placing a much greater emphasis on the separation of the public and private than the Whigs. The Democrats' stress on the inclusion of white men from all social classes in the political process tended to mean that they were much less willing to accept women as participants.[17]

There was little continuity between the two periods of heightened female partisanship, however, and the 1820s represented a transitional period during which the continued acceptance of women's political activism came under attack. During the Revolution and the period following it, women took an active part in politics, but in the shifting political landscape of the early nineteenth century, they gradually became marginalized. In the first decades of the new nation, some women seized the opportunity presented by this period of political experimentation to engage in political discussion. Among them were women such as Judith Sargent Murray who were imbued with the confidence that resulted from being a member of the ruling classes, and who eagerly asserted a public and even partisan identity. Other women who were not part of the ruling elite were equally confident in expressing their political views. Considering themselves to be public actors, entitled to participate in the political life of the new nation, they did not recognize their sex as a bar to public engagement.[18] A new class of women emerged, interested in and seeking to influence politics directly, who were happy to embrace the title of "female politician." Although they were often criticized for doing so, these women acted as independent political agents, with their own opinions, and they were prepared to make their own political choices. They expressed themselves in writing but occasionally also in public speeches.[19]

As political parties developed during the 1790s, women actively supported them. But as parties emerged, the fluidity that had marked the first years of the new republic began to disappear as political opinions solidified and became organized around the two parties. Increasingly, the parties began to focus on the vote as the central feature of the political process, and that had an impact on women. The Republican Party in particular sought to ease women out of politics as they concentrated on expanding white manhood suffrage—a development that took place over the course of the early decades of the nineteenth century. Where economic and social status might previously have given some women a voice in the political sphere, the vote from which they were excluded on the grounds of their gender became the only marker of citizenship that mattered.[20]

The partisan conflict that characterized the emergence of the Republican and Federalist Parties also affected the ways in which women's participation in politics came to be regarded. For as party divisions became increasingly rancorous and threatened to undermine the fragile republican experiment and split families and communities, the country seemed to be on the verge of civil war.[21] In the face of this strife, newspaper editors, political leaders, and even the party rank and file began to criticize women who had acted as female politicians and taken an interest in electoral politics. They urged these women to withdraw from party politics and instead to serve as peacemakers, and concentrate on repairing social and political bonds. Instead of acting as an independent political agent, a woman's role was to be a mediator among male partisans, ensuring domestic tranquility and exercising only indirect influence on politics through her husband and family. Efforts to exclude women from political participation were remarkably successful, and women turned their attention to other means of expressing their commitment to the common good. "Whig Womanhood" of the 1840s represented a brief resurgence in women's political participation following two decades during which they had gradually been excluded from electoral politics.[22]

Nevertheless, the exclusion of women from party politics was neither a complete nor quick process. Throughout the 1820s there were still signs that women's political participation was welcomed, although it was to be limited. During the election of 1828, John Quincy Adams's supporters opened up the possibility of women's participation in politics by suggesting that the private and public spheres were intimately linked, and the morality of the private sphere should govern the public. The Jeffersonian tradition was, by contrast, much less willing to allow women to participate in party activities and influence party policies. The Jacksonians emphasized the distinction between the public and private spheres, thus excluding from partisan involvement women who might have rallied to Jackson's cause.[23] Jacksonian women were not easily deterred, however. Even after the election, they tried to assert their authority in political life, using many of the arguments about female moral superiority that were later to define Whig womanhood.[24]

Anne Royall, like many of the women who had been politically engaged in the early years of the new republic, entered the political sphere assuming her right to operate as an independent political actor. Her reluctance to declare herself for one party or the other during the elections of 1828 should be understood in the context of efforts by editors and politicians to bar women from politics. Arguments that sought to define women as nonpolitical by nature, and that used the phrase "female politician" as a term of abuse, clearly had an impact on her willingness to admit to any party loyalty, particularly when such criticisms were directed at her. Equally editors who referred to her as a "Jackson Man," or who used the pages of their newspapers to push her to declare her politics, recognized her political engagement and tried to label her as absurd or even unfeminine.[25] Although she tried to maintain a stance of disinterest in partisanship, she was unable to completely disavow all interest in politics. Moreover, her continued campaign against the entry of the evangelicals into politics made it difficult for her to convince her contemporaries that she was anything other than a political woman, and a Jacksonian.

In the summer of 1829, when charges were brought against her by members of an evangelical congregation in Washington, Royall was quick to denounce it as a new attack by the Presbyterians. It was proof, she maintained, of a conspiracy against her triggered by her exposure of their dangerous schemes. But to many of her contemporaries it was an attempt to limit her activities, as a political woman and one whose anti-clericalism was a significant irritant to the evangelical movement.[26]

For a few months in the spring and early summer of 1829, Royall rested from her travels in Washington. She was almost sixty years old and had been on the road intermittently for the last six years. Washington had become her home between tours, and it was there that she wrote her books and prepared them for printing. She lived on the second story of a building on Capitol Hill, from where she commanded a good view of the neighborhood. Its location also allowed her to visit Congress easily to view its proceedings, and to examine the books in the Library of Congress. Between the end of January and May 15, she wrote several volumes and, by her own reckoning, published 3,500 copies.[27] She quickly found, however, that in the vicinity was a congregation of "missionaries" and a Sunday school occupying a building she referred to as the Engine House. Her relationship with them was rancorous, for she saw many of their activities as a deliberate attempt to provoke her.[28] Her reaction was true to character—she retaliated by shouting abuse at them.

This particular congregation was determined to curtail Royall's campaign against them. On July 6, 1829, the grand jury entered the U.S. Circuit Court in Washington with a presentment against her, the result of a complaint by a number of "respectable" citizens belonging to the Engine House congregation. They charged that Royall had used "opprobrious and indecent language to respectable females and Gentlemen when on the publick street, whilst going to publick worship." Moreover, she had uttered "other malicious and false sayings and writing such as Thief, Villain, Hypocrite, etc. etc. to the Great annoyance of Females; and citizens of the Capitol Hill and to the disturbance of Said Good people in the discharge of their religious duties."[29] She had also shouted insults at the Sunday school teachers as they passed her windows on the way to the church, frightening some of them to the extent, that one newspaper noted, "Some of the young ladies were actually afraid to pass. Nor could they come within hearing, without having themselves outraged by language, to which no delicate female could listen."[30]

The charges were the result of an immediate grievance. The members of the congregation found Royall's caustic comments and verbal abuse insufferable. They were an affront to their sensibilities, and they were particularly indignant about the insults directed at the women of the congregation. Both those who brought the charges and the editors who commented on them highlighted the contrasts between the supposedly delicate feelings of the young women attending church on Capitol Hill and their tormentor's aggressive and seemingly unfeminine behavior. The tactic of labeling a woman as unfeminine was not uncommon among evangelicals. These women, and men, used the ideology of femininity as a weapon to police the behavior of other women that they considered to be too radical or that threatened to undermine their own purposes. It deflected criticism from their own activities and enabled them to question the propriety and morality of others.[31] The attack on Royall as unfeminine challenged her morality and excluded her from the notion of middle-class respectability this group held up as the standard. Ostensibly this prosecution was less concerned with the nature of Royall's opinions as expressed in her writings than with her disorderly behavior in the public arena of Capitol Hill. It was, nonetheless, a way in which to discredit Royall in the eyes of her readers and potential readers. She was to be brought under control as an unruly woman—one who did not conform to the understanding this congregation had of proper female behavior, an understanding they assumed was the standard for all "respectable" people.[32]

Royall's conduct on Capitol Hill was not the only aspect of her activities under scrutiny. By the summer of 1829 few commentators could ignore Royall's national reputation as a writer with forceful opinions on the nature of the evangelical threat. Many understood that in bringing charges against her, the "respectable" citizens were launching an attack that had all the appearance of an attempt to silence her assaults on the evangelicals, and she herself saw it in those terms. Her own account of the events leading up to her trial accused the prosecution of being part of a wider conspiracy to silence her, because they feared her influence in the new Congress. She cited incidents of boys throwing stones at her house and doubtful characters calling at her lodgings to besmirch her character. She claimed that the members of the congregation then attempted to "convert" her by praying and singing hymns under her windows at night. These efforts failed to silence her, and she concluded that the prosecution was the next line of attack.[33] Amid her attempts at self-justification and efforts to portray herself to her readers as the innocent victim in her encounters with the evangelicals, there is some evidence that she was being deliberately goaded by members of this congregation. In July 1829, at the time of her trial, she wrote a letter to the clerk of the court accusing those who had brought the charges against her of equally unruly behavior: "This old one C is always around my house & annoying me with all sorts of noise & so far did he go evening before last that he came to my own door & not in the street & threatened my life & I am about to have measures taken to bind him to his good behavior & therefore appeal to you what steps to take. I have no peace of my life from the whole gang."[34] Her torrents of abuse against the Engine House congregation were, in her eyes, a reaction to provocation. Such was her reputation, however, that commentators were more concerned with Royall's behavior than that of her opponents.

Few of the newspapers commenting on the trial expressed much surprise that a complaint had been brought against Royall. Several indicated that the charge was long overdue: "All decent people will be happy to hear that impudent Virago, Anne Royall, is at last in a fair way to meet her deserts."[35] Some regarded the occasion as an opportunity to mock Royall and bring levity to their reporting, by suggesting their astonishment that a jury having had the charges presented to them had "sufficient courage" to bring a court case against her. As one editor noted with heavy irony, "It required no ordinary share of animal, as well as moral courage, in any three and twenty men to make so daring an attack upon the rights of this belligerent authoress. She might have indulged herself in any reasonable latitude, in her invasions of the public peace with impunity, for nothing less than an extraordinary course of outrages upon the feelings and usages of society would have screwed up the courage of any jury to the sticking point of a presentment."[36] Even the most sympathetic of editors believed that she had brought a prosecution on herself: "Thus it is with great geniuses in all ages—Galileo, the starry Galileo, was imprisoned for his wisdom, Tarso was the tenant of a cell, and Columbus sighed in a dungeon. Why then should Anne Royall hope to escape the general doom of genius?—It is inherent in her destiny, and a concomitant of her greatness."[37]

Although many editors were entertained by the prospect of a trial in which Royall took center stage, it was unclear what she was to be charged with. What was needed was an indictment that would compel Royall to give security for her good behavior, but as one newspaper noted, "The U.S. Attorney seems in as much perplexity to frame an indictment against her which will stand."[38] Nor, some editors taunted, were they convinced that the grand jury would have the temerity to bring a charge against Royall, given her formidable reputation. As one editor quipped, "She marched into Court, demanded the names of the Jurymen, and so frightened the poor fellows, that not one of them dared to acknowledge himself concerned in presenting her."[39]

Despite such supposed concerns, the following week the grand jury came up with an indictment that arraigned Royall on three counts for offenses committed on June 1, 1829. Collectively they charged her with having disturbed the public peace. The first accused her of being "an evil disposed person, and a common slanderer and disturber of the peace and happiness of her quiet and honest neighbours"; the second with being "a common scold and disturber of the peace"; and finally with being "a common brawler and sower of discord."[40] Such was her reputation for belligerence that a rumor quickly spread that she had decamped, a frightened marshal having warned of her impending arrest. Royall's appearance in court to face the charges swiftly contradicted such reports.[41] Her counsel entered a plea of not guilty to the second count but demurred on the other two counts. After some deliberation, Judge William Cranch dismissed these two charges, and Royall stood trial only on the charge of being a common scold.[42]

The charge of "common scold" had a long history in English common law but had been little used in the United States after independence.[43] A scold was defined by English law as "a troublesome and angry woman who, by her brawling and wrangling among her neighbours, doth break the public peace, and beget, cherish and increase public discord."[44] Such women had always existed. Before the mid-sixteenth century the ecclesiastical and manor courts in England had jurisdiction over scolding women. The punishment had been penance or a small fine, but the authorities had not been much concerned by such women. By the middle of the sixteenth and into the early seventeenth centuries, however, the problem of disorderly women became an increasing source of worry, as rapid social and economic changes led to fears of an impending breakdown in social order. The preoccupation with female offenses against public order and patriarchal structures reflected these fears and more specific concerns about gender relations in this changing world.[45] While very occasionally men were presented for scolding, both in England and the English colonies in North America, the charge of common scold was considered a female offense—one seeking to punish violators of the gender hierarchy that bolstered social order. Increasingly the punishment for it, and one reserved exclusively for women, was the ducking stool.[46]

An offense reflecting early-seventeenth-century English concerns with proper gender behavior entered the statute books of many of the American colonies as they were established.[47] After independence, it remained on the books of a number of states, including Maryland from which the District of Columbia drew its laws, but prosecutions were sufficiently rare as to provoke comment in the newspapers. There had, though, been cases in Massachusetts, New York, and Pennsylvania. Indeed, the attorney general of Philadelphia County had found records of cases, in the years immediately prior to the revision of the Pennsylvania Penal Code in 1790, in which the plaintiff had not only been convicted of the offense but had been sentenced to a ducking. Moreover, the sentence was carried out.[48] A more recent Pennsylvania Supreme Court case in 1825 had overturned the conviction of a woman named Nancy James as a common scold because the sentence of ducking was deemed by the court to be a cruel and unusual punishment and thus not permissible under the Pennsylvania constitution.[49] Nonetheless, this and other cases in Massachusetts and New York established that scolding was still an indictable offense in some states. The lawyers advising the grand jury in Royall's case might have been aware of these other incidents, but, significantly, they were not mentioned in any of the reported legal arguments at Royall's trial.[50]

None of the earlier common scold trials attracted the kind of press attention engendered by Royall's case, but there was enough novelty value in such cases to cause comment. These earlier trials suggest that the indictment of common scold had much more to do with a woman's general reputation than with any particular incident, and as a result, there was little defense against the charge. The general expectation was that all women scolded; those who were charged with being common scolds were out of the ordinary. As one Minty Graham discovered, "Abundant evidence of her [Graham's] scolding is stated to have been produced, but the jury returned a verdict of *not guilty*. It is related that they expressed conscientious scruples about convicting her as a common scold, when it was proved that she was an uncommon scold."[51] The women charged with being common scolds in the early republic were from diverse backgrounds, and it is not always clear why and who brought the charges against them. For instance, Elizabeth Bowlan, who was convicted and fined in Boston in August 1813, was brought to court by her neighbors. She was of a low social status, and the incident in 1813 was not her first offense. Nancy James of Philadelphia, on the other hand, was an African American woman; who brought the charges is unclear.[52] Although not used with any regularity, the charge of common scold was still on the statute books of many states and it was available as a means to control the behavior of women considered to be unruly.

Despite these earlier cases, the indictment, together with the identity of the accused, provoked considerable interest in the trial, as Royall noted: "The Court House was crowded, as the trial was the first of the sort ever tried in the United States, and excited much interest."[53] While the charge was not as unique as either Royall or some historians have asserted, it must have taken a considerable amount of research to identify. Given the nature of the grievances against Royall, there were few options available to the grand jury, for the complaints were of such a general nature that many alternative charges were unenforceable.[54] Even so, Royall claimed that the arraignment was simply untenable: "Every legal man will be astonished, that the Grand Jury of our metropolis, should be so ignorant as not to know these charges could not be brought before them." For, she maintained, "A drunkard, or an abandoned woman infesting the streets can be committed to the workhouse as a common nuisance; but no such thing is cognizable by a Grand Jury; and had I been one of those characters, I should have been safe enough, as they are too popular on Capitol Hill or any other hill in the city."[55]

In the early nineteenth century, women were seen in the courts much more rarely than men, but the most frequent crimes for which women were arrested, tried, and convicted were public order offenses such as drunkenness, idle and disorderly conduct, prostitution, and vagrancy. Traditionally, the family and church had corrected these transgressions. Only on rare occasions were the perpetrators brought before the courts, but as American society underwent rapid change in the early nineteenth century, the courts intervened more often. In the more anonymous urban world, where crime rates seemed to be increasing, disruptive behavior of any kind threatened to undermine the social order. Moreover, the agents of the evangelical revival increasingly sought to ensure their dominance and to impose their own ideals of behavior on the wider society, by defining a new code of morality. It became the duty of women, as their closest allies, to maintain the social order and uphold the new moral codes. As these evangelicals began to shape a stricter code of female morality, certain crimes (particularly those of sexual misconduct) were defined as exclusively female. A range of behavior from lewd and lascivious carriage, stubbornness, and disorderly conduct, to adultery and fornication brought women into the courts. Consequently, the ratio of female to male convictions was much closer for public order offenses than for other crimes, such as those against the person or property.[56] These convictions for public order offenses and sexual misconduct, which tended to be brought against working-class women, sought to ensure that all women upheld the social order. Otherwise, it was feared, unruly women might undermine the very basis of society.[57]

Newer categories of exclusively female offenses were not appropriate to the complaints against Royall. The grand jury's decision to indict her as a common scold drew on a much older, but still specifically female, charge. Together with the two charges of being a common slanderer and common brawler, the indictment would empower the prosecution to ensure that the trial focused on Royall's behavior as a disorderly woman.[58] Moreover, the common scold charge allowed the court to investigate a woman's general reputation, not just a specific incident. Royall's wider conduct was therefore under scrutiny. It cannot have escaped the notice of the jury, any more than the newspaper editors, that by 1829 Royall was a notorious figure. Few observers believed that she was on trial *only* for her offenses against the members of the Engine House congregation.

Finally, after a number of delays, the case came to trial. The charge itself occasioned some difficulty since it was unusual, and the lawyers were uncertain what a "common scold" was, as one editor quipped: "The opinion of one of the authorities quoted is, that the person so designated must be *always* scolding. If so, we need look no further for the perpetual motion, after a single conviction grounded on that authority."[59] Some also questioned whether Royall's behavior really merited the charge. She did not scold continuously, they argued, nor was she loud all the time. The same editor went on to say, "According to some of the witnesses, Mrs. Royall, although frequent in her verbal exhilarations, was not *always* loud, but on the contrary, has inflicted some of her linguadental severities in a very soft tone, and with a very smiling countenance, coming up, in fact, to the poet's description, and show that she can smile, and smile, and murder while she smiles."[60]

Much of the newspaper coverage of the trial reflected their editors' existing perceptions of the defendant. Only a few reported directly, but even where the editor relied on an account copied from another newspaper, he often added his own comments. Some saw the trial merely as an amusing interlude when there was little else to report: "For want of something more worthy of your sprightly and various columns, I send you some account of a trial which has excited some interest, and occasioned some gratification among the lovers of the ludicrous."[61] For others it was of interest because it seemed that Royall was effectively being brought to trial for all her past attacks on those who did not agree with her, or who had not bought her books. Among these were the editors who believed that Royall was finally being brought to account for her "impudent" attacks on the evangelicals.[62] For still others there were much deeper implications to the trial, because of Royall's associations with the recently inaugurated Jackson administration.

Drawing on assumptions that Royall had influence with members of the new administration, a number of editors claimed that the prosecution was revenge for the defeat of the Adams administration: "Mrs. Royall, we more than suspected, was a Jackson *man*, and since the overwhelming defeat that our party sustained in the last presidential contest, there can no longer be any doubt either of her sentiments or their effects upon the citizens; and prettily the Adams men and women at Washington are revenging themselves of her."[63] Royall did little to dispel such notions, and she was quick to endorse Andrew Jackson's moves against the spoils system. Her influence seemed to be confirmed when some commentators noticed that certain members of the Engine House congregation who had been officeholders under the Adams administration had been replaced by Jackson appointees. Their subsequent appearances as witnesses for the prosecution at her trial strengthened suspicions that they were taking revenge on Royall for her political connections. Speculation about her influence among members of the new government was heightened still further when she called as her own witnesses Secretary of War John Eaton and a number of officers of Congress. Reports that Jackson himself was to be a character witness on her behalf came to nothing, however, as he declined to appear.[64] The suggestion was an attempt to cast doubts on Royall's moral character, given the slurs against both Andrew and Rachel Jackson during the election campaign. The apparently close connections with the administration allowed opposition editors to link Royall with Jackson's supposed immorality and the riotous behavior of his supporters.[65]

Conjecture about her connections diminished as the trial began and commentators focused on the spectacle to come. Witnesses for the prosecution testified that Royall had been acting in a manner designed to provoke the members of the Engine House congregation.[66] While some accounts continued to see the amusing aspects of the incidents described by the witnesses, others saw her slanders as outrageous and offensive—though the specifics of what Royall was alleged to have said were never spelled out. Critics drew a contrast between the delicate feelings and benevolent character of the daughters, wives, and mothers of the complainants, who were the victims of her verbal abuse, and the vulgarity of Royall's attacks. One account observed, "But these smiles all vanished on the examination of the first witness for the prosecution, who testified to outrages on the female part of his family, so gross and abominable, that a general feeling of indignation put every thing of the ludicrous to flight." The victims had done nothing to upset Royall, he contended, but that did not stop her invective: "None of the family had done aught to provoke the virago; yet she had not ceased to pour out on every one of them torrents of the most coarse, vulgar and obscene language, until they could not appear even at the windows of their own house." Other witnesses claimed that her real crime was her abuse of female members of the congregation, "(for had she confined her attacks to men alone, the prosecution would never have been undertaken), and that both in the public street and in their own houses."[67]

Another observer highlighted the contrast between the respectable women she had abused and Royall's own behavior, though he had a greater sense of the farcical nature of the complaints: "Many of the respectable citizens who reside on Capitol Hill appear to have been prodigiously annoyed by this gifted dame, whom Petruchio would have found harder to tame than Kate the Curst and an universal terror of her, except among the boys, infects that whole region. . . . They testified sundry wicked sayings of their tormentor—which although they relaxed the features of the bench and bar, will perhaps be found insufficient to relax the sterner countenance of justice."[68] The prosecution was determined to justify the charges and emphasize Royall's vulgar and unfeminine behavior. In their eyes Royall was abusive, and her offence was particularly odious because her insults were directed at the women in the congregation. Moreover, she had invaded the privacy of these women's homes, as well as insulting them on the public streets. The men of the congregation clearly had a duty to protect their women from this virago. They believed that Royall needed to be stopped because she threatened to undermine the social order and disrupt the peaceful activities of the evangelical congregation—a situation made worse because, as a woman, she should have been supporting the evangelical cause, not attacking it.

Royall's own witnesses did little to contradict the impression given by those for the prosecution. While Secretary Eaton testified that Royall had not been guilty of any misconduct in his presence, her other witnesses caused the court to dissolve into laughter as they described how she shouted at people from her window, and "slandered" one witness by calling him an "exemplary man" and another by describing him as a handsome man: "Why there's Mr. Waterston, she says in the same book that he and Joe Gales are two of the handsomest men in Washington; now I leave it to all the world if *that* is not a slander."[69]

Throughout the trial Royall conducted herself with dignity and good humor. She sat quietly next to her lawyer, taking notes, apparently as much amused by the proceedings as some of the other observers.[70] Although her reputation for belligerency and verbal abuse was being rehearsed before the court, none of the accounts of the trial suggests she conducted herself with anything other than propriety. Nonetheless, the trial and the reporting of it, as well as Royall's own demeanor during the hearings, highlight the complexity and ambiguities of her claims to be a respectable woman. Even if the complaints against her were an exaggeration and probably did not merit a prosecution, in the eyes of her accusers her disregard of their sensibilities and the challenge she represented to their ideas of proper female behavior deserved to be punished. To them, Royall's conduct embodied the antithesis of the newer constructions of middle-class femininity that they and the other supporters of the evangelical revivals were trying to establish at this time. In bringing the prosecution against her, the Engine House congregation sought not only to deal with the immediate problem of Royall's abusive outbursts but also to isolate her from her readers and supporters. Moreover, by emphasizing the differences between Royall's behavior and that of her victims, they sought to define acceptable middle-class femininity in their own terms. For in portraying the female members of the congregation as pious, virtuous, passive, and in need of protection, they could be labeled as undeniably respectable, in contrast to Royall's aggression, vulgarity, independence, and above all irreligion.

If the leaders of the congregation used the trial as a means to warn against female independence and promote their own ideology of femininity, Royall had other concerns and was not especially troubled about feminine propriety. During most of the trial her attorney conducted the case without interference from his client, but before the jury was asked to decide on their verdict, Royall stood up to address the audience in the courtroom.

Drawing on the same language she had used in her books and presuming that the charges against her were a response to her more general attacks on the evangelicals, she took the opportunity to reiterate her earlier warnings. The prosecution had been brought by her enemies, she proclaimed, and the proceedings were a "blot on the country which ages will not wipe out." Those who had brought the charges were part of a wider conspiracy to silence her, for "these are the same men who have persecuted me with increasing rancor since I began to expose their impositions on the people. In one instance they made an attempt on my life—I mean the same sect—and with pens steeped in gall, have hunted me from one end of the Union to the other." If the jury allowed the prosecution to succeed, she warned, no one would be safe from their machinations. "Let them once get the wedge in, and the Judge on the bench, and the President in his seat, may tremble for their liberty. I hope, therefore, gentlemen," she concluded, "that you will meet these encroachments upon our civil and religious rights like freemen. Give this dangerous sect a precedent, and our liberty is gone."[71] Representing the prosecution as part of a much larger conspiracy to overthrow American liberties, she tried to have the charges dismissed as spurious. They were an attempt by these dangerous elements to silence her, she contended—the very elements she had been seeking to expose through her books and on her travels. In her mind, the "priests" would stop at nothing to impose their power.

The public in the shape of newspaper editors paid little attention to her admonitions about an evangelical conspiracy. While she asserted her right to a public forum for her opinions, neither the editors nor the jury responded to her injunctions. One editor dismissed her caution airily: "Your fancy must add the graces of emphasis, gesture and expression of countenance, the collection of which made up the rich but unavailing eloquence of the persecuted Cassandra of our age. . . . Alas for the fate of posterity—her appeal was unavailing."[72] The jury returned a verdict of guilty. As Royall noted, "It was said they were all Bladensburg men!"[73] The trial was not over yet, for on receipt of the guilty verdict, her attorney, a Mr. Richard Coxe, moved for an arrest of judgment and a new trial, and she was released on a security of $100.

Coxe's plea to have the verdict overturned was straightforward—the only punishment available for a common scold was to be ducked, and this penalty was inappropriate. It would allow the offender the privilege of scolding with impunity once the sentence had been carried out and encourage other women to scold as much as they liked with the knowledge that they could only be punished once.[74] The case should therefore be dismissed. The prospect that Royall might be ducked induced a flurry of excitement among the newspaper editors, as they ridiculed Royall and the potential consequences of her sentence: "We believe common scolds may be punished by being ducked three times,—but neither law nor custom prescribes the period of submersion; leaving that to be determined by circumstances. In Mrs. Royall's case, perhaps from two to four hours will be thought long enough for her to remain under water."[75]

In the event, Royall was not ducked, although she claimed a ducking stool was constructed at the Navy Yard for that purpose.[76] Coxe's argument that the ducking stool was an obsolete sentence in England and had never been in force in America proved to be conclusive. But nor was the case dismissed. After much deliberation, followed closely in the newspapers, Judge Cranch delivered his judgment. He dismissed each of the defense's objections, and drawing on various legal authorities, he concluded that "ducking is only a *part* of the punishment under the common law; and if it be not in force, there are other punishments yet in store, for the discretion of the Court." He overruled the motion in arrest of judgment and sentenced Royall to pay a fine of $10. To ensure her continued good behavior, he demanded that she give sureties to the sum of $250 for the period of one year. She stood committed until these securities were given.[77]

Predictably, Royall was incensed at the outcome of her trial, accusing her persecutors of having interfered with the judge and jury.[78] Both the nature of the charge and the defendant's reputation for invective, however, suggest that the guilty verdict was entirely appropriate in the circumstances. Royall may have been correct about the real reasons for the prosecution, but her enemies had outmaneuvered her and there were no grounds for appeal. The charge of common scold, which might have appeared archaic, had been carefully chosen to trap her. Its focus on what might constitute unacceptable public behavior for a woman translated an antiquated charge into a useful instrument to control a woman who sought to undermine the evangelical cause and its efforts to shape a new ideology of middle-class femininity. While Royall might justify her forthright behavior because of the danger she believed the country was in from her accusers, there was no denying that she had disturbed her neighbors' peace by her tirades and might, as a consequence, be regarded as a common scold.

As soon as the judgment was delivered, John Coyle, one of those who had brought the original complaint against her, complained of a further outrage against him. An evening or two earlier, he alleged, Royall had assailed him and called him a hypocritical old scoundrel. In the view of the prosecuting attorney, this made it all the more important that Royall should be treated severely. But she was not to be browbeaten and countered by denying the charges and claiming that Coyle had been guilty of an outrage against her, "by assuring her that her time was short." No doubt tired of the episode, the court concluded that the complaints cancelled each other out and ordered an end to the matter. Royall was released, accompanied by an officer, to find sureties for her bail.[79] For many who had followed the trial the sentence was an anticlimax after the long debate over whether Royall should be ducked. A number of editors concluded that the court had been too lenient and that members of the public would feel cheated by the judgment. Others expressed their disappointment that the entertaining spectacle was over, for Royall had played to her audience to the last.[80]

If some editors were disappointed in the outcome of the trial, others believed that she had received her due: "Thus has Mrs. Royall *fallen,* in the pride of her *old age;* and but few there are who shed a single 'tear of sorrow.' . . . She has fallen—and we did not anticipate it—*peace be to her literary ashes.*"[81] Many hoped that her conviction would put an end to her activities and discourage their fellow editors from patronizing her, for the editors were themselves "much to blame for puffing up and encouraging this ridiculous old bedlam."[82] But if some editors thought the episode was over, they had misjudged the interest in the trial and the fate of its star.

Immediately after the trial editors began to speculate about who would pay the fine and stand security for Royall, since she did not appear to have the means herself. Several suggested that her securities were to be Secretary Eaton; Major William Lewis, the second auditor; and Dr. William Jones, the postmaster of Washington. All were members of the Jackson administration, again emphasizing Royall's links with that group. Alongside the conjectures, hostile editors were loud in their condemnation of those who continued to support her. One editor maintained that to pay Royall's fine was to derogate from the dignity of the high offices these gentlemen held. Another leapt to her defense, however, claiming it was only to the credit of such gentlemen "to have prevented the incarceration of an aged woman, the wife of a revolutionary officer *and a mason,* by entering as her bail on such an occasion."[83] Eventually two newspapermen intervened on her behalf, or so it was said, for "the honor of the press, and gallantry of the profession."[84] Although she had made enemies among those editors infuriated by her behavior, Royall still had supporters. Nor did newspaper interest in her diminish much once the trial was over—she remained newsworthy.

The Engine House congregation and their allies no doubt intended that the trial and conviction should silence Royall. Few believed this would be the result, and Royall soon made it clear she would not remain quiet, despite the injunction on her to keep the peace for a year. Within a month of the end of the trial she was already advertising her second volume of *Mrs. Royall's Pennsylvania* to include an appendix containing a sketch of "the famous Trial of Anne Royall."[85] Nor were her subsequent books more temperate or any less sparing of the evangelicals—if anything they were even more vituperative in their attacks on the "blackcoats."

The trial did little to moderate Royall's conduct. Despite the emphasis during the trial on her behavior as an unruly woman, she still insisted on her right to voice her opinions on public affairs in the public sphere. She denounced the legal proceedings as an outrage and a slur on the American justice system: "The odium of this infamous persecution, blackens the very face of humanity, and will remain an eternal blot on the American character."[86] She continued to insist that her trial was part of a much wider conspiracy by the "priests" to undermine the free republican government and to remove all in the way of their attempts to pass laws to impose Sabbath observance and stop the mails on Sunday.[87] Her pride was hurt by the conviction, but the lesson she drew from her prosecution was that the government and Congress should redouble their efforts to ensure her persecutors did not achieve their purposes or gain influence in government.[88]

By the late 1820s, women who, like Royall, maintained their right to voice their opinions in public were increasingly criticized. Those who continued to participate in political activities therefore did so within certain limits. Jacksonian women, like Whig women a few years later, insisted on their female moral superiority as the basis of their participation. They also emphasized that they were "disinterested" political participants—as women they were only interested in lending their morality and dignity to their party's cause.[89] Royall used none of the rhetoric of female moral superiority, and indeed disparaged the concept. She was outspoken, critical, and forceful in her political participation. She also entered the political public sphere without regard to social conventions, making her opinions known both through print—in her books but also through letters to newspapers—and in verbal attacks on the "Presbyterians" in taverns and stagecoaches, and sometimes on the public streets. She continued to assert her right to express partisan political opinions even though women who did so were gradually being marginalized and denigrated as "political women."

To many newspaper editors, though, Royall's status as a woman who espoused a party line in public presented difficulties. Certainly some of them regarded her outspokenness and willingness to comment on public and political affairs as unsexing her, but other more friendly writers insisted on her womanliness by portraying her as the dignified widow of a Revolutionary War officer and Mason.[90] Both groups sought to frame Royall's behavior according to their own conceptions of how a respectable middle-class woman should behave, but those conventions were neither stable nor certain in the 1820s.

Royall's trial and conviction as a common scold can be understood at a number of different levels, but it was ultimately an attempt by her enemies to diminish her. For while the Engine House congregation may have been acting to deal with an immediate grievance, the wider evangelical community clearly saw the prosecution as an opportunity to be rid of a more longstanding problem. Anxious to curtail her activities, they believed that by prosecuting Royall they would undermine support for her by exposing her as vulgar, ridiculous, and possibly mad—a lower-class woman who should be excluded from respectable society.[91] But the discussion in the newspapers prompted by Royall's trial suggests that her behavior was of interest to many others besides the evangelical community, and that the evangelicals were not able to dominate opinion. For although often framed in slightly different terms, her conduct and prosecution as a common scold acted as a focus for debate among a number of competing groups about how women should behave and what their level of involvement in public life should be.[92]

7 · The Female Politico as Newspaper Editor

In early December 1831, Anne Royall published the first issue of her newspaper, the *Paul Pry*, from her premises in Washington City. Acting as the editor and writer of much of its material, she produced a newspaper every week for over twenty years until shortly before her death in October 1854. Both the *Paul Pry* and its successor, *The Huntress*, reflected the often idiosyncratic views of its editor, developing the themes and political standpoints that she had earlier made public in her travel books. Increasingly she concentrated on an audience that consisted of members of Congress and inhabitants of the Federal City, but she maintained a determined following in the country and among some other newspaper writers. Keeping to a different schedule and with a more focused audience, she commented on national politics and the workings of the federal government to a much greater extent than she had done in her books.

To Royall the publication of a newspaper was the logical successor to her books. It enabled her to maintain the public presence she had accomplished through her books and tours, but in establishing herself permanently in one city, she avoided the need to be constantly on the move. Moreover, by publishing a newspaper every week she was able to react more quickly to political events, while at the same time it provided her with a medium for her pen portraits. It also afforded her a forum to express her political opinions without impinging on her private life. For, having experienced the consequences of provoking the evangelicals, she may have been wary of stirring up the kind of reaction that women like Frances Wright engendered in conducting lecture tours and appearing on public platforms. A newspaper put her at one remove from her audience, or at least from the audience with which she was not personally familiar.[1]

As efforts to exclude women from politics persisted into the 1830s, and ideas that women were inherently nonpolitical began to gain ascendancy, there were still women who continued to assert their right to a political voice. Some of these women rationalized their activism in terms of their gender, arguing that their supposed moral authority impelled them to act with other women to reform the nation.[2] Others, who have been referred to as female politicos, maintained an active role in politics without reference to their gender. They were more concerned with partisan politics than they were with female collective activism. This latter group largely ignored the changing political landscape that focused on expanding white male suffrage across the social classes at the cost of all female political participation. Rather than accepting that women had no recognized role in electoral politics, these women continued to voice their opinions, often in the face of criticism from both men and other women.[3]

Always more interested in proclaiming her own opinions on partisan politics than being part of a community of women, Royall nonetheless continued to pay lip-service to the idea that women should not be involved in politics. Her first editorial in the *Paul Pry* reflected her attempts to appear disinterested, as she proclaimed, "Our course will be a straight forward one, as heretofore; the same firmness which has ever distinguished our pen, will be maintained." But she insisted that she was above partisan politics: "To this end let it be understood, that we are of no party, we will neither oppose nor advocate any man for the Presidency. The welfare and happiness of our country is our politics." Despite such declarations she continued to take an active role in partisan politics with little reference to her gender, participating from the sidelines in the generally rancorous politics of antebellum Washington.[4]

By the late 1820s, Royall had become a significant figure in the United States. She was well-known both for her travels and the books she wrote about them, and although many newspaper editors and private individuals disparaged her views and behavior, it was difficult to ignore her. The furor created by her trial as a common scold, and the fact that it was reported across the nation, suggests that people were interested in and held strong opinions about her. While few openly acknowledged her political influence, her editorial presence in Washington from 1831 until her death in 1854 was frequently remarked upon, with one editor suggesting that "it is generally admitted that Madame Royall publishes more *truth* in her *Paul Pry* than any other editor in Washington."[5] Country editors also considered her newspaper sufficiently important to request exchange relationships with her.

Even before she decided to start a newspaper, Royall had begun to hint at the reasons why traveling, researching, and writing travel books no longer had the appeal they had once had. By the end of 1830, she had completed her tour of the United States, having visited all those areas accessible by stagecoach. Although she continued to travel even after she commenced her newspaper, this tended to be only along familiar and well-traveled routes such as the one between Washington and Boston.[6] With some justification she may well have felt that she had exhausted the possibilities for writing and selling the kinds of books she had been producing to this point.

By 1831 there were other reasons why travel was no longer so attractive. She was sixty-two years old and had lost the agility she had enjoyed when she first started to travel. Increasingly she portrayed herself as a martyr to the cause of enlightening her readers. She made it clear that she was making considerable sacrifices on their behalf in order to satisfy their demands for her books. She highlighted the difficulties in maintaining the pace of traveling, visiting, and receiving guests while at the same time trying to keep up her writing and itinerary. Her unrelenting schedule was exhausting, she protested, especially in the heat of the South, for it allowed little respite: "A quadruple heat to contend with—the heat of the climate—the rapidly approaching season, and my 'quick time' travelling, of course, the pleasure of my friends at Columbia, as well as my own, was actually sacrificed to this polar star of my tour."[7] Although she continued to enjoy the attention she received on her tours, she found it tiring and claimed to be relieved to retire to a quiet room at the end of the day.

She was also more easily frightened than she had been, especially when she encountered hostile receptions in several of the towns she visited during her southern tour. She used such encounters to warn her readers of the dangers posed by her enemies, maintaining that she was the victim of unprovoked attacks. Her growing notoriety made it difficult to pass through a town without exciting a reaction, but these could be unpredictable and occasionally violent. In St. Louis she became so alarmed by her reception in certain parts of the town that, with the aid of some sympathizers, she left the place secretly in the dead of night.[8] She made it clear to her readers who she held responsible for her poor treatment in St. Louis, but her experiences there had clearly shaken her. The injuries she received as a result of her encounter with the "missionary" in Burlington, Vermont, and the incidents in Charlottesville and St. Louis made her more wary of potentially violent situations. Consequently, when she was assaulted in Pittsburgh in late 1830, she concluded she was putting her personal safety at risk by traveling to certain parts of the country.[9] By the time she had completed her southern tour and returned to Washington, she had been harassed on several occasions, she was physically exhausted, and she was tired of constantly traveling.

Difficulties in financing her travels also persuaded Royall that she should discontinue her extensive tours of the country. Until the end of her southern trip, she had managed to pay for her travels through a combination of book sales and the generosity of stagecoach companies and her patrons, including the Masons. These sources had already begun to dry up before she set out on the tour, partially as a result of the publicity surrounding her trial. Moreover, her habit of abusing all those who refused to treat her in the manner she demanded was starting to have an effect. Her attacks on stagecoach proprietors in the pages of her books meant that they stopped subsidizing her travels. Consequently, her transport became more expensive and risky. Although she did not admit to a loss of sales, she encountered increasing setbacks in distributing her books. Unprepared to acknowledge she was at fault, she blamed her problems on the "missionaries," accusing them of influencing the booksellers and causing their unwillingness to take her books. As she noted in her *Southern Tour,* the evangelicals were prejudicing her livelihood, "and because I had independence enough to expose their vile robbery, every bookseller, who is known to sell my books, from Maine to New Orleans are assailed, when they go to New York, with such language as this, 'She ought not to be encouraged—she is the enemy to religion—she is an enemy to God.'"[10]

It was, then, for a number of reasons that Royall decided to shift her literary endeavors from books to another print media—a weekly newspaper. The recurrent need to support herself financially meant that she had to find a new source of income, although she continued to sell her books in the cities of the Atlantic seaboard and to send them to booksellers further afield while demand lasted.[11] Despite her need for the money, she persisted in maintaining that her aim in publishing was not a pecuniary one—she had a much higher purpose in writing her books. "It will be asked then, what encouragement I have to write? and how I am able to publish at all," she revealed. "To the first, I answer, I do not write from profit or for fame. I write for the benefit of my country, and to please my friends. The books are read and have done good; thus my object on this point is realised."[12] She professed a similar aim in publishing her newspapers.

The rapid expansion in print culture that had been underway since the American Revolution was well established by the time Royall began to publish her newspaper in late 1831. The exploitation of cheaper methods of printing meant that the number of newspaper titles produced in the United States rose from just 200 in 1801, to 375 in 1810, and 2,546 in 1850. The frequency of their publication also increased. In 1801, most of them had been weeklies, but by midcentury a much higher proportion were printed daily.[13] While the most successful were able to boast high circulation rates, especially in the larger cities, many struggled to keep afloat, and newspapers merged or went bankrupt as frequently as new ones appeared.[14] The increase in literacy rates meant there was a sufficient demand for newspapers by the second quarter of the nineteenth century to sustain any number of new newspapers and periodicals. The expansion in print matter catered to a wider readership than had previously been the case. Whereas in the late eighteenth century, newspapers had been the preserve of gentlemen and clergymen, the new print culture of the 1830s had a mass appeal to both sexes and all classes. Royall was uninterested in appealing to this large popular audience, who were attracted by the sensational penny press. Rather, she aimed at the more traditional readers of economic and political news found in the large-size newspapers, produced for regular subscribers rather than the more spontaneous purchasers of the penny press.[15]

The early-nineteenth-century explosion in print culture also encouraged the entry of new writers into the field. The world of print culture provided fresh opportunities for women. Publication allowed them to broaden their influence, and this occasionally extended into the public sphere of politics. Women might be excluded from electoral politics, but this did not stop them from publishing and expressing their opinions in print to audiences beyond their own firesides.[16] Like Royall, many female authors wrote books, but others contributed articles, poems, and stories, often anonymously, to the new periodicals and newspapers. A few became proprietors or editors of their own periodicals, most notably Sarah Josepha Hale, who edited

Godey's Lady's Book for many years, and some like Royall edited newspapers.[17]

In becoming the editor of her own newspaper, Royall joined a tradition of female printers and editors that dated back to colonial times.[18] Many of these female editors were carrying on the family business, inherited from their husbands or fathers, and had served at least informal apprenticeships under them. Consequently, they often had considerable knowledge and experience of the printing business.[19] Although Royall had no such experience, she had spent several years negotiating a path through the world of book publishing and had a close acquaintance with many newspaper editors from whom she had received substantial support. She was therefore confident in her ability to set up her own paper.[20]

Royall joined a body of female editors who varied quite markedly in their editorial purpose. During the 1820s and 1830s, some female editors of periodicals—newspapers as well as magazines—aimed deliberately at a female readership. Proclaiming in their titles that their publications were specifically, or even exclusively, for women, this literature frequently promoted newer ideas about "woman's special nature" and helped in the development of a female culture. By the 1830s there were also female editors who aimed at a mixed audience, but who nonetheless believed that men and women were different and had different interests.[21] But not all female editors acted self-consciously to emphasize the gendered nature of their enterprise. While sporadically acknowledging the idea that women's role was primarily domestic, some of these women acted in a quite contrary manner, playing an active part in the political sphere.[22]

Few female newspaper editors could avoid the subject of politics altogether. Occasionally such women tried to remain aloof from expressing their own political opinions, while others were little more than the name on the masthead making only a minor contribution to the editorial aspects of the newspaper.[23] Others used their positions to advocate greater civil and political rights for women, including the right to vote. There were still others who, like Royall, took the role of a female politico in editing their newspapers. These women assumed a right to participate in political life without reference to their gender, and were rarely interested in pushing for women's suffrage—many of them actually denigrated the idea that women should become involved as voters in electoral politics.[24]

Throughout her career as a writer, Royall had generally paid only lip-service to increasingly dominant social conventions that tried to exclude women from politics. Despite attempts to label her as a "political woman" and hence to marginalize her, she continued to voice her political views.[25] As a newspaper editor she no longer tried to deny that women could express political opinions, although she persisted in drawing a distinction between political agency and partisanship.[26] Occasionally she would insist on maintaining an anti-party stance, but this was largely a rhetorical device. Even the most partisan of politicians adopted this distancing of themselves from party politics at times, and Royall followed their lead. While claiming that her only politics was the welfare of her country, she remained a Jacksonian for much of her editorial career. Her decision to launch a newspaper in the political capital of the nation signaled that she no longer even attempted to hide behind a fiction of disinterest in politics.

Washington had been Royall's home since leaving Alabama in 1823, and had been the base from which she set out on her travels. It was, therefore, the natural place for her to establish a newspaper. Much of her patronage came from the congressmen, senators, and officeholders who inhabited the federal city, and they, together with a number of newspaper editors scattered across the country, continued to be her chief supporters. These people also provided her with the main source of the news she reported in her newspapers. Her first editorial, however, was written from Boston, where she had been collecting subscriptions for her new project. The tone of the editorial assumed a familiarity with her audience and with the milieu of newspaper editors: "The time has at length arrived when *we* have to make our *congee* to the public. We had some thought of calling up Mr. Walsh or the Pink, to write a neat little debut, but here (in Boston) we whiled away the time, and have to call in the aid of our printer to patch up something for us in the shape of a NEWSPAPER. We therefore forward a few outlines of *our* course to Washington, where we shall soon appear in our own proper person."[27]

The *Paul Pry*, like many other newspapers published at this time, contained little reporting but was a mixture of materials taken from other newspapers—sometimes acknowledged and sometimes not—excerpts from novels, and editorials and comment written by the editor. At first it did not contain advertisements, but gradually these began to appear.[28] So too did letters from readers, usually praising the publication but occasionally criticizing it, providing the editor with an opportunity to lash out at her detractors. In an early number of the newspaper, she asked her readers for advice about what to include in the paper.[29] The responses she printed two or three weeks later reveal a great deal about why her readers subscribed to the *Paul Pry*. "Some of our friends complain we do not season high enough," she divulged. "Throw in more cayenne Mrs. R. we want something relishing." Clearly her opinionated stance, acerbic style, and willingness to abuse all those who crossed her appealed to a large part of her audience. Consequently, she quickly dismissed those who merely asked for more news from Washington, recognizing that she was more likely to secure sales from those who enjoyed her characteristic style: "Our paper is small; the weather is cold; times are hard; our fire is low; our candle is dull; but, we will send over to our neighbour, New Jersey, by stage, for a little more cayenne."[30] Among those who responded to Royall's request were a group who suggested that she cease attacking the Christian religion. Rather than acting on their request, this group became one of the chief targets of Royall's "cayenne."

The *Paul Pry* enabled Royall to carry on a public dialogue with the editors of other newspapers whom she considered to be friends. Since she first began her travels on the eastern seaboard, she had counted some of the New York editors among her greatest supporters, and local newspaper editors were usually her first port of call when she arrived in a town. Few editors failed to notice her presence in their town in the pages of their newspapers, though their comments were not always friendly.[31] Most ceased to follow her movements once she left town, but the *New York Enquirer*, in particular, had taken a great interest in her travels and publications, though many of its printed comments gently poked fun at her.[32] It was therefore to the New York editors Colonel William Leete Stone of the *Commercial Advertiser* and Major Mordecai Noah of the *Morning Courier and New York Enquirer* that Royall turned when she required a "neat little debut" for her new project. One of them apparently obliged, and the recommendation was duly printed in one of the early numbers of the *Paul Pry*: "The numerous works which have appeared before the public under the editor's name, are sufficient evidences of her industry, and her powers of observation and description," the writer began, but readers were to be warned that Royall was to be no supine printer of pleasantries: "If she has been severe on some portions of the community, it is only because she believed that they deserved to be exposed in their true colors. The truth shall always be discovered in her observations and remarks, being unwilling for the sake of pleasing a few, to insert unjust encomiums, or to withhold merited commendation. *'Be just and fear not.'* is her motto; and with that sentiment for her guide, she fearlessly comes before the public, as an editor of a weekly paper."[33]

Her readiness to be portrayed as fearless and an enemy of those who peddled false pieties was also apparent in the other recommendations she published in her newspaper. In the first few issues of the *Paul Pry,* she printed several comments from editors who noted the appearance of the new newssheet. While she chose to publish those editorial opinions that were generally favorable, occasionally the comments were not entirely flattering and could hardly have recommended the paper to genteel society—that she printed them suggests she wished to cultivate her prickly reputation. A notice reprinted in *Paul Pry* from an otherwise unidentified newspaper, for instance, served to remind people of Royall's incendiary style: "Mrs. Royall is the Hannibal of the age, and in our opinion could, if she pleased, split rocks without vinegar. Let her be patronized. The world is a mere booby, and has no more taste for *Belles Lettres* politics than an oyster has for apple dumplings, if it neglects this opportunity of throwing in a stick or two of kindling wood to the great brush-heap. . . . If Paul Pry is suffered to languish for lack of patronizing nurture, we shall despair of literature."[34] She presumably chose not to reprint the unfavorable notices, and the editors who did not approve of the project tended to ignore the new publication. Others were simply dismissive. One New Hampshire editor censured Royall's new enterprise by flatly noting, "Mrs. Royal has commenced her threatened newspaper at Washington, called the 'Paul Pry.'"[35]

Reactions to the advent of her newspaper mirrored earlier responses to Royall's books and behavior, but also echoed wider social concerns. A reading public who were no longer limited to the eastern elite meant that newspapers reached a more diverse audience than they had done previously. Editors, too, particularly those who supported Jackson in the 1820s, revealed a growing democratization of the press. Their social backgrounds as well as their editorial stances were frequently the subject of attack by Jackson's opponents, who condemned the "vulgarity" of the new editors with their rough-hewn western manners and absence of social refinement.[36] Attitudes toward Royall's newspaper suggest that many regarded her, and those who read her papers, in the same light.

Royall's reputation predisposed many editors to look unfavorably on her new project. For others, however, it was the very absence of finesse and Royall's confrontational style that appealed to them. As the editor of the *Baltimore Patriot,* a longtime supporter, noted of the *Paul Pry:* "It is well charged with original matter, and that so far as we have examined, appears to possess that same peculiar spicing, which has contributed to extend the circulation of the various literary productions from the same pen."[37] Most subscribers to Royall's newspaper were aware that it was likely to reflect the same viewpoints, in the same style, as her books. They must also have suspected that she would continue to pour scorn on the evangelicals and express her admiration for Andrew Jackson. Although some people might claim they would not subscribe to her newspaper until they knew what her politics were to be, it was obvious enough where her sympathies lay.[38]

Editors had been significant agents in the revival of party spirit in the 1820s, and they continued to play a key part in the formation of broadly based mass parties in the decades that followed. The volatile political atmosphere of the early 1830s was partially of their making, and consequently an editor who expected to sell his newspapers could not remain above party conflict.[39] Although she remained on the margins, Royall became a participant in these political debates, maintaining her earlier sympathies with the Jacksonian party.[40] In the early years of her newspaper career she did not openly electioneer for a particular political party, as many of her male colleagues did, but her choice of causes to support or criticize revealed a high level of partisan commitment.

Royall used the *Paul Pry* as a platform from which to run political crusades, developing the methods she had used in her travel books. Impatient at the apparent unwillingness of some male editors to act quickly against threats to the country's liberties, she occasionally reminded them of their duties. Through the pages of her newspaper, she denounced their inaction and claimed that, because of it, she was forced to act herself: "We flattered ourselves upon taking hold of a paper, we would have it in our power to gratify our humor, and amuse our friends with chit chat—table talk—city anecdotes—and all that sort o'thing, when lo! we are (shame to gentlemen editors) compelled to gird on the sword and take the field to defend our country's civil and religious rights." Showing little reluctance to enter the political arena, she pilloried certain male editors, suggesting that it was their cowardice which had led them to deceive the country by supporting the Bank of the United States. With a sense of almost personal betrayal, she railed against those politicians and editors who had taken loans from the bank or who had refused to denounce it: "We find ourselves on the field of battle, and in the VAN of our brother editors—all having fled, or hid behind barns, churches and ditches. But the greatest number has jumped behind a great marble building in Chesnut Street, Philadelphia, called the United States Bank!!!! A few, however, stick close to our side; how long they will do so is dubious, for since Lewis McLean and Noah has deceived us, we put *no faith* in *man.*"[41]

Royall's denunciation of the editors and politicians who had gained favorable terms on loans from the Bank of the United States followed closely the criticisms of the institution made by Andrew Jackson and his supporters. While not all of the president's political allies shared his suspicions, increasingly hostility to the bank defined Jacksonianism. In his first annual message, Jackson condemned the bank as unconstitutional and denied that it had any useful purpose to serve, and he made similar pronouncements in subsequent annual messages. The administration gave ambivalent signals, however, for many of Jackson's cabinet members and appointees were its supporters.[42] Royall did not share in their hesitation. She had been a fierce critic for some time, seeing it as a source of corruption. She asserted that it drained the whole country of its property and forced men to sell their consciences or starve. She was particularly concerned about its effect on the independence of the press, believing that many editors had been bought up.[43] Jackson's attack on the bank therefore met with Royall's approval, even if it lost him support elsewhere.

The depth of Royall's own distrust of the bank was revealed in her willingness to censure those editors who had received loans from it on favorable terms, especially those who altered their editorial line accordingly. She was prepared to break friendships over the issue, she announced, even with those like Noah of the New York *Courier and Enquirer,* who had been longstanding friends and supporters. Noah's objections to her criticisms met with a swift response in the *Paul Pry:* "We never denyed his kindness to us, when we were a destitute and persecuted stranger. But we put no private friendship—no individual obligations in competition with the liberty of our country." She went further: "The man who advocates the Bank of the United States is a public enemy to his country, and the Major having first broken the treaty of amity between us, by joining the enemy, the fault is not ours." Having roundly condemned Noah, she insisted that, poor as she was, the bank could not buy her.[44]

Royall continued to excoriate the pro-bank editors as its supporters attempted to secure its re-charter in Congress. She attacked the bank itself through the pages of her newspaper, not simply for its corruption but because much of it was owned by foreigners, particularly English shareholders. Occasionally she printed the speeches made in Congress by the bank's critics, endorsing them and adding her own comments.[45] If anyone had doubted that she was a Jacksonian, her reaction to his veto of the re-charter bill in July 1832 made her position very clear. His action raised him to new heights in her estimation as she praised him for his bravery and patriotism. In her opinion, he became, as he had been when she first saw him in Alabama, a hero: "The veto of the President has raised him to the highest pinnacle of honor. It has placed him amongst the most magnanimous sons of America, and proves to the most sceptical the sterling integrity of the man!" As she told her readers, his actions had saved the United States yet again from the machinations of those who would destroy its liberties: "This noble act must endear him to the poor man whom he has so nobly defended against the encroachments and oppressions of the rich! It must not only endear him to every virtuous American, but render him the admiration of Europe. Our liberty upon the very brink of distruction! It is well we had a President who regardless of every selfish motive, activated by pure love of country, once more stretched out his arms to save it!"[46] For Royall there was no doubt that Jackson's veto of the bank re-charter was essential in protecting American liberties.

Anxious to portray herself as the defender of the American people against a "set of men, who have long since shaken hands with honor and principle—the very basest of mankind," Royall added her voice to the attacks on the bank and its supporters. Her rhetoric of tyranny and corruption was not very different from that of other Jackson supporters as the coalition around him began to shape itself into the Democratic Party. She put her own stamp on her attacks, however, denouncing the bank as a tyrannical force, acting in total disregard of public opinion. It slandered the president and the people of the United States, she wrote, and refused to answer the charges against it of "Bribery, Corruption, Fraud and Extortion."[47] It offended her sense of patriotism, but she also began to position herself as the defender of "ordinary" people. Thus she challenged the wealthy and aristocratic who were, she claimed, putting their special interests above those of the only true republicans, the people of the United States. Echoing Jackson's own rhetoric in his attack on monopoly and privilege, she also reflected her interest in the ideas of the Workingmen's Party, whose proceedings she frequently cited in the *Paul Pry*.[48] But she had not lost her independence, and although she was a Jacksonian on most issues, she still felt able to criticize Jackson's administration.

In early 1834, Royall identified three parties that, in her opinion, had designs adverse to the liberty of the people of the United States: the Bank of the United States, the "Church and State Party," and the "Office Holders."[49] Her suspicions of the Church and State Party were longstanding, and she continued her attacks on evangelicals and propagators of what she called "money religion." She continued to publish exposés that revealed the sums of money the "missionaries" had extorted from the poor and misguided, but she also warned her readers of the dangers posed by their new ventures. Their plans to "convert" the "people of the Valley" and establish temperance societies came under censorious scrutiny. But whereas both the Bank of the United States and the Church and State Party were by the mid-1830s old targets, and ones she shared with many other Jackson supporters, her pursuit of officeholders was a new undertaking. Moreover, it was one aimed at those in Jackson's own party who sought to short-circuit the electoral process. As she explained, "By Office-Holders, we do not mean, nor never did, every man that holds an office, or a contract, or a clerkship, under the Government, as many of them are known to us to be honorable men, and staunch friends of the people. But when we speak of Office-holders, we mean a political party, who would sacrifice the liberty of the country, at the expense of the Electoral Franchise, to use that power, which they now have to establish a family nobility, and life salaries in this country."[50]

In this she shared Jackson's avowed policy of rotation in office of federal employees. He had raised the issue in his first annual message in 1829, when he provided a lofty rationale to justify the removal of his predecessor's political establishment and replacement by his own appointees. If public officials were not regularly rotated out of office, he argued, they would breed corruption. For officers had begun to regard their offices as a "species of property, an engine for the support of the few at the expense of the many."[51] Moreover, Jackson contended, the monopolizing of offices by an entrenched group of haughty officials gave the impression that their duties could not be carried out by ordinary, intelligent men. Thus, Jackson aimed to democratize the executive offices while also fulfilling his political purpose of removing those he believed had stolen the presidency from him in 1825.[52] In reality Jackson only replaced about 10 percent of federal appointees during his presidency, but many of them were high profile, and the policy attracted widespread criticism.[53]

While Royall applauded Jackson for his removal of lazy and greedy officeholders, especially those she accused of being "blueskins" (evangelicals), she was also appalled by those who sought to take their places. Like many others, she was dismayed by the numbers of office-seekers who came to Washington and the poor quality of some of the patronage appointees.[54] Through the pages of her newspaper, she fulminated against the corrupt officers, advising her readers of their offenses.[55] But although she joined Jackson in attacking the corruption of some government officers and calling for their removal, she began to scent a still more dangerous aspect of the entrenched civil service—their attempt to perpetuate their power by perverting the electoral process. Martin Van Buren's nomination to the vice presidency and his acknowledgment as Jackson's successor particularly worried her. It was in her eyes a conspiracy by the officeholders to circumvent the usual means of electing a president. Although she claimed not to have any personal animosity against Van Buren, like other erstwhile Jacksonians, she began to abandon her support of Jackson's party in the last years of his presidency as it appeared likely that Van Buren would be crowned as his successor.[56]

Many other editors who had been keen Jackson supporters in the early years of his presidency voiced strong criticisms of him as he failed to live up to their expectations. He remained the "old hero" to Royall for much longer than he did to many others. She was extravagant in her praise of him in his destruction of the bank and believed that the Nullifiers, that is, John C. Calhoun and other supporters of Nullification, acted from hatred of the president—the majority of Nullifiers, she charged, would see the United States "reeking with blood" in order to get their revenge on Jackson.[57] But she too began to waver in her loyalty over the issue of corruption in certain government departments, and she became very defensive about her continued support for the president. In response to jibes from other editors, she was pressed into asserting that she was still a "Jackson man," but she had her reservations: "We go beyond General Jackson in democracy, if that be what they mean," she bristled. "Does it prove that because we are opposed to a combination of corrupt office holders, who are aiming to saddle themselves and their relations upon the people by buying up the press, that we are not a friend to General Jackson?"[58] Even she began to suggest some disillusionment with the president when he failed to act to stamp out corruption in the Post Office department.

Royall had a particular interest in the affairs of the federal Post Office. Her travels had given her an intimate knowledge of how the mail routes worked, and she claimed a familiarity with the regulations governing the duties of local postmasters and the delivery of the mail. She also depended on the mail to deliver her newspapers to subscribers outside Washington and therefore relied on its efficiency for her livelihood. Political interference in the Post Office became obvious as local postmasterships were used as patronage posts, and it began to have a detrimental effect on the workings of the mail. When John McLean was replaced as postmaster general by a political appointee, William Barry, many people began to protest that this would open the door to fraud, widespread inefficiency, and cuts in service.[59] Royall was highly suspicious that local postmasters were being replaced by "blueskins," "missionaries," and others seeking to undermine American liberties. As a consequence, she argued, her newspaper was suppressed in many parts of the country. She frequently filled the columns of her newspaper with complaints from her subscribers who were not receiving their newspapers through the federal mail. These complaints alternated with her own protests that corrupt postmasters were deliberately waylaying and failing to deliver the papers.[60]

Royall's deep disappointment in Jackson became very apparent when, faced with a plea from the people of New Orleans that he should deal with fraud in the federal Post Office, Jackson supported the actions of his postmaster general rather than answering his critics. Barry's stewardship of the Post Office was, in Royall's eyes, far too corrupt to be excused. Thus while she intimated that pernicious influences were at work on Jackson, her belief in him rapidly began to fade: "And whether he be under the influence of Kitchen or Parlour Cabinet, we are constrained to say, he is no longer the Gen. Jackson he once was and we fear there is some grounds, for they report that he considers Mr. Van Buren as the heir apparent."[61] Jackson's acknowledgment of his vice president as his successor seemed to Royall the final betrayal. For, she argued, Van Buren was the nominee of the officeholders, and the general's recognition of him as his heir apparent was tantamount to establishing hereditary officeholding at the highest level. As a consequence, although she rejoiced in the defeat of the Whigs in the Ohio elections of 1834, whom she understood to be "the Bank party and purse-proud aristocrats," she began to lobby for an alternative to Van Buren as her own favored candidate.[62]

By the mid-1830s, Royall had long since ceased to pretend that her sex prevented her from having an active voice in political affairs, but to use her newspaper openly as a forum from which to lobby for a specific presidential candidate was something new. She maintained that she did not wish to act in a partisan or authoritarian manner, but since hers was the only newspaper "devoted exclusively to the people, in this city," her hands were tied, and "we have, in relation to this step, only complied with the wishes of our patrons—by whose advice we have been governed."[63] Imitating the position of many male politicians, she pronounced that it was only because of the extraordinary circumstances of the time that, reluctantly, she felt it incumbent upon herself to get involved in matters that were not really part of her sphere. Hiding behind the artifice that she was only defending the American people, she told her readers, "We have always said we would never meddle with the Presidential question, our peculiar business being chiefly that of exposing corruption, and guarding the rights of the people; and it is at their instance we announce Judge WHITE as their candidate, and having done so, we hope they will carry out their wishes themselves, and let us remain untrammeled."[64]

Despite her protestations and pleas to "remain untrammeled" by such partisan issues, in the months leading up to the elections of 1836 Royall became fully involved in the presidential question. She quickly abandoned the stance that she was merely voicing the wishes of the people and instead openly promoted her own opinions. She denounced Van Buren's candidacy and extolled the virtues of first Judge Hugh L. White of Tennessee and then the military hero William Henry Harrison, the Whig candidates. Like the Whigs, Royall portrayed Van Buren as dishonest and in league with elements dedicated to thwarting the will of the people. She blamed Van Buren for the corruption and intrigue in Jackson's government, and asserted that Jackson's nomination of Van Buren as his chosen successor was a danger to the liberties of the American people. In contrast, she advised her readers, both White and Harrison were the candidates of the people, unsullied by the machinations of Van Buren's supporters.[65]

Royall's public desertion of the Jacksonian cause and her overt entry into the presidential campaign did not pass without comment. As they had done in the past, a number of editors sought to ridicule Royall and her attempts to intervene in partisan politics. Believing that it was not acceptable for women to express independent partisan political views, they aimed to undermine any influence she might enjoy.[66] Some did so simply by ignoring her pronouncements, but others made it clear her opinions were not to be taken seriously. They tried to belittle her concerns by poking fun at her. In doing so they emphasized her status as a widow and sought to insinuate that her interjections would end if she were under the control of a husband. Thus at least one editor portrayed the differences she had with Van Buren as a lovers' tiff to be patched up easily, incidentally ridiculing him too: "It is evident that Van Buren must conciliate the good lady forthwith, or his hopes of the Presidency will be disappointed. The aspirant to the Presidential Chair is a *bachelor.* Mrs. Royall is an engaging *widow.* Here be the means of reconciliation—and it is wonderful that the sharp-sighted politician does not employ them."[67]

Other editors sought to both elevate and deride Royall's verdicts at the same time. They gave an apparent legitimacy and importance to her desertion of the Jacksonian cause, while simultaneously disparaging the notion that Royall had any influence at all. This kind of rivalry among editors, and the often spiteful exchanges that appeared in their newspapers, were common in the highly partisan atmosphere of the antebellum period.[68] Royall's gender and her reputation for tolerating no opposition gave the editors an easy target. Accordingly, one could remark sardonically that Van Buren should be careful of her displeasure: "The Magician was never in danger before. His star begins to pale. The Whigs must indeed be put to their trumps, when they have recourse to so formidable an auxiliary."[69] Moreover, once she began to endorse Harrison's candidacy for the presidential office in 1836, editors began to use her support to add to the gender-based slurs already aimed at him. Harrison was dubbed the "Petticoat Candidate" because of his alleged cowardice during the War of 1812 and "Old Granny" due to his age—Royall's backing gave opposition editors still more artillery with which to attack him. As one editor quipped, "Mrs. Anne Royall comes out lustily in support of Gen. Harrison, because the democrats abuse him for wearing *petticoats.* She thinks it an indispensable article for all *old* grannies, and will not quietly look on and see him defeated on that account. Verily, the old General has become the 'Pet of the Petticoats.'"[70]

Ignoring such reactions, Royall continued to berate Jackson and Van Buren, warning her readers of the dangers they posed to American liberties. She was also quick to respond in kind to the scorn of the male editors. Remarking that she had been called a "Petticoat Editor" by the *Harrisburg Reporter,* her riposte was swift: "We shall only add, that a petticoat patriot is at least equal to a trouserloon traitor."[71] She was equally fast in defending Harrison's reputation and comparing his courage to Van Buren's inaction during the War of 1812. It was Van Buren who was the coward, she asserted, not Harrison: "Instead of shouldering his musket as General Harrison did, and meeting the foe hand to hand, he was doing every thing in his power to discourage and thwart those who did defend the country. Traitor like he opposed the defense of the country, and skulked like a coward!" In a final assault on Van Buren's manhood, she added, "His conduct in those perilous times would have disgraced an old woman!"[72]

But Royall was not a natural Whig. She was opposed to their views on the bank, disliked their elitism, and vociferously attacked the evangelicals, anti-Masons, and nativists who made up core elements of the Whig constituency.[73] Her advocacy for the Whig candidates in the election of 1836 was less an embrace of the ideology of the emerging Whig Party than a rejection of what the Jacksonian party had become. She sought to persuade her readers that Jackson had changed, and had fallen under the influence of hypocrites and knaves. Nowhere was this more apparent than in his nomination of his successor, proof, she claimed, that Jackson had become a despot—an accusation she restated as she ceased publication of the *Paul Pry* and relaunched it as *The Huntress* in December 1836.[74]

The decision to stop publishing the *Paul Pry* and to relaunch it with a new title seems to have been a largely economic one. Royall had been finding it increasingly difficult to collect subscriptions from distant readers, and so she decided to cut her losses and begin a new newspaper. She had also been persuaded by her friends that *Paul Pry* was too trivial a title for a serious paper.[75] She did not explain why she had chosen the name originally, but there are some indications of her reasoning. *Paul Pry* was the name of a play written by the English playwright John Poole, which had been staged in New York in 1826. The name gained popular currency during the late 1820s on both sides of the Atlantic. It told the story of a man who was irrepressibly curious, and it may explain why Royall chose it for the title of her newspaper.[76] The title gave no hint that the editor was a woman, nor did it give any suggestion of the paper's editorial stance. The play also revealed, however, that its protagonist was an inveterate eavesdropper prone to interfering in other people's business, and this may well have persuaded Royall that the title unnecessarily lowered the reputation of her paper. Consequently, when she relaunched it in 1836, she chose a new name.

In naming her newspaper *The Huntress*, Royall wanted it to be more immediately identifiable with its editor. She aimed to present herself and her paper as fearless in pursuit of their quarry and ready to hunt down corruption in politics and religion. The old title, she suggested, was too evocative of gossip and "chit chat." Besides, she claimed, she had often ridden to the chase as a young woman, so *The Huntress* reflected both the purpose of the paper and the qualities of the editor. With many of the same flourishes with which she had embellished the earlier newspaper, on December 3, 1836, she launched *The Huntress*. Expressing her thanks to those who had helped in the past, she opened her first editorial with the hope that "the Huntress makes her humble and respectful courtesy to day; though she appears in a plain, simple dress—yet she trusts, 'for the sake of old Lang Syne,' she will not be totally eclipsed by her more wealthy contemporaries."[77]

The new title, like its predecessor, was a four-page newspaper and contained similar materials. It followed a standard format throughout its existence. Royall generally filled its front page with a serialized novel reprinted from another newspaper or magazine—occasionally she would print congressional proceedings but only when no suitable fiction was available.[78] The back page contained advertisements, frequently for hotels and stagecoach and steamboat companies, but also for schools, patent medicines, and local businesses, such as would be found in other newspapers. Those pages sometimes also contained poems sent to the editor, anecdotes, and witticisms, generally of a lighthearted nature. The middle two pages contained the substance of the paper: editorial matter, news stories and comment, and items gleaned from exchange newspapers. It was in these pages that Royall expressed her opinions but also continued her habit of producing "pen portraits" of members of Congress and their wives as each new Congress met. She would similarly print letters to the editor, acknowledge the receipt of a new exchange paper, and use the columns to wage campaigns of various descriptions, including opposing corruption in federal departments, deploring the cruelty of Indian removal, and encouraging the provision of education for all. But like the *Paul Pry*, much of the column space in *The Huntress* was dominated by political comment.

With her customary nod toward non-partisanship, Royall claimed for *The Huntress* what she had professed to be the purpose of the *Paul Pry*. The new paper would expose corruption, hypocrisy, and usurpations in all. She also gave some indication of her political preferences—she was in favor of states' rights and against the Church and State Party.[79] She lost little time in alerting her readers to the dangers posed by that party and the so-called missionaries, not only in their activities in converting "the citizens of the Valley" but their continued involvement in what she called "Money Religion"—the concentration on raising money rather than acting as Christians. She made it very clear that she did not approve of Van Buren's election, and she continued to criticize him.[80] The editorial stance of *The Huntress* differed little from that of its predecessor, although her partisanship became more subdued as election fever subsided.

Even though her partisanship was for a time muted, Royall continued to write about and engage in national politics through her newspaper, paying little attention to any adverse reactions she received from other editors or from her own readers. In the election of 1840, as she had done in the presidential contest of 1836, she extolled the merits of the Whig Party candidate, William Henry Harrison, and denigrated his opponent.[81] Her reasons for doing so differed quite markedly from those of the many other women who backed the Whig cause and were encouraged by the party to do so in the election of 1840. This election and that of 1844 saw a brief interlude in the more general tendency toward excluding women from partisan politics, as the Whig Party created a new space for women interested in politics. As many of its leaders were active in evangelical religion, it particularly attracted those women who had embraced ideas about female religiosity. The association between the Whig Party and the kinds of reform and benevolent activism with which many women were also involved was a further spur toward their support of the party. Furthermore, the party actively sought out politically interested women, hoping that their endorsement would lend the moral authority which they understood women to represent. With the decline of the Whig Party, however, women were once again marginalized by the political parties as the Whigs' opponents, the Democrats, focused on appealing to white men of all classes.[82]

Royall's interest in the Whig Party was of a different nature. Her concern was with effecting the defeat of the party in power because of the corruption it seemed to encourage, rather than in actively promoting the Whigs.[83] She greeted Harrison's election in 1840 warmly, and mourned his death shortly after his inauguration, but quickly became disillusioned with his successor when he did not act decisively against the officeholders.[84] Her focus remained on party politics rather than with the issues that prompted many other women to take an interest in politics. Moreover, she was highly critical of those women who sought to influence politics through their benevolent and reform activities.

By the 1830s many women had become involved in civil society.[85] They were active in benevolent societies and social reform, joining associations of other women in attempting to tackle the great moral issues of the day—temperance, moral reform, and abolitionism. For most of these women evangelical religion influenced and encouraged their activism. These activities brought women into a public sphere from which they sought to shape public opinion and the national political agenda while stopping short of organized politics. It was these forms of participation in civil society that Royall particularly despised.[86] She did so because she associated these female organizations and their activities with the "missionaries." Throughout her career as a writer and newspaper editor she had been strident in her denunciation of those women who had flocked to the evangelical cause, chased after "priests," and gave all their money to the "missionaries." By contrast, she professed to believe that women should be modest and retiring, and should act with charity and kindness toward the poor.[87] In her eyes, women's participation in petition campaigns or meetings to encourage reform, especially where they also involved male evangelicals, were inappropriate and unfeminine. Not only did these women forward the missionaries' plans to establish control but they were deviating from their "proper" role in society. Her criticisms of women who were active in benevolent and reform organizations often sounded like those of other critics who labeled these women as "unfeminine," but her perspective was a quite different one.

Occasionally benevolent women used the accusation of "unfeminine" behavior as a means to distance themselves from other evangelical women whose cause they considered too radical or unpopular. By doing so they tainted both the women and their cause with the charge of immorality and sought to dissuade women from pursuing reform. Catharine Beecher, for instance, attacked anti-slavery women over what she regarded as the impropriety of organizing abolitionist petitions to Congress, despite her own part in the petition campaign against Indian removal several years earlier. While she believed women had an important part to play in reforming the nation, she felt female influence should be indirect and not include direct lobbying of Congress. She was still more offended by the "brazen front" and "unfeminine" and immoral behavior of a woman like Frances Wright, whose opinions on religion and women's place were anathema to Beecher.[88] She might similarly have accused Royall of impropriety and indelicacy because of her anti-evangelicalism, and certainly the evangelicals were quick to use such allegations against Royall. Ironically, Royall seems to have been willing to appropriate the same language to criticize women involved in reform activism. Indeed, her targets were occasionally the same as those of more conservative evangelical women.[89]

Royall frequently expressed her disapproval of other women's activism. Thus she complained that the women of New England were lost to delicacy and modesty, acting like "swaggering dragoons" as they gathered signatures on petitions to Congress to further their causes. She was particularly judgmental of those women who openly espoused the anti-slavery cause—a movement with which she had very little sympathy or patience. In the early days of the *Paul Pry*, she had reacted with disdain when the editor of the *Genius of Universal Emancipation*, Benjamin Lundy, suggested exchanging newspapers. She announced that she would have nothing to do with anyone who wished to excite bloodshed and sedition. Making clear her position on abolition, she accused Lundy of hypocrisy and advised him to mind his own business and allow the people of the South to do likewise. Moreover, she condemned William Lloyd Garrison, the editor of the *Liberator*, as a fanatic, and concluded that he was probably insane.[90] Her attitude toward the women who advocated the abolition of slavery displayed similar sentiments.

Denouncing abolitionist women for appearing at public meetings and addressing mixed audiences, Royall adopted many of the same tactics as other critics of abolitionism. Like them she suggested that abolitionist women were acting outside their sphere and meddling in activities that were not appropriate to their sex. She argued, "If these women had any respect for their sex, they would attend to their own business, and let the men attend to state affairs, and if they cannot and will not, let them change clothes with the females."[91] But her condemnation of these women as unfeminine and indecorous was also a way to mask her own hostility to the abolitionist cause and to the evangelical religion these women espoused.[92] Thus she focused on the absurdity of women delivering public anti-slavery lectures as a means to censure abolitionism. She singled out Abby Kelley and Lucretia Mott, two leading female abolitionists, for particular criticism, joining with a fellow editor in denouncing Mott for "the unseemly, unfeminine and indelicate exhibition she has been lately making of herself before the world, on the subject of slavery, the rights of women and other old maidenish crotchets and idiosyncracies."[93]

Her reaction to the emergence of a women's rights movement was equally hostile. Seeing no necessity for women to demand any more rights than those they already possessed, she poured scorn on the whole idea of calling conventions to discuss women's grievances. The women's rights advocates were, she suggested, a symptom of the country's degradation and the "the climax of stupidity." Predictably she associated these women with the missionary and abolitionist movements, and condemned the whole women's rights movement as a farce.[94] But if Royall criticized the activities of female abolitionists and women's rights advocates as unbecoming their sex, her reaction to dress reform and the introduction of the Bloomer costume—modeled on Turkish pantaloons to give greater freedom of movement—elicited still swifter condemnation. She remarked, "In regard to the thing itself, we think it indelicate, unbecoming, and highly inconvenient: it makes the woman look the most disgusting of nature's works and must be doubly so in the eyes of men." Challenging the idea that the costume was, in the opinion of some doctors, actually good for the health, she exclaimed, "Is there no medium between corsets and immodesty—cannot corsets be dispensed with without forfeiting delicacy, modesty, and all that is estimable in the virtue and dignity of woman." Even dress reform was, in her eyes, the product of the missionaries' pernicious influence and their aim to undermine American liberties.[95]

In her condemnation of other women who sought to exercise political influence through their reform associations, Royall aimed to set herself apart from these women and their causes. In many senses she had very traditional views of how other women should behave, believing that they should defer to men in public affairs. In this respect, she adopted similar views to those of the more conservative evangelical women. But she could see little reason to modify her own conduct, arguing that her public interventions were necessitated by the threat to American liberties posed by the very groups who were seeking to reshape women's roles. Thus, while ready to judge other women by narrow criteria as to what constituted appropriate female behavior, she was unhappy to be treated in the same way. In the eyes of many male editors, there was little difference between her conduct and that of the women she criticized. Although she adamantly opposed the abolitionist and women's rights causes, Royall was still seen by many as a "political woman" involved in areas of public life not usually considered the province of women.[96]

On several occasions during the 1840s, male editors associated Royall with other women who had gained reputations for being opinionated and forthright in their public pronouncements. The editors aimed to ridicule these women in the hope of belittling their opinions. Thus they paid little attention to the fact that Royall was of a very different political persuasion—the editors were more interested in emphasizing the absurdity of women being involved in politics of any kind. So in October 1840, a Connecticut editor published his idea for an "Independent Ticket" for the presidential race. It included the actress Fanny Elssler and the abolitionist Abby Kelley, as, respectively, nominees for president and vice president, with Royall and a number of abolitionist and otherwise prominent women as electors. They were to run on a platform of "Petticoat Government—The Only True Form of Republicanism."[97] Similarly, during the 1848 presidential contest, another editor sardonically voiced his fears that Royall and Abby Folsom would run against "the Old Bachelor's Ticket."[98] The fact that Folsom was an abolitionist and women's rights advocate, known for her disruption of public meetings and therefore the focus of Royall's own disapproval, mattered little. Neither editor was interested in drawing a distinction between the politics of these women, for in these editors' eyes, they were all equally outspoken, disruptive, and consequently unfeminine.

Undisturbed by or unaware of such jibes made by unsympathetic editors, Royall brusquely asserted that she would have nothing to do with the ludicrous idea of women's rights. She did not acknowledge the restrictions placed on women by society, nor did she regard the franchise as necessary for women to gain a political voice. She assumed the right to be an active agent in national and partisan politics, and she was satisfied with the influence she was able to wield through her newspaper and her access to members of Congress. To her the vote would diminish that influence, and so, like the later anti-suffragists, she rejected the suggestion that it would give her a greater voice in the affairs of the country.[99] From her own perspective she had rarely found her gender a barrier, believing that she could discuss what she liked in her newspapers without reference to her gender except when it was useful to her. Her position as editor of a newspaper gave her a forum from which she could broadcast her political views. Occasionally she used it to criticize other women for being unfeminine when they created roles for themselves in civil society, but at the same time, she attracted opprobrium for acting as a "female politician." Such a position meant that she was frequently the subject of other editors' ridicule, and many might have joined with the editor who described her as "the editress of a filthy, straightout eight by ten paper."[100] Although perhaps few took her opinions completely seriously, her newspaper was not ignored.

8 · The Widow of a Revolutionary War Officer

In July 1848, Peter Silvester, a Whig representative from New York, felt it necessary to speak on behalf of a "modest and retiring class of persons, unable to help or provide for themselves, and who have been cast by adversity and misfortune upon the protection and charity of their country."[1] The persons he was referring to were the widows of Revolutionary War veterans for whom he was seeking pensions. But he was not their only advocate. Since the early 1830s, Anne Royall had also been campaigning forcefully for such a pension. Her claim was on the basis that she was the widow of "William Royall deceased, who served as Captain during the whole of the Revolutionary War."[2] But although she occasionally voiced her support for the wider campaign for widows' pensions, she only did so when it helped to further her own project. Moreover, unlike the other Revolutionary War widows for whom Silvester spoke, her reputation as a virago and common scold with uncompromising views meant that she could claim to be neither modest nor retiring. As had been true throughout her career, Royall was assertive and dogged in her determination to secure a pension based on her husband's war service. Using the columns of her newspaper as well as personally lobbying members of Congress, she forced her demands on her readers and the representatives of the United States.

Royall identified herself as the widow of a Revolutionary War officer early in her career as a writer. After the loss of her inheritance and the social rank her husband's wealth had afforded her, her status as the widow of one of the "revolutionary worthys" enabled her to claim a degree of social respectability denied her by her poverty.[3] Her husband's rank as a major at the end of the war, and his patriotism as a member of the Continental Army, offered Anne Royall, as his widow, a degree of social respect and status. It also provided her with a promising source of funds, for with the passage of the federal Revolutionary War Pension Act of 1818, there seemed to be a possibility that her husband's war service might qualify her for a pension. As she settled in Washington and began her newspaper, she started a campaign to secure herself such a pension. Using her newspaper as her forum, she proclaimed that it was the government's duty and it was the *right* of all widows of Revolutionary War soldiers to receive pensions for their husbands' patriotism and sacrifice, indeed that theirs should be one of the first claims on government expenditure. But although her most strident demands were framed in the language of entitlement, when she found it useful, she also drew on ideas about the dependence of widows and their need for the charity and protection of their country. Like Congressman Silvester, she recognized that the portrayal of women as dependent and submissive, herself included, was a necessary prerequisite for gaining a widow's pension.

Royall began campaigning for a government pension in recognition of her husband's service because she needed a more secure form of income. Since the decision of the courts against her in the case of *Roane v. Royall et al.*, her finances had been unstable. Her travel books had provided a sufficient income, enabling her to support herself, but the sales were unpredictable and did not produce riches. She frequently complained that rather than being profitable, her book sales produced considerable losses: "On all the works I have published, I have *not* been able from sales to pay for the paper, much less the printing. The frauds of agents, insolvencies, losses by sea, thefts by the post-offices, have exceeded my credits an hundred per cent."[4] While some of her protests were designed to deflect any censure she might receive from those who believed no respectable woman would admit to writing for pecuniary reasons, she also found it useful to plead poverty.

At least some of the sales she had made were prompted by charitable impulses, as a means to support the poor widow of a Revolutionary War officer.[5] Moreover, she assured her readers, the problems caused by her crusades meant that it was only through the munificence of her supporters that she was able to write her books: "The second 'how I am able to publish at all,' is answered at once by the aid of my friends, by private donations bestowed on me for food, clothing, fuel, etc, but of which comforts I deny myself, to pay my debts. I live in a house upon humiliating charity, without furniture." Only the leniency of her creditors allowed her to publish, she maintained, and even then she was dependent on the goodwill and generosity of her printer: "My printer, William Greer, hard as the winter was, with an expensive family, advanced money to pay the hands for two octavos." Above all, "the kindness and liberality of Washington City and Congress (all but the godly) have enabled me to publish."[6] Depicting herself as dependent on the charity of her supporters and the patience of her creditors, she emphasized the importance of her work and the ways in which she was appreciated. People aided her, she suggested, because they recognized her part in alerting Americans to the dangers posed to their liberties.

Royall found it useful to preserve the appearance of being impoverished and dependent, but the evidence also suggests that her pleas of poverty were not entirely disingenuous. For many women in the early republic, scraping together sufficient money and other resources to feed, house, and clothe themselves and their families was a constant struggle. Many of them took paid work, when they could obtain it, but it was rarely sufficient for wages were frequently below subsistence, especially for women. Consequently, they relied on a variety of strategies to survive, such as pooling resources with family members or neighbors. Occasionally, they asked for charity. When there was no work, or if illness prevented them from working, they resorted to the almshouse where they could at least expect shelter and food. Such grinding poverty seldom allowed these women to accumulate any savings, and an economic downturn, illness, or even old age could spell disaster. Royall's poverty was not of this nature, but she still had to exercise numerous stratagems in order to achieve an income regular enough to keep free of debt and enable her to produce her newspaper. She had many resources that enabled her to do so, and though she was not able to achieve the level of comfort in which she had lived as a married woman, nor the material refinements to which the emerging middle class aspired, generally she was able to meet her personal expenses and maintain an independent household.[7] Nonetheless, her constant pleas of distress and her vociferous gratitude for the charitable handouts she received indicate that, in her eyes at least, a life of poverty was a very real prospect if she lost the support of her "friends."

Beneath the tales of hardship, Royall was a fairly astute businesswoman, and she missed few opportunities to maximize her income. Even after she had decided to stop traveling, she continued to pursue the sale of her books. As she had previously, she did this through a mixture of cajolery and bullying. She wrote to acquaintances asking them to chase up booksellers and encouraging them to buy her books. For instance, in 1831, she enjoined the magistrate of police in Albany, "May I ask you dear Cole to present my respects to the Dear Rev Lacy & say to him my Southern Tour 1st & 2nd vol is at Mr Littles & that I wish him to name it to his friends & to Travellers & do you do the same. Tell him there will be two more volumes at least."[8] In an accompanying note to her bookseller in Albany, she revealed the difficulties she had in delivering her books and obtaining payment for them when she was not able to do so in person: "NB Can you no how in the world get the books or the money from Dr (somebody) at Schenecktady do try I think you sent there Write me if you know."[9]

Such personal correspondence and direct communication with her booksellers remained her chief means of chasing up sales, but it was not always very successful. She had to rely on the good will of others, and on the smooth operation of the postal service and transportation. Occasionally, too, disaster struck, as when a bundle of books addressed to customers in Camden, South Carolina, was destroyed in a fire—an event that was noted unsympathetically by a number of newspaper editors: "Dreadful literary calamity. The whole bundle of Mrs. Royall's Southern Tour, intended for her subscribers in this town, was burnt in the La Fayette hotel, in the late distressing fire at Fayetteville. We have heard of nothing like it since the destruction of the Alexandrian library."[10]

As she concentrated her efforts on her newspaper, Royall used similar tactics to market her new enterprise. Again she used personal acquaintances, many of them Freemasons, to chase up subscriptions and maintain a network of readers, some of whose names she could barely remember: "Be so kind present my best respects to his Excellency Governor Marcy & ascertain from him whether it be agreeable to him for me to continue my paper," she requested of Colonel Stephen Van Rensselaer. "Also to Mr Knawer (I think though I am not certain of the name I remember the man very well one of the more amiable men in the state) cashere of some bank in your city. Do be so kind continue some means to inquire of them whether I must continue or not & to send me the needful as early as convenient."[11] She also published notices in her newspaper to encourage recalcitrant readers to remit their subscriptions.[12]

In Washington she called on members of Congress and other public men to encourage them to buy her paper. Absorbed in the business of writing and publishing, for the first time Royall admitted to requiring assistance with her enterprises. She delegated some of her tasks to a friend, Sally Stack, who helped to collect subscriptions and deliver the newspapers around Washington. From time to time she would also send Stack on longer trips to gather outstanding sums. On these occasions Royall would ensure that Stack was properly equipped with letters of introduction to those who had aided Royall on her own travels, as well as a word of explanation. Thus she addressed a Mr. Sanderson of Philadelphia, "Being hard pressed for the needful our mutual friend Sally is going as far as New York where I have something due me & she calls on her way upon a few of my friends in your city, some of whom owe for the present year." In order to impress upon him the urgency of Sally's journey, she continued, "As the time is short when the 3rd year of the Paul Pry commences & the weather is growing cold those gentlemen in Philadela who may feel disposed to aid me the ensuing year will hardly make the time an objection."[13]

Besides acting as her assistant, Sally Stack became an important part of Royall's household once she had decided to settle in Washington. The story she told of their meeting and friendship was characteristic of Royall. The two women had met, she recalled, when Royall first arrived in Washington, a penniless and friendless stranger. Sally had taken her in and allowed her to live in the boardinghouse she ran for six months "without fee or reward."[14] When Stack herself met with misfortunes, Royall helped her out, and the two became mutually supportive friends, with Stack acting as assistant and helpmeet. Since both women were widows, sharing household expenses and dividing some of the tasks involved in producing the newspaper made sense. The friendship also provided Royall with the emotional support and practical help that enabled her to continue her newspaper career as she grew older, though it does not appear to have been the kind of emotionally intense relationship that some women experienced.[15] It also provided Sally with some benefits, for it gave her an outlet for her energies beyond those of domesticity. Royall interpreted the situation somewhat differently, believing that loyalty caused Stack to stay: "She is now comfortably situated and might live without work, upon the labor of the boys she raised. *But* nothing can induce her to leave me."[16] Stack took on many of the jobs Royall was no longer willing or able to do. She acted as messenger, debt collector, and business manager, as well as importuning members of Congress and officeholders for subscriptions and other kinds of material aid.[17]

With Stack's assistance and through the help of others, Royall was able to keep her newspaper going, occasionally requesting paper and type, and even cast-off printing presses from her fellow editors.[18] But the newspaper did not bring in much of an income. Delinquent subscribers, the practice of exchanging newspapers, and thefts as well as having to rely on the federal mails meant that Royall, like many other newspaper proprietors at the time, probably did little more than cover her costs.[19] As she grew older, her pleas of poverty became more frequent, and her newspaper contained many notices chasing subscribers for money—at one point she threatened to publish a list of the worst offenders. The economic slump of 1837 hit her hard, and in July 1838, she informed her readers that she had been forced to take measures to cut down her expenses, announcing that she would end her southern exchanges and that "I have also reduced my rent from $9 to $6 per month, by giving up my kitchen."[20] But she persisted in publishing her paper despite dwindling returns, because she believed that it had a purpose to serve. As had been the case with her books, she assumed, possibly with some justification, that her newspaper was one of the few independent voices in the country, and as such was important in defending the liberties of the American republic. As a crusading editor, her newspaper was a forum for her political views and for the occasional exposé of corruption, but *The Huntress* also served as a platform from which Royall campaigned for a pension that was proving increasingly important for her survival.

Royall campaigned for a pension and monetary compensation for her husband's service during the Revolutionary War on more than one front. One line of action was to petition Congress privately to claim the back pay she believed should have been paid to William at the end of the war. The other was to broaden her demands and press publicly for a government pension that might extend to all widows of Revolutionary War veterans. In doing so she drew on a wide range of arguments to justify her claim and persuade Congress of the validity of her cause. It was not unusual for a widow to petition for personal relief, but her wider campaign to push for legislation to provide the widows of veterans with pensions was not a common undertaking for a woman. She was not alone, however, in seeking financial aid from the federal government. American society had already begun to recognize its debt to the Revolutionary generation and had started to grant aid to certain elements of the Revolutionary forces.[21]

Debates about pensions and bounties for those who fought on the patriot side in the Revolutionary War had begun even before the war ended. The discussions had been caught up in wider arguments about the nature of the patriot armed forces and the implications of the republican belief that it was the duty of a citizen to provide military service.[22] Although there were some categories of soldiers whose right to receive a pension was accepted with little opposition, for others the issue was hotly debated. Soldiers and sailors who had been disabled in the service of the United States were compensated by a law passed by the national Congress in 1776, but attempts to award pensions simply on the basis of military service were much more contentious.[23] In the minds of many, pensions were associated with placemen and were contrary to republican principles. They feared too that volunteers would be attracted only by the benefits, and that the wrong kind of men would be recruited. Suggestions that the officers of the Continental Army should receive half-pay pensions in order to compensate them for their sacrifices of property and fortune were greeted with similar outrage. Pension advocates, however, eventually overturned these objections, and a compromise bill passed the Continental Congress in May 1778.[24]

The measure did not satisfy the officers, and they continued to agitate for lifetime pensions. Congress resisted, but in 1780, under pressure from the army, they were forced to concede and, in the face of bitter opposition, allowed for half-pay to officers for life. They also extended the benefits to the widows and orphans of Continental officers who met the requirements of the earlier act.[25] The promise of a pension, which had seemed to army officers merely the proper and honorable public recognition of their contribution to independence, was to prove short-lived. As the war ended, the issue again became a matter of public debate, and in March 1783, Congress withdrew the pension, instead awarding officers commutation certificates worth five years' full pay. There was no money to pay them, and by the time the new federal government could do so, many officers had sold their commutation certificates to speculators for a fraction of their value, leaving many feeling cheated.[26] Agitation continued into the first decades of the republic, and veterans flooded Congress with private petitions seeking public assistance and what many of them saw as "remuneration as an expression of national honor and gratitude."[27] Increasingly they made their claims in legalistic terms, employing rights-based rhetoric, but Congress continued to reject their appeals.[28]

Attitudes toward veterans of the Revolution started to change in the aftermath of the War of 1812, and popular sentiment began to portray them as heroes and patriots.[29] In this climate and with a budget surplus, President James Monroe urged Congress to pass a measure that would give federal aid to impoverished Revolutionary War veterans. Despite considerable opposition to the idea of pensions based only on military service, in March 1818, Congress passed the Revolutionary War Pension Act. It allowed pensions for life to veterans of the Continental Army who had served for at least nine months, were in reduced circumstances, and were in need of support from their country. In 1820, Congress introduced a means test to address some of the criticisms of the act and to resolve the ambiguities that had led to many more claims than had been anticipated.[30]

The Pensions Act committed the federal government for the first time to playing an active role in the lessening of poverty. It created a "programmatic benefit" for certain groups of worthy citizens, establishing an exclusive group of those entitled to or deserving of federal aid.[31] Consequently, veterans gained a new, esteemed cultural status. Americans embraced and celebrated the elderly soldiers of the Revolutionary War as the symbols of the patriotic Revolution that defined their national identity. As Congress showed its willingness to mark the national debt of gratitude by compensating those who had fought for American liberties, so during the 1820s Americans came to embrace their veterans of all classes, as heroes and patriots.[32]

Royall's insistence on her husband's membership in this newly honored class was a product of this changed environment. Her status as the widow of a Revolutionary War officer had been helpful on her travels in attracting customers for her books and occasional charity, but it did not provide her with a federal pension. The Pension Act of 1818 had created an exclusive group of those considered worthy of government aid, but it also produced groups of those not deemed deserving. Among these were women. There was no explicit pension legislation for widows, and they were left to make claims under the provisions of various bills entitling widows to the half-pay for seven years of an officer killed on military duty.[33] By treating veterans as a class, the Pension Act had dealt with the vast majority of petitions to Congress from impoverished veterans seeking individual aid. Grievances remained, however, for the act did not resolve the issue of the promise made to officers in 1780 of half-pay for life, nor did it fulfill the contract implied by these officers' acceptance of commutation certificates in lieu of five years' full pay. The matter was to come before Congress several times during the 1820s.[34] While the Pension Act might have stemmed the flow of petitions from veterans, it did not do the same for petitions from soldiers' and officers' widows, among them Anne Royall.

The right to petition Congress had been established in the first meeting of the new federal Congress, but it was a much older right. The practice of petitioning began with an individual requesting of his (or her) ruler redress of a personal grievance. The petitioner was to take the humble role of a supplicant and acknowledge the superior status of the body to which the petition was addressed. In the new republic, citizens were expected to present their concerns to the legislature, and Congress was required to respond.[35] It was also one of the few political rights women had, for Congress was obliged to receive and respond to their petitions, as much as to men's, no matter what the subject of the request. By the 1830s women had begun to use the petition as a collective means to influence public opinion on political issues, gathering signatures to press for reforms such as the abolition of slavery. For the majority of women, however, it remained a means by which an individual could seek redress for a personal grievance.[36] Royall, like many other supplicants, initially sought a pension by means of petitioning.

Encouraged by President John Quincy Adams, in 1828 Congress passed an act that aimed to settle the matter of half-pay benefits for those officers who had served to the end of the Revolutionary War. While it granted pay for life to the surviving officers and soldiers of the Continental Armed Forces, it made no provisions for the widows of deceased veterans.[37] Nonetheless, it offered some hope to those widows like Royall who sought recognition for their husbands' war service. This legislation may well have prompted Royall to embark on a campaign to persuade Congress of the justice of her claim. On May 3, 1830, Richard Johnson of Kentucky presented Royall's petition to the House of Representatives.[38] In the conventional language of a petitioner, she submitted her request: "Anne Royall, widow of Major William Royall, deceased an officer of the army of the Revolution, praying that the accounts of her deceased husband may be settled, and that the sum due may be paid to her." The petition was referred to the Committee on Revolutionary Claims, but nothing seems to have come of it—perhaps because the committee had no powers to deal with claims made in such vague terms.[39] Legislation to expand the pension system was stalled by debates over the tariff.[40]

Royall was undeterred. By 1832 she had settled in Washington and was editing her newspaper, but she was also keeping a close eye on legislative proceedings every time the question of extending Revolutionary pensions to new groups came up. Maintaining a high profile during the congressional debates, she also lobbied individual members of Congress. After the defeat of an amendment that might have extended benefits to the widows of veterans, in June 1832, she wrote to Tristam Burges, who had been chairman of the Committee on Revolutionary Pensions in the previous Congress, demanding his support: "Was it not cruel in Messrs. Foot & Holmes—was it not savage to shut out revolutionary widows!!!—If you have a heart & ever knew want of bread & clothes you must feel these men were Brutes. Mr. Webster was my friend & tried to have us taken in." Although he was not a Jacksonian, Royall still expected to receive Burges's sympathy and influence. She assumed that he would work for a general Revolutionary widows' pension law and also support a private bill for relief. "I have a private petition before the Hubbard Committee," she stressed. "May I ask you to say to Hon. Hubbard if he has a spark of humanity to have me placed on the pension list till next winter at least."[41] Her need for relief overcame partisan political boundaries.

Pensions for Revolutionary War veterans was not a specifically partisan issue. As president, both John Quincy Adams and Andrew Jackson had supported the principle of extending veterans' pensions to new groups, and neither the Jacksonians nor the anti-Jacksonians took a party stance on the issue. Certainly there were divisions in Congress, but these were frequently sectional in nature, rather than political.[42] Royall did not choose her sponsors because of their party affiliations but rather for their personal support. For while Richard Johnson of Kentucky, her original patron, had been an obvious choice because of his involvement in the Sunday mail issue, her subsequent sponsors were less clearly associated with her political interests. She sought assistance and influence where she could find it, since in her early campaigns to secure compensation for her husband's service it was a private matter. Like other widows in a similar situation, she acted as a supplicant seeking the benevolence of Congress.[43]

Despite an atmosphere in Washington that was increasingly favorable to the notion of aiding those who had fought for their country's independence, Royall continued to have difficulties in obtaining relief. In January 1833, the petition she had presented in June of the previous year was referred by the House of Representatives to the Committee on Revolutionary Pensions. As a measure of the complexity of such claims, on February 14, 1833, the Committee on Revolutionary Claims passed Royall's petition on to the Committee on Military Affairs.[44] A few days later the committee reported on the two aspects of Royall's petition—her entitlement to Major Royall's commutation award and her request for a widow's pension. The committee outlined the dilemma they faced in granting her a widow's pension. While they had every sympathy, they declared, they were powerless to act

> As to a pension to the widows of those who served in the revolutionary war, the committee will frankly state that, while they cannot recommend a special law for any particular widow of a particular officer, yet from the high merit and high claims of the widows of those who achieved our independence, it is worthy of the most serious consideration whether a general provision ought not to be made for all the surviving widows, such as has been made for the surviving officers and soldiers of the revolution, by which general provision the said Anne Royall would, of course, be embraced.[45]

Any recompense on this front would require further lobbying from Royall.

The committee's report on the private claim suggested there was rather more immediate hope of redress from that direction. While the committee had no jurisdiction over pensions or claims arising from Revolutionary War service, "yet they are not backward in expressing a decided opinion, that, if the petitioner can prove that her husband had any just claim against his country for rations or services at his death, that the claim, with interest, ought to be paid to the person entitled to receive it."[46] Notwithstanding Royall's personal acquaintance with many members of Congress, and her well-established claim to be the widow of a Revolutionary War officer, in an environment where Congress was concerned about fraud and the abuse of the pension system, Royall too had to provide the necessary evidence. Meanwhile, her claim was referred back to the Committee on Revolutionary Claims.[47]

In order to establish her claim, Royall had to provide evidence of her husband's service in the Continental Army and his entitlement to commutation pay. The Virginia service records were notoriously incomplete, and so she had to find other means to prove his record. The process was a lengthy one, and it required a certain amount of application. Moreover, she would also have to present a further petition. As she observed in her newspaper, other matters were more pressing, and both she and Congress had been preoccupied with other things: "We were so intensely engaged that session, in particular on the Bank and Tariff questions, and not wishing to take up one moment of the time of Congress during their short session, till these points were settled, our petition was laid too late." The delay allowed someone to find the missing papers, however, enabling her to pursue her claim with the necessary evidence.[48]

The discovery of the papers proving William Royall's service may well have been related to the presentation by John Tyler of a petition to the Senate on January 9, 1834. This was a petition offered by Elizabeth Roane. Now a widow herself, she laid claim to Royall's commutation money.[49] In her petition, Roane, "the only surviving heir at law of Captain William Royall of the War of the Revolution," stated that he had not only served for the duration of the war, but that "during his lifetime he never received the Commutation of Half-Pay promised to him by the Resolves of Congress of the 22nd March 1783." She presented as evidence of that service the papers by which he had been allowed bounty lands by the state of Virginia—no doubt the papers Anne Royall had believed were lost.[50] Whether Roane had intended to claim the commutation money entirely for herself as part of her uncle's estate is unclear, but her petition was quickly linked with Royall's, and the two were dealt with together by Congress.[51]

Despite continued concerns about the nature of the evidence available as proof of William Royall's service, the Senate committee reported favorably on the case. So-called parol testimony, which allowed for the confirmation of service by those who had served with the applicant, was often treated with suspicion after such a long time. In this case, the committee accepted it. As the report noted, "Such testimony must be relied upon, or great injustice will be done to individuals."[52] They did not allow interest, however, "because the committee do not believe interest ought to be allowed in any such case, unless application had been made in due time, and the evidence furnished to the Government that the officer was entitled to receive the principal." The bill presented with the report passed into law on June 30, 1834. It allowed for the payment of five years' full pay to the widow and heirs of Captain William Royall, to be apportioned according to the Virginia laws for the distribution of the personal estate of persons dying intestate. The sum of $1,200 was paid to Anne Royall, but not without further inquiries into her status.[53]

Royall's persistence had gained her a portion of her husband's commutation money. Her petition had succeeded in an atmosphere where Congress accepted the principle that the promise made to officers at the end of the Revolutionary War should be honored. Once this principle had been established, the justice of claims like Royall's was recognized, as long as the evidence to prove entitlement was available. As Royall discovered, however, since it was money that had been due to William Royall, it was a debt that could be claimed by his estate and was therefore subject to the laws of inheritance. As his widow, Anne stood to inherit William Royall's claim, but so too did his heirs. The sum she received did not satisfy her for, she argued, it had done little to solve her financial difficulties. She was soon seeking additional means to supplement the income she received from publishing her newspaper.[54]

Her initial efforts were concentrated on further petitions to gain interest on the commutation money, a tactic closely shadowed by Elizabeth Roane. Congress remained reluctant to accede to the request, though Royall persisted over several years. From time to time the debates over her private claims for interest were reported by newspaper editors, who noted the amusement had at her expense among some members of Congress.[55] For the most part, opposition to her petitions reflected a more general antipathy to claims for interest.

Her petitions met with varied responses in Congress, but the committee consistently denied her interest on the commutation pay because the evidence was so flimsy: "This testimony, uncorroborated by other circumstances, is clearly insufficient to establish a claim to a large amount," they maintained, "and which, had it been due, might easily have been obtained fifty years before."[56] Its conclusions were the same as for other claimants of this class, but Royall objected strongly. The interest was merely a part of the sum owed to William Royall for his services in the war, she argued. Any attempts to suggest the money should have been claimed years ago were clearly unjust and absurd, as the claimants were not then in need.[57] She persisted with her petitions. Seeking the backing of her readers, she commented tartly, since Congress was so liberal with the public money for other purposes, there was no reason why they should not grant her the interest due to her, "that is, provided Congress will only be so kind, and so condescending, and above all, so *just,* as to allow us the balance of our MONEY."[58]

Frustrated in her attempts to resolve her financial difficulties, Royall began to campaign on other fronts. Drawing on the now widespread veneration of Revolutionary veterans, she sought to extend sympathy for the suffering soldier to the suffering widow.[59] She began by commenting privately on the cruelty of excluding widows from the 1832 Pensions Act, but quickly extended her audience by expressing similar views in the more public forum of her newspaper: "It, therefore, rests with the present Congress to atone for the cruelty and injustice of their predecessors," she declared, "in leaving for the last what ought to have been done first, and so far as it may be in their power, wipe out this blot upon our boasted New World!"[60] In 1836, she argued in support of a rumored bill to extend pension provision to Revolutionary widows, emphasizing the great need of "aged and indigent widows" whose hardships should not be ignored because of concerns about the costs of such a program. Besides, she insisted, Congress had been incompetent in allowing the heirs of veterans to claim commutation pay—they were mostly young and able to earn their own living. By contrast, the widows were old and incapable of working—the two cases should be kept separate, she believed.[61]

In trying to persuade her readers, and through them Congress, of the worthiness of the widows' claims on the public purse, Royall used arguments that drew on ideas about the nature of widowhood. Her rationale was neither new nor unusual. It derived from assumptions about women's dependency that had long existed. A man was expected to protect and provide for his wife and children—his death did not, in theory, end his widow's state of dependency or need for protection. Increasingly by the early nineteenth century, the image of the poor widow became sentimentalized, and at a time when poverty was often believed to be the fault of the individual, the widow became the notable exception.[62] Poor widows were some of the first objects of charitable and benevolent societies established in the growing towns of the new republic, often encouraged by clergymen and run by women.[63] Such assumptions about the claims of widows on the community became part of the public discourse of the early nineteenth century, but charity was a private affair, and Congress had no part to play in providing for widows' welfare. It meant, therefore, that support for widows was inconsistent and uncertain. Royall sought to persuade Congress that it was the legislature's duty to provide for one particular group of widows, those of Revolutionary War soldiers.

Her reasoning developed from and was echoed by some of the debates in Congress and the press. She argued that it would be an act of justice by Congress to grant pensions "to those widows whose husbands risked their lives to secure to them the blessings of freedom."[64] Drawing on longstanding ideas that wives, and by extension widows, deputized for their husbands, Royall could see no difficulty in claiming the patriotic actions of the Revolutionary soldiers for their widows. For the soldiers had put their lives and property in danger to fight for liberty for the whole country, and it behooved those who had benefited from their sacrifices to protect their suffering widows and orphans. Since the veterans themselves were receiving the largesse of a grateful country, so too should their widows.[65]

Royall was not alone in using such arguments. Members of Congress utilized similar sentiments. In January 1827, during a debate in the House of Representatives over extending pensions to new groups, one congressman emphasized the inadequacy of existing provisions for widows: "Now, Sir, what does the poor widow get out of this million of dollars? she, whose brave companion, after unrivetting the chains of his country, has gone to the narrow house of the dead, and can no longer defend her, what does she get? One hundred dollars a year; the poor pitiful sum of one hundred dollars a year; and this for five years only: then she must die, or fall back again upon her own resources."[66] By the end of the 1820s, a growing number of members of Congress, including those involved in the Committee on Revolutionary Claims, were coming to the conclusion that there should be some general provision for the surviving widows of Revolutionary veterans.[67]

Movement on behalf of the widows was slow. The first Pension Act that included provision for widows was passed on July 4, 1836, granting half-pay to the widows or orphans of men who had died of their wounds in the military service of the United States. It also extended pensions to the widows of Revolutionary soldiers if they had been married before their husbands left the army at the end of the war.[68] As such the act only included a limited number of widows, and further attempts in early 1837 to extend the pensions to all widows of Revolutionary officers and soldiers stalled in Congress. Royall greeted the failure with contempt: "Well, the House Committee were all apparently willing to pass the bill. O, Mrs. R. just bring the bill from the Senate and we will pass it, and so perhaps they would, had not Mr. CARR give them too much CHAMPAIGNE to get them to vote for his bill." She stormed against Carr's bill claiming that it wasted money on providing messenger boys for Congress.[69] Gradually Congress passed acts that extended pension legislation to include those widows married after the end of the war, initially to marriages that had taken place before January 1, 1794, by an act passed in July 1838. It took another ten years before the widows of veterans who were married before January 2, 1800, were included. Royall had to wait until July 1848 before she could claim a pension, since there was no evidence she had been married before November 1797.[70]

Increasingly Royall came to see a pension for Revolutionary War widows as a right, and one that Congress should recognize speedily. Pinning her hopes on a general pension bill that would extend the earlier act to include those widows of veterans married after the end of the war, and on a bill that would allow interest on commutation pay, she berated Congress for not doing its duty. As the protector of the republic and the agent of the people, she scolded, Congress should be ashamed at keeping the widows' money for so long, or spending it on profligates: "We ask, will Congress, to whom the people have committed the ark of their safety—Congress, that high and dignified tribunal of the nation—stoop so low as to *defraud* the helpless, the poor and the aged widow, out of the means of procuring a cup of cool water upon a sick bed, or of smoothing her dying pillow."[71] Thus, far from being a supplicant, as she had been in her petitions to Congress, Royall used her position as the editor of a newspaper reaching many members of Congress to bully and cajole them into aiding the suffering widows of those to whom they owed their liberty.

She quickly saw a connection between Congress's failure to pass such a bill and its willingness to spend money on "unworthy" items. Returning to the issue frequently, Royall commented at length and in elaborate detail on the corrupt manner in which Congress spent the people's money: "Whatever profligate or idle renegade wants money (and what profligate does not want money, and takes all he can get) has nothing to do but come to Washington and bring a bundle of books, pamphlets or maps; or pens or post-paper, or any notion he may conjure up," she claimed, "and he will find a ready market in Congress hall, the proceeds of which will last him till next session comes round, when he comes again—whilst the aged widows and poor orphans of the *revolutionary war* are left to struggle in poverty and want."[72] While officeholders were granted large salaries, and were able to find jobs for their children, she continued, members of Congress "REFUSE TO PAY THE WIDOWS and the ORPHANS of the men to whom they owe the proud name of UNITED STATES CITIZEN." In her eyes, such profligacy was akin to the tyrannical actions of English kings, and she called for the impeachment of those involved.[73]

She did not campaign out of altruism, however, for she had a very clear vested interest in any pension legislation—a fact underlined by the irritation she voiced in her editorials: "God knows what ailed Congress this time! they did *pass the bill,* which was originally got up by our friends for our benefit. But unfortunately, it did not extend to our case by one or two years. . . . Some say there was too much Brown Sherry, too much everything but the right thing."[74] Nonetheless, she could see the advantages of waging an aggressive campaign on behalf of all excluded war widows through her newspaper, for an inclusive bill would surely gain more support in Congress.[75] But although she tried to persuade Congress of the importance of extending the pension legislation to new groups, Congress was not easily persuaded. In Royall's eyes it was simply a question of justice for all veterans' widows, as, she argued, they were equally entitled to the gratitude of their country. She refused to recognize the distinction that Congress had drawn between those who had married before the war and those who married afterward.[76]

Congress cited financial restraints as the reason for their reluctance to extend pension provisions to widows married after the end of the war, but there were other considerations which suggest that there were points of principle at stake. Many of these concerns were raised during a debate over the particular case of a veteran's widow whose marriage did not take place until 1813. One speaker argued that the date had not been extended beyond 1794 because any widow married after this date was too young to have experienced the difficulties of the Revolution herself. Nor would she have suffered the hardships caused by the absence of her husband or fiancé—suggesting that it was the widow's own experience which qualified her for a pension. Another representative questioned whether it was within the powers of Congress to grant pensions purely out of sympathy or justice toward the intended recipients. Eventually Congress agreed that a widow should receive a pension not because of her own birth before or after the Revolution, but on account of her husband's service during the Revolution. The only remaining argument against extending pensions to all veterans' widows was the cost.[77] Accordingly, Congress established the principle that women should receive pensions only because of their marriage to a veteran. Consequently, women received pensions solely because of their relationship to men who were considered worthy by the state. Widespread assumptions about the widow's role gave her an entitlement from which women who may well have played a much greater personal role in the Revolutionary struggle were excluded.[78]

Royall's own arguments for Revolutionary widows' claims on the benevolence of Congress were more simplistic than the arguments aired by Congress. She believed that Congress, as the representative of the people, owed a debt to those who had fought for their liberties during the Revolution, and by extension to their widows. She was not alone in this. Many other women presented private petitions for individual relief before Congress, though rarely did they publicly articulate their rationale nor extend their concerns beyond their own needs.

Newspaper editors, when they commented at all, accepted almost universally the principle that the widows of Revolutionary veterans were a worthy cause. Thus they noted with approval the passage of the various acts that extended pensions to widows, as for instance a New Hampshire editor who commented on the 1838 Pension Act: "Such a law as this was demanded by the exigencies of the somewhat numerous class of aged females, to whom its enactment will bring the means of obtaining those comforts and conveniences indispensable in the evening of life. We rejoice in that sense of justice and gratitude which prompted its passage."[79] The claim of suffering widows to federal pensions became so much a part of the public discourse that when in the early 1840s the term of the act of 1838 expired, several editors demanded its renewal because otherwise those "few feeble and white-haired old women" who had depended on the pension for their comfort would find it difficult to obtain the necessities of life.[80] Later, when Congress renewed the act, the editor noted that the claim of the widows was "meritorious and equitable," and to have refused them would have been a gross injustice. He concluded that the quick passage of the act reflected honor on the country, for "it will gladden the hearts of a number of deserving and aged widows, who were actually destitute of the means of procuring the necessities of life, and would have been under the inevitable necessity of seeking refuge in the Almshouse, had not Congress afforded them relief."[81] The editors seemed to be uninterested in the plight of those Revolutionary widows who were still not included in the provision of the act—the principle had been accepted, and there was no further discussion. The support of Revolutionary soldiers' widows, together with the veterans themselves, had been accepted as a legitimate burden on the federal government.

For Anne Royall the campaign for a pension continued for some years. When she finally became eligible for a pension in July 1848, however, she hardly acknowledged it in her newspaper.[82] It meant that her public pleas for help diminished in number. Nonetheless, her sense of justice and belief that she was owed interest on her husband's commutation pay continued until her death. As her health deteriorated and she found it more difficult to meet her financial obligations, she once again petitioned Congress for the interest on her husband's commutation pay.[83] Outlining the part William Royall had played in the Revolutionary struggle and the financial costs it had put him to, she claimed the interest on his behalf: "He never received a dollar the whole seven years though entitled to 10 rations per day and bore the expenses of the Virginia line to Hillsborough N.C. was robbed by the Tories of two fine horses—servant—one hundred pounds in specie." In case Congress did not fully recognize his heroism, she continued, "But twice the interest would not be equivalent to what he did & what he suffered & bore his own expenses the whole war! At one time while passing between the lines alone he was surrounded by the british light-horse & only saved his life by making the Masonic sign."[84] Only her death in October 1854 allowed the congressional committee to which the petition had been referred to discharge the case.[85]

In obtaining a pension in 1848, Royall gained some financial security but also the recognition and respectability she had long claimed of being the widow of a Revolutionary officer, a class of women honored and made worthy by their association with their patriot husbands. While the impact of her campaign to press for the passage of legislation gradually extending pensions to new groups of Revolutionary War widows cannot be easily measured, her influence cannot surely have been ignored. Her paper was read by many members of Congress, and she was frequently a visitor to Congress, making her a well-known public figure and one whom few members wished to cross. Drawing on longstanding ideas about the nature of widowhood and the willingness of the post-Revolutionary generation to recognize their debt to the soldiers of the Revolution, she produced a rational and persuasive argument to convince Congress to provide pensions to their widows. It was an argument that, ironically, rested heavily on nineteenth-century ideas of women's dependency and need for protection, factors that had hardly been at the forefront of Mrs. Royall's own career.

Conclusion

Anne Royall was eighty-five years old in 1854. Her increasing infirmity meant she was unable to collect subscriptions for her newspaper in person and had to rely on the help of others. Moreover, Sally Stack was ill and not in a position to help. As a consequence Royall hardly ventured out and quickly fell from public view. On July 24, 1854, she acknowledged she was no longer able to edit and publish her newspaper, and in her editorial of that date, declared it to be the last edition of *The Huntress*. She lived for only a few more months. In the final number of her newspaper, she reiterated old themes and pleaded once again for the support of her readers, claiming that for the first time since she had come to Washington, she was unable to pay her rent. Echoing her newspaper statement, she petitioned Congress, complaining that her pension was not enough to live on.[1] Insisting on her poverty, she gave as evidence her mounting debts and her reliance on the benevolence of her friends. After the demise of her newspaper, her health deteriorated rapidly, so that the announcement of her death on October 1, 1854, caused little surprise: "Royall. Yesterday morning, the 1st instant, Mrs. Ann Royall at a very advanced age."[2]

Royall might have died in poverty, but she did not die forgotten or in obscurity. The announcement of her death prompted the publication of notices and obituaries in newspapers around the country. Some recalled her visits to their towns many years before, while others related a story of her life; still others simply reprinted the announcement from another paper. One remembered, "She was a remarkable woman twenty years ago; wielding a sarcastic, and often bitter pen, as a domestic tourist through the

United States, and flourishing at a time when this sort of literature excited unusual attention."[3] Several provided her with a romantic background with scant regard for veracity: "Mrs. Royall was born in Virginia, and at an early age was stolen by the Indians, with whom she continued until she had seen fifteen summers in the western part of that state. After her release, she met with Capt. Royall, who became her husband; and then it was that she first acquired the rudiments of an English education having graduated, as it were, in the free school of nature."[4]

Royall could still invite controversy. In assessing her life in their obituaries, editors displayed a degree of ambivalence. The editor of the Washington *Evening Star* observed, "She was a woman of considerable literary attainments and benevolence, and of strict integrity, although somewhat peculiar in her views."[5] The editor of the *Fayetteville Observer,* on the other hand, was more colorful in his recollections, noting that she was remembered for "the blowing up she gave every body and every thing," while an Ohio editor recalled that she "was somewhat conspicuous upon the public stage during the administration of Gen. Jackson."[6] A longer obituary, which appeared in several newspapers, tried to offer some balance and commented that she was "vehement and violent in her antipathies, and the expression of them," but "she was equally warm in her friendship for those she favored, though from her peculiar ways of manifesting her likings, few, indeed, courted her affectionate regards. To the hour of her death she preserved all the peculiarities of thought, temper and manners, which at one time rendered her so famous throughout the land."[7]

The insistence by those who looked back on Royall's career that she was eccentric and possessed peculiarities of thought, temper, and manners, disguised the exasperation, resentment, and anger she had prompted at the height of her career. She had divided her contemporaries, some of whom accepted and even encouraged her forceful opinions and, by buying her books, helped to alleviate her financial difficulties. Others were repulsed by her attacks on the evangelical leaders and their cause, and sought to diminish her influence by marginalizing her. In both cases, reactions to her indicated the controversial character of her views. Sometimes they resulted in violent confrontations, especially during the 1820s. Such episodes highlight the intensity with which the evangelical leaders fought their battles to Christianize America, and their persistence in trying to nullify opposition. They were acutely watchful of any criticism from women, as they endeavored to gain the approbation of the emerging middle class for their notions of womanhood. Their portrayal of Royall as an enemy of religion, and their prosecution of her as a common scold, aimed to convince other women of the intrinsic truth of their way of thinking. The apparent lessening of their attacks in the 1830s and 1840s suggests that by then, the evangelical leaders believed they had marginalized her, and that they no longer considered her to be a cause for concern. By then, too, they had persuaded a significant number of middle-class women to embrace religiosity, and they had achieved hegemony for their ideals. The association of femininity with piety and morality had become widely accepted.[8]

Even if by the early 1830s the evangelical clergy believed Royall no longer posed a threat to their plans, she remained a constant critic. She also maintained influence as the editor of her own newspaper in Washington, and continued to divide her contemporaries as some bought her paper and others regarded it as a scurrilous publication. Moreover, she retained her public presence, using her newspaper as the forum through which she broadcast her opinions on the issues of the day. Paying little heed to efforts by political leaders to exclude women from party politics, her newspaper reflected her support for Andrew Jackson as president and her frustration at what she saw as his successor's failures. As a political woman she attracted both the opprobrium of those who believed women should not be involved in politics at all, and the vilification of those who disagreed with her political views. But although she occasionally attempted to disguise it by claiming her disinterest in politics, she remained a highly partisan and individualistic woman, asserting her right to a political voice with little regard to her gender. She had no interest in being part of the community of women engaged in reform and benevolent associations. Unlike her own, their political engagement was framed in gendered terms and focused on lobbying for specific causes rather than the electoral politics that were at the center of Royall's concerns. Moreover, she was deeply suspicious of these women's close connections with the evangelical cause and vocal in her criticisms of anti-slavery and women's rights advocates. But her attacks on these women were very different from those of some of their other female critics. Assuming her own right to a political voice, her condemnation focused on the causes in which these women were involved, rather than their demands for the right to speak as women.[9]

Her abrasive style, political viewpoint, and persistent attacks on the evangelicals meant that during her lifetime, Royall provoked controversy. Although the intensity of reactions to her had dulled by the time of her death, she was still capable of stirring fervent responses. But if contemporaries were divided in their opinions of Royall, since her death in 1854, writers of various descriptions have attempted to assess her significance, and in doing so continue to echo some of the earlier disagreements.

Newspaper columnists in the late nineteenth century tended to reflect the views of Royall's contemporaries. More recent writers, on the other hand, have tried to see her in broader terms, but as was true while she was alive, she has remained a source of fascination. In the years after the Civil War, columnists from as far afield as San Francisco; Bismarck, North Dakota; and Chicago hailed Royall as the "original Washington female correspondent" and mother of "personal journalism." Few were complimentary, and some, echoing her contemporaries, emphasized what they regarded as her masculine qualities.[10] For instance, a *Washington Post* columnist characterized her as "a rough old customer, a regular Suwarrow in petticoats. . . . She was too terrible for ridicule; she wielded a sharp pen; she had stout lungs and a formidable voice, which was perfectly masculine, commanding eyes, compact form, a Coriolanus carriage, and when angry was dreaded by her victims as if she were a Hyrcanian tigress."[11]

As Washington's local, as well as national, newspaper, the *Washington Post* has consistently taken an interest in Royall, reflecting changing assessments of her historical significance and perhaps also a more general transformation in attitudes toward women in the public life of the federal city. At the end of the nineteenth century, when there were still those who could remember her when she was alive, the *Post* columnists continued to regard Royall as a "holy terror" with a pen "as venomous as a rattlesnake's fang."[12] Gradually attitudes toward her softened, and instead of seeing her as terrible, abusive, and a disgrace to her sex, she became an eccentric, although one journalist in 1899 believed her to be "an advocate of the rights of her sex long before Susan B. Anthony and her followers took up the fight against the common enemy—man." At the time, this was not a recommendation.[13] By the first decade of the twentieth century, *Washington Post* journalists had begun to recognize Royall as a pioneer woman journalist. Moreover, one reported, she was "not so black as painted."[14] As female journalists became more conspicuous in Washington, opinions of her became more admiring. She was portrayed as the "policewoman of truth," whose newspaper with "fiery truthfulness and knifelike probings of the public and private affairs of men and women" sought out corruption in government and paved the way for other women in journalism.[15] In the years since World War II, the *Washington Post* has continued to relate stories of her but has been less certain of how to categorize her. Columnists have tended to emphasize the picturesque and unconventional qualities of her career, and although they suggest some admiration for her determination to root out corruption, in the 1970s at least, one columnist felt it necessary to make her more accessible to his readers by placing her in a more modern context: "She was the great gossip back when the reward for gossips wasn't their very own television show."[16]

She has, however, been the subject of a number of radio plays. Between 1935 and 1953, CBS and then NBC broadcast a drama series sponsored by the DuPont chemical company called the *Cavalcade of America.* It included plays that covered a range of themes celebrating American innovation, patriotism, and courage. Alongside programs about George Washington and Abraham Lincoln, there were features on Lincoln's mother, Nancy Hanks, and Jane Addams of Hull House. Royall was the focus of three plays: one broadcast in February 1940, another in May 1942, and the final one in November 1944. Starring well-known actresses of the day and revolving around her trial as a common scold, each of the broadcasts portrayed Royall as a patriot and defender of American liberties. She was depicted as battling against corrupt and malevolent forces in her struggle to protect the rights to freedom of speech and freedom of the press. Describing her as a "remarkable woman" and one who "risked everything to defend the principle of freedom of speech," Royall had become an American hero, a crusader against corruption in government, and a fighter in defense of "truth." Reflecting the values the broadcast companies and their sponsor wished to encourage as the United States joined the battle against the Axis Powers in World War II, Royall was celebrated as a passionate defender of the right to speak the truth openly. She became an example of the enduring greatness of the American spirit, and of the triumph of courage and honesty over adversity. Although her sharp tongue was not forgotten, she employed it for the good of America.[17]

If these broadcasts rehabilitated Royall for a general radio audience, over the course of the twentieth century a number of popular and scholarly writers have sought to bring her before the reading public. The handful of short popular biographies of her, mostly found in collections of themed biographies, reflected a growing acceptance of women in public life and the desire to recognize female pioneers in certain professions.[18] Although these works varied in their assessments of her career, they invariably focused on her trial as a common scold. Echoing later disputes over the role of religion in public life, one early biographer claimed that "the trial proved one of the most laughable travesties in American legal history," arguing that the Scopes Trial in Tennessee paled in comparison.[19] Over the years, other writers have been equally fascinated by this episode in her life, and have used it as a reflection on Royall's character to illustrate, variously, her fanaticism, her outspokenness, her eccentricity, or her heroism in the face of tyranny.[20] Although often acknowledging her sharp tongue and idiosyncratic style, these writers helped in the development of her reputation, from her nineteenth-century portrayal as a nuisance to the advocate for civil liberties she has become in more recent times.

This process has been helped by a small number of book-length biographies, which have received coverage in the press and on the radio. Collectively they have uncovered many more details of Royall's life than had previously been known, and brought her writings to a modern audience. Although more nuanced than the shorter writings or radio plays, they have contributed to the shaping of her reputation as a somewhat eccentric, forthright woman who spoke in defense of American liberties.[21]

Royall continues to fascinate, and she retains a place in popular memory as reflected in the columns of newspapers and the electronic media. The story about her which seems to resonate most is that of her sitting on John Quincy Adams's clothes and interviewing him as he stood naked and embarrassed in the Potomac River. Its telling and retelling suggest an ongoing admiration for a feisty woman who could put the president of the United States in a position of total discomfiture. Alongside this story, she is characterized as a pioneer woman journalist who developed the technique of interviewing politicians and other public figures, but who was also a fearless investigative journalist who rooted out and exposed government corruption. Interestingly, what is left out of almost all of these popular stories about her is her persistent fight against the agents of the evangelical revival.[22] Different interest groups have taken her story to meet their own needs, among them feminists who have adopted her as a pioneer women's rights advocate who paved the way for women in public life—an irony given Royall's own strident views on the subject of women's rights.[23]

What is also left out is a recognition of the sheer length of her life, her resilience, and her capacity to keep the interest of her contemporaries for so long. Royall did not become a public figure until she was in her mid-fifties, but for the next thirty years, she was seldom out of the public eye and remained the focus of considerable attention, particularly from fellow newspaper editors. Although she was rarely at the very center of public affairs, she succeeded in engaging audiences almost until her death. Her sharp pen and willingness to pursue issues unremarked upon by other writers inspired both detractors and sympathizers. On the one hand, there were those who were so offended by her that they tried to silence her, and on the other, supporters who enabled her to influence public opinion sufficiently to open the doors of politicians and public officials to her. Her descriptions of those same politicians and public figures, in either glowing or abusive terms, depending on the way they treated her, fascinated and repelled her readers, but they also sustained her public profile. Thus, she remained noteworthy, aided by her own efforts at self-promotion and a determination to maintain a public presence. Even as she grew older and more restricted in her movements, she continued to attract attention and an enduring circle of supporters.

Royall was significant not just as a public woman. As the author of nine books of travel writing together with the *Letters from Alabama,* and perhaps even her novel, she made a notable contribution to the literature of her time. In them she created a particular style of writing that appealed to a popular audience, keen to learn about the country in which they lived and who enjoyed her gossipy approach. The "pen portraits" of individuals, while they annoyed her detractors, were read eagerly by many others. Although the books are highly opinionated, and some contemporaries censured them as inaccurate, they gave descriptions of people and places; captured patterns of speech, culture, and behavior; and offered an understanding of political and historical events that the foreign travel writers who visited her country did not depict. Moreover, she probably saw, and certainly wrote about, more of the United States than the vast majority of her fellow Americans who took the "fashionable tour" but ignored much of the rest of the country.

Since her death Anne Royall has been remembered both as a feminist and a pioneer woman journalist. Neither of these is a characterization Royall herself would particularly applaud. She was not interested in the "advancement" of women and could not understand the need for women's rights, since she believed that women already had all the rights they needed.[24] As an editor she claimed to advocate no party in politics, nor sect in religion, but aimed to expose corruption, hypocrisy, and usurpation in all.[25] Clearly she was not free from partisanship in either politics or religion, but she used her newspaper as a platform for several campaigns believing that they would preserve American liberties. Although she was often laughed at, few of her fellow editors ignored her, and many had a grudging respect for her. As one contemporary editor observed, she was a woman who certainly could not and cannot be passed over lightly: "Mrs. Royall is pretty extensively known throughout the country, as the authoress of two or three volumes, in which she has contrived to give as many hard raps as she has herself received during the chequered scenes of her life. Mrs. Royall is a woman of no mean talents, at least in the particular line in which she chooses to exert herself, as many a 'galled jade' can testify." But it was her reputation and public presence for which this editor believed she would be remembered. As he concluded, "She is a perfect nightmare to many of the luckless wights who have fallen under her vengeance, and a source of endless amusement to those who are fortunate enough to escape the venom of her tongue and pen."[26]

Notes

Introduction

1. "Morgan Found at Last," *Carolina Observer,* July 3, 1828. On the Morgan kidnapping, see Bullock, *Revolutionary Brotherhood,* 277–80.

2. "John Neal's Description of Mrs. Royall," *Essex Gazette,* May 10, 1828.

3. "Morgan Found at Last," *Carolina Observer,* July 3, 1828.

4. Basch, "Marriage, Morals, and Politics"; Freeman, *Affairs of Honor;* Zagarri, *Revolutionary Backlash.*

5. The scholarly literature on the subject is immense. For an early interpretation of women's roles in the early nineteenth century, see Welter, "Cult of True Womanhood." See also the critique of separate spheres by Kerber, "Separate Spheres, Female Worlds," and Scott, "Gender as a Useful Category." For more recent discussions, see the essays by Mary Kelley, Julie Roy Jeffrey, Laura McCall, and Carol Lasser published collectively as "Redefining Womanly Behavior in the Early Republic: Essays from a SHEAR Symposium," *Journal of the Early Republic* 21 (Spring 2001): 71–123.

6. On women and the economy, see the chapters by Catherine Kelly and Amy Dru Stanley in Hewitt, ed., *A Companion to American Women's History,* 100–116, 193–205. On politics broadly and narrowly defined, see Zagarri, *Revolutionary Backlash,* 7–8.

7. Kelley, *Learning to Stand and Speak,* 5–10.

8. Lasser, "Beyond Separate Spheres"; Jeffrey, "Permeable Boundaries"; Baker, "Domestication of Politics"; Hewitt, *Women's Activism and Social Change;* Ginzberg, *Women and the Work of Benevolence;* Jeffrey, *Great Silent Army of Abolition.* On the question of civil society more generally, see John L. Brooke, "Consent, Civil Society, and the Public Sphere in the Age of Revolution and the Early American Republic," in Pasley et al., eds., *Beyond the Founders,* 207–50.

9. Branson, *These Fiery Frenchified Dames;* Rosemarie Zagarri, "Gender and the First Party System," in Ben-Atar and Oberg, eds., *Federalists Reconsidered,* 118–34; Klinghoffer and Elkis, "'The Petticoat Electors.'"

10. Varon, "Tippecanoe and the Ladies, Too"; Zboray and Zboray, "Whig Women, Politics and Culture."

11. Allgor, *Parlor Politics;* Varon, *We Mean to Be Counted.* See also Sacher, "'Ladies Are Moving Everywhere'"; Fredrika J. Teute, "Roman Matron on the Banks of Tiber Creek: Margaret Bayard Smith and the Politicization of Spheres in the Nation's Capital," in Kennon, ed., *Republic of the Ages,* 89–121; and Zboray and Zboray, *Voices without Votes.*

12. Zagarri, *Revolutionary Backlash;* Branson, *These Fiery Frenchified Dames;* Ginzberg, *Untidy Origins.*

13. Ginzberg, "Hearts of Your Readers"; Cott, *Bonds of Womanhood,* 128–59.

14. Ginzberg, "Hearts of Your Readers," 195–201; Ginzberg, *Women and the Work of Benevolence,* 23–35; Wood, "'One Woman So Dangerous.'"

15. Zagarri, *Revolutionary Backlash;* Zboray and Zboray, *Voices without Votes,* 1–16.

16. See Janet L. Coryell, "Superseding Gender: The Role of the Woman Politico in Antebellum Partisan Politics," in Parker and Cole, eds., *Women and the Unstable State,* 84–112. Women were involved in a wide range of activities that took them into political activism. See Baker, "Domestication of Politics."

17. Teute, "Roman Matron on the Banks," 94. Some of the early notices of her book include "Travels of a Lady," *Essex Register,* June 15, 1826; "Mrs. Royal," *Salem Gazette,* August 18, 1826; and "Mrs. Royall," *Baltimore Patriot,* August 23, 1826.

18. Hewitt, *Women's Activism and Social Change,* 17–23; Ginzberg, *Women and the Work of Benevolence,* 1–10.

19. *Essex Register,* August 23, 1827. On more sympathetic comments, see Royall, *Black Book,* 2:118–19.

20. See, for instance, "Mrs. Ann Royal," *Arkansas Gazette,* August 7, 1833; "Female Biography," *New York Spectator,* March 12, 1834; and "A New Age," *Baltimore Sun,* August 11, 1837.

21. The most important works include Porter, *Life and Times of Anne Royall;* Jackson, *Uncommon Scold;* and James, *Anne Royall's U.S.A.* More recent explorations include Maxwell and Dunlevy, *Virago!;* Beasley, "Anne Royall"; and Earman, "An Uncommon Scold."

22. Cohen, *Murder of Helen Jewett,* 152–86; Varon, *We Mean to Be Counted,* 26–27, 74; John, *Spreading the News.*

23. The story appeared frequently in the *Washington Post* and is noted by Royall's biographer: James, *Anne Royall's U.S.A.*, vii–viii.

24. One of the earliest appearances of the story is "Monument to Anne Royall, the Mother of 'Yellow Journalism,'" *Washington Post,* May 2, 1909.

25. James, *Anne Royall's U.S.A.*, vii.

26. The item appeared in "Ceremony," *Aurora and Pennsylvania Gazette,* November 6, 1829; *Salem Gazette,* November 10, 1829; and *Farmers' Cabinet,* November 14, 1829. It bore the byline *Colonial (U.C.) Advocate.* Adams's habit of taking an early morning swim in the Potomac is recorded in his diary. John Quincy Adams, "Diary in Abridgement," December 1, 1821–December 31, 1838, Reel 36, entry for May 21, 1825, Adams Family Papers microfilm, Massachusetts Historical Society.

1. A Frontier Childhood

1. Royall, *Pennsylvania,* 2:178, 180, 181; Watson, *Liberty and Power,* 17–18, 78–79.

2. On Turner's frontier thesis, see Nobles, "Breaking into the Backcountry," 641–42. Royall, *Pennsylvania,* 1:212. See also Royall, *Sketches,* 187–88, and Royall, *Southern Tour,* 3:132–33, 163–64.

3. "Mrs. Anne Royall," *New-Hampshire Gazette,* September 18, 1827.

4. The date and place of her birth are usually accepted as June 11, 1769, at Baltimore, but the evidence is very sketchy. Sarah Harvey Porter used this date in the first biography of Royall, which has no references, and the date has been accepted as correct by other biographers. Porter, *Life and Times of Anne Royall,* 18. Royall herself merely suggested on an early visit to Baltimore that she expected to be patronized there because it was her native *state.* Royall, *Black Book,* 1:100. Her year of birth can be calculated from her pension certificate, signed on September 8, 1848. The June date is given by Royall herself: "Health of the Editress," *The Huntress,* January 21, 1854; Pension Certificate, September 8, 1848, Anne Royall's Pension Claim.

5. Royall named her parents in Royall, *Letters from Alabama,* 85, and Royall, *Black Book,* 1:308. The name Newport appears on the marriage bond entered into by William Royall. Marriage Bond between William Royall and Anne Newport, November 15, 1797, Botetourt County Marriage Bonds, 1770–1815. The biographers who delved most extensively into Royall's family origins were Porter, *Life and Times of Anne Royall,* 17–30, and James, *Anne Royall's U.S.A.,* 3–21.

6. Paul John Eakin, *Fictions in Autobiography: Studies in the Art of Self-Invention* (Princeton, NJ: Princeton University Press, 1985), 5–6, 20–21; Elizabeth W. Bruss, *Autobiographical Acts: The Changing Situation of a Literary Genre* (Baltimore: Johns Hopkins University Press, 1975), 11–13.

7. Royall, *Black Book,* 2:118–19.

8. Hinderaker and Mancall, *At The Edge of Empire,* 170.

9. Bushman, *Refinement of America,* 383–88; Nobles, "Breaking into the Backcountry," 642.

10. "Mrs. Royall," *Essex Gazette,* July 28, 1827.

11. "Providence," *Literary Cadet and Saturday Evening Bulletin,* June 17, 1826. Whether the pipe was real or metaphorical is unclear.

12. Young, "George Robert Twelves Hewes." Both Porter and James sought to provide an explanation for Royall's failure to talk about her father, as explained in note 14 below. Porter, *Life and Times of Anne Royall,* 18–19; James, *Anne Royall's U.S.A.,* 10–11, 389–92n. On married women's status, see Basch, *In the Eyes of the Law,* and Lebsock, *Free Women of Petersburg.*

13. Royall, *Letters from Alabama,* 85.

14. Royall, *Pennsylvania,* 2:217. Some of her earlier biographers have suggested that the reason Anne's family moved to western Pennsylvania was because her father was a Tory, who, having lost his property, wished to escape further retribution by moving to the frontier. There is little evidence to support this interpretation, and it seems unlikely given the timing and choice of location. Lucille Griffiths, "Anne Royall: Tireless Traveler and Common Nuisance," in *Letters from Alabama, 1817–1822, by Anne Newport Royall,* ed. Lucille Griffiths (Tuscaloosa: University of Alabama Press, 1969), 19; Porter, *Life and Times of Anne Royall,* 18–19.

15. Hinderaker and Mancall, *At the Edge of Empire,* 80; Faragher, *Daniel Boone,* 9–30.

16. Hinderaker and Mancall, *At the Edge of Empire,* 122–23, 154–55; Jack D. Warren, "Introduction," in Bartlett, *Keeping House,* xiv–xv.

17. Hinderaker and Mancall, *At the Edge of Empire,* 150–55.

18. Ibid., 155–57.

19. Royall, *Pennsylvania,* 2:213, 217–18. There are no records of a William Newport taking out a patent on land at this time in Westmoreland County, Pennsylvania.

20. Warren, "Introduction," xvi–xvii; Nobles, "Breaking into the Backcountry," 648.

21. A range of historians have made such assumptions, among them Daniel Blake Smith, "'This Idea in Heaven': Image and Reality on the Kentucky Frontier," in Friend, ed., *The Buzzel about Kentuck,* 83–85; Eslinger, ed., *Running Mad for Kentucky,* 37; Cashin, *Family Venture,* 44–49; Warren, "Introduction," xix–xx; Nobles, "Breaking into the Backcountry," 650; and Bartlett, *Keeping House,* 3.

22. Faragher, *Daniel Boone,* 49–50; Norton, *Liberty's Daughters,* 13–15.

23. Peavy and Smith, *Women in Waiting.*

24. The absence of her father from Anne's memories suggests that he was frequently away from home, for unspecified reasons, leaving her mother to run the homestead.

25. Royall, *Letters from Alabama,* 86.

26. Faragher, *Daniel Boone,* 46–50; Ulrich, *Midwife's Tale, passim;* Royall, *Letters from Alabama,* 84–88; Royall, *Pennsylvania,* 2:211, 215.

27. Royall, *Letters from Alabama,* 88.

28. Royall, *Pennsylvania,* 2:206–9; Royall, *Letters from Alabama,* 84–86.

29. Royall, *Pennsylvania,* 1:223.

30. Ibid., 2:215.

31. Ibid., 2:206, 198.

32. Ibid., 2:211.

33. Albert, *Frontier Forts of Western Pennsylvania,* 290–94; Hinderaker and Mancall, *At the Edge of Empire,* 155–58; Bamberger, *Short History of Westmoreland County,* 47; Boucher, *History of Westmoreland County,* 1:85–86; Abernethy, *Western Lands and the American Revolution,* 93–97, 109–13; John B. Frantz and William Pencak, "Introduction: Pennsylvania and Its Three Revolutions," in Frantz and Pencak, eds., *Beyond Philadelphia,* xxiv.

34. Hannastown Resolutions, as quoted in Albert, *Frontier Forts of Western Pennsylvania,* 295–96, 294; Bamberger, *Short History of Westmoreland,* 48; Frantz and Pencak, "Introduction," xvi–xvii; Gregory T. Knouff, "Soldiers and Violence on the Pennsylvania Frontier," in Frantz and Pencak, eds., *Beyond Philadelphia,* 171–93.

35. Royall, *Pennsylvania,* 2:33n; Young, "George Robert Twelves Hewes," 567–70; Knouff, "Soldiers and Violence"; Griffin, *American Leviathan.*

36. Royall, *Letters from Alabama,* 154–55.

37. Royall, *Pennsylvania,* 2:211, 218–19; Royall, *Letters from Alabama,* 86–88.

38. Royall, *Pennsylvania,* 2:206.

39. Ibid., 2:200.

40. Royall, *Letters from Alabama,* 154 55.

41. Royall, *Pennsylvania,* 2:37. Earlier biographers suggest that William Newport died or disappeared earlier than this, and that it was her stepfather, a Mr. Butler, who was killed at Hannastown. The fragmentary evidence seems to suggest that Mary Newport had not remarried at the time of the firing of Hannastown. See James, *Anne Royall's U.S.A.,* 16–21; Porter, *Life and Times of Anne Royall,* 29–34; and Application for Warrant by Mary Newport, February 28, 1785, Land Records, Original Warrants, Westmoreland County, Pennsylvania State Archives, Harrisburg.

42. Michael Huffnagle to President William Moore, July 1782, in Hazard, ed., *Pennsylvania Archives,* 9:596.

43. David Duncan to Mr. [James?] Cunningham, Member of Council from Lancaster, July 30, 1782, in Hazard, ed., *Pennsylvania Archives,* 9:606–7; "Extract of a Letter from Westmoreland County, 16 July," *Independent Gazetteer,* July 27, 1782; Griffin, *American Leviathan,* 172–74.

44. Huffnagle to Moore, July 1782, in Hazard, ed., *Pennsylvania Archives,* 9:596.

45. Ibid.; General William Irvine to President William Moore, July 25, 1782; Lieutenant Colonel Edward Cook to President William Moore, September 2, 1782, both in Hazard, ed., *Pennsylvania Archives,* 9:595, 629.

46. Royall, *Pennsylvania,* 2:23.

47. There is little evidence to suggest what happened to the Newport family after the destruction of Hannastown, but this seems a possible scenario given that Anne's sister remained in the area and married a local man. See ibid., 2:213–18.

48. List dated February 28, 1785, Application for Warrant, February 10, 1785–March 29, 1785, Pennsylvania State Archives; Warrant by Mary Newport, February 28, 1785, Land Records, Original Warrants, Westmoreland County, Pennsylvania State Archives; Munger, *Pennsylvania Land Records,* 65–66, 141.

49. Westmoreland County, Mary Newport, 406½ Acres, Land Records, Surveys, Book C179, Pennsylvania State Archives. The map of Newport's survey shows her tract surrounded by those of several other women who, given the legal status of women at the time, could only have acted as *feme sole* if they were widows or single women over age twenty-one. See Salmon, *Women and the Law of Property.*

50. Patent Enrolled September 12, 1801, P46, 206, Land Records, Patent Books, Pennsylvania State Archives. This date of remarriage, which is later than that suggested by James, would explain why Royall never mentioned her stepfather—she never met him. James, *Anne Royall's U.S.A.,* 18–19, 392.

51. Waddell, *Waddell's Annals,* 332. This possibility is raised by James, *Anne Royall's U.S.A.,* 22–23.

52. Royall, *Sketches,* 91.

53. The farming and possession of land might suggest this status, though it would seem that Mary Newport only gained a legal title to the land after her husband's death. List dated February 28, 1785, Application for Warrant, February 10, 1785–March 29, 1785, Pennsylvania State Archives; Warrant by Mary Newport, February 28, 1785, Land Records, Original Warrants, Westmoreland County, Pennsylvania State Archives.

54. Kierner, *Beyond the Household,* 17–19.

55. Lewis, *Ladies and Gentlemen on Display;* Chambers, *Drinking the Waters;* Kierner, *Scandal at Bizarre,* 106.

56. Royall, *Black Book,* 1:249–50; Harris, "The Colonial Royalls of Virginia." Various land transactions can be traced through the pages of the County Court Order Books for Amelia and Chesterfield Counties. For comparisons in wealth, see Main, "The One Hundred." On slaveholding in Amelia County, see Kulikoff, *Tobacco and Slaves,* 153.

57. Will of Richard Royall, April 2, 1774, Amelia County Will Book 2, 1771–80, 253; Will of Richard Royall, October 8, 1774, Amelia County Will Book 3, 1780–86, 220–21; Will of Elizabeth Royall, October 25, 1777, Amelia County Will Book 2, 1771–80, 340.

58. William Royall, Capt., Certificate 6165, Military Certificates, No. 3, 1811–78, Virginia Land Office, 28, card index, Library of Virginia, Richmond.

59. Royall, *Sketches,* 89–90; Main, "The One Hundred."

60. Kulikoff, *Tobacco and Slaves,* 157–61; Inventory of William Royall's Property, March 22, 1813, Monroe County Will Book 1, 1799–1817, 269–73.

61. See, for instance, Monroe County Order Book D-2, 1811–13, 1, 181, 195, 213; Morton, *History of Monroe County,* 201–10; and Kulikoff, *Tobacco and Slaves,* 421–22.

62. Brown, *Good Wives, Nasty Wenches,* 253.

63. Smith, *Inside the Great House,* 128–29; Brown, *Good Wives, Nasty Wenches,* 253–60; Kulikoff, *Tobacco and Slaves,* 252–55; Kierner, *Beyond the Household,* 113–16.

64. On the sexual vulnerability of white and black female servants in planters' households, see Block, *Rape and Sexual Power,* 63–74; Kierner, *Beyond the Household,* 10, 17–18; Smith, *Inside the Great House,* 69–71, 130–50; and Kulikoff, *Tobacco and Slaves,* 252–55, 259–60. Anne Royall was certainly the subject of such allegations. See Bill of Complaint of James Roane and Wife, Elizabeth, of Charles City, June 20, 1814, *Roane v. Royall et al.*, Box 235, Clerk's Office, Augusta County Circuit Court, Staunton, VA (hereafter Box 235), and "Mrs. Ann Royall," *Western Virginia and Kenawha County Gazette,* September 20, 1826.

65. Deposition by Charles Dew, September 13, 1815, Box 235; Deposition of John Lewis, July 18, 1814, Box 235; Affidavit of James Thompson, July 27, 1814, Box 235; Deposition of John Shaver, July 18, 1814, Box 235. Each of these is endorsed, "excepted to being without authority wholly inadmissable."

66. Royall, *Letters from Alabama,* 224–25; Anne Royall to Thomas Jefferson, June 20, 1824, Thomas Jefferson Papers microfilm, reel 54, series 1, September 20, 1823, to March 12, 1825, Manuscript Division, Library of Congress (hereafter Jefferson Papers). On Virginian hospitality, see Isaac, *Transformation of Virginia,* 302–5.

67. There are passing references to her married life in Royall's books, but she never fleshes these out. Royall, *Sketches,* 20, 80; Royall, *Black Book,* 1:249–51; Royall, *Southern Tour,* 3:224–25, 235–37. Other glimpses into the marriage can be seen in Separate Answer of Anne Royall, October 30, 1814, Box 235; Deposition of Anna Malvina Gardner, October 1814, Box 235; and Deposition of Mary Butler, September 6, 1815, Box 235.

68. Inventory of William Royall's Property, March 22, 1813, Monroe County Will Book 1, 1799–1817, 269–73. On the importance of material goods to the notion of refinement, see Bushman, *Refinement of America.*

69. Royall, *Letters from Alabama,* 99–100; Royall, *Pennsylvania,* 1:199–200, 219.

70. Royall, *Southern Tour,* 3:60.

71. Kierner, *Beyond the Household,* 102–10; Royall, *Letters from Alabama,* 88–90, 95–100.

72. Royall, *Pennsylvania,* 2:178, 181.

2. The Widow and the Court Case

1. "Mrs. Anne Royall," *New-Hampshire Gazette,* September 18, 1827.

2. Details of William Royall's landholdings can be found in Box 235.

3. Monroe County Will Book 1, 1799–1817, 222.

4. Carr and Walsh, "The Planter's Wife," 542–63; Kierner, *Beyond the Household,* 12–13.

5. Salmon, *Women and the Law of Property,* 141–84; Gundersen and Gampel, "Married Women's Legal Status"; Kulikoff, *Tobacco and Slaves,* 188–89; Kierner, *Beyond the Household,* 12–13; Lebsock, *Free Women of Petersburg,* 42–47; Wood, *Masterful Women,* 29–31.

6. Lebsock, *Free Women of Petersburg,* 42–47.

7. Snyder, *Brabbling Women,* 123, 142; Kierner, *Beyond the Household,* 12–13; Kulikoff, *Tobacco and Slaves,* 188–89; Gundersen and Gampel, "Married Women's Legal Status," 119; Wood, *Masterful Women,* 31–33.

8. Isaac, *Transformation of Virginia,* 88–94, 317–20; Dayton, *Women before the Bar,* 1–14; Brown, *Good Wives, Nasty Wenches,* 277–82; Sturtz, *Within Her Power,* 30. For Royall's own description of a court day in Monroe County, Virginia, see Royall, *Sketches,* 33–35.

9. Monroe County Court Order Book 1, 1811–13, 372; Monroe County Will Book 1, 1799–1817, 222; Deposition of Isaac Hutchison, July 12, 1814, Box 235. On Mary Butler's residence in the Royall household, see Deposition of Mary Butler, September 8, 1815, Box 235.

10. Monroe County Court Order Book 1, 1811–13, 372, 384; Separate Answer of William S. Archer, August 20, 1813, Box 235; Royall's Executrix Bond, March 18, 1813, Royall Family Papers, Archives Division, Virginia Polytechnic Institute and State University (hereafter Royall Family Papers).

11. Lebsock, *Free Women of Petersburg,* 120–29; Kulikoff, *Tobacco and Slaves,* 189–90; Wood, *Masterful Women,* 15–34.

12. Lebsock, *Free Women of Petersburg,* 120–29; Wood, *Masterful Women,* 15–34; Wilson, *Life after Death.*

13. Monroe County Superior Court Order Book, 1809–14, 188; March 20, 1811, Monroe County Order Book D-1, 1811–13, 24; Separate Answer of Anne Royall, October 3, 1814, Box 235; Lebsock, *Free Women of Petersburg,* 120–25. On women's business experience, see Wood, *Masterful Women,* 15–34.

14. Kirsten E. Wood, "'The Strongest Ties That Bind Poor Mortals Together': Slaveholding Widows and Family in the Old Southeast," in Coryell et al., eds., *Negotiating Boundaries of Southern Womanhood,* 135–57; Lebsock, *Free Women of Petersburg,* 26–27, 118–20; Wilson, *Life after Death, passim.*

15. Wood, *Masterful Women,* 90–93; Inventory of William Royall's Property, March 22, 1813, Monroe County Will Book 1, 1799–1817, 269–73; September 20, 1814, Monroe County Order Book E, 1813–17, 86.

16. Deposition of Christopher Shawver, September 5, 1815, Box 235; Depo-

sition of James Wylie, April 8, 1816, Box 235; Deposition of John Lewis, July 15, 1815, Box 235.

17. Separate Answer of Anne Royall, October 3, 1814, Box 235; Answer of Anna Malvina Gardner, October 3, 1814, Box 235; Kenawha County Land Tax Lists, 1811–13; Royall, *Sketches*, 50; Stealey, *Antebellum Kanawha Salt Business*, 16–18.

18. Separate Answer of Anne Royall, October 3, 1814, Box 235; Separate Answer of William S. Archer, August 20, 1813, Box 235; Deposition of Major Andrew Beirne, September 13, 1815, Box 235.

19. Mann, *Republic of Debtors*, 128–39.

20. Ibid., 134–35, 260–61.

21. Ibid., 133–39, 260–61; Kulikoff, *Tobacco and Slaves*, 127–31; Isaac, *Transformation of Virginia*, 247, 251.

22. Separate Answer of Anne Royall, October 30, 1814, Box 235; Royall, *Letters from Alabama*, 108. These four slaves appear in the inventory of the Monroe County property, but another two female slaves and the child of one of them appear in the appraisal of William Royall's estate in Kanawha County. Inventory of William Royall's Property, March 22, 1813, Monroe County Will Book 1, 1799–1817, 269–73; Appraisement of W. Royal, Decd., June 27, 1813, Kanawha County Deed Book D, 1812–17, 171.

23. Stealey, *Antebellum Kanawha Salt Business*, 16–17.

24. Articles of Agreement between Ann Royall and Anna Malvina Cowan, and William Hensley, August 14, 1813, Kenawha County Deed Book D, 1812–17, 82; Lebsock, *Free Women of Petersburg*, 126–28.

25. Royall, *Sketches*, 44.

26. Indenture between Patrick Keenan, and John Reynolds and Ann Royal, August 9, 1813, Kenawha County Deed Book D, 1812–17, 75–78; Ann Royall Account of the Estate of William Royall, October 3, 1814, Box 235; Various Notes and Receipts, Box 235; Stealey, *Antebellum Kanawha Salt Business*, 119. For widows' enterprises, see Judith A. Ridner, "'To Have a Sufficient Maintenance': Women and the Economics of Freedom in Frontier Pennsylvania, 1750–1800," in Eldridge, ed., *Women and Freedom*, 167–90.

27. Bill of Complaint of James Roane and Wife Elizabeth of Charles City, June 20, 1814, Box 235.

28. Ibid.

29. Kulikoff, *Tobacco and Slaves*, 173–75; Smith, *Inside the Great House*, 191, 243–44. That Joseph Royall had received his portion of his father's estate is suggested by Indenture, May 1768, Amelia County Deed Book 10, 1768–69, 28, and Articles of Agreement, February 17, 1773, Chesterfield County Deed Book 7, 1772–74, 361–63.

30. Will of Richard Royall, April 2, 1774, Amelia County Will Book 2, 1771–80, 253; Will of Richard Royall, October 8, 1774, Amelia County Will Book 3, 1780–86, 220–21; Will of Elizabeth Royall, October 25, 1777, Amelia County

Will Book 2, 1771–80, 340. Joseph seems to have had two children: a son, Joseph, as well as a daughter, Elizabeth. See *Richard Randolph v. Joseph Royall, Son and Heir at Law of Joseph Royall, Decd.*, August Court 1777, Chesterfield County Order Book 6, 141.

31. Joseph Royall Appointed Guardian of Elizabeth Royall, Orphan of Joseph Royall, February Court 1779, Chesterfield County Order Book 6, 203; Elizabeth Royall, Orphan of Joseph Royall, Decd. in Acct. with Joseph Royall Her Guardian, Chesterfield Will Book 4, 78–79; Elizabeth Royall Making Choice of Benjamin Branch as Her Guardian, June Court 1783, Chesterfield County Order Book 6, 436. It seems likely that Joseph Royall was Elizabeth's brother, who must have died in early 1783.

32. Deed, April 6, 1804, Charles City County Deed Book 5, 1803–16, 77; Indenture, May 21, 1798, Charles City County Deed Book 4, 1789–1802, 401–4; Indenture, March 12, 1801, Chesterfield County Deed Book 15, 1800–1802; James Roane, List of Inhabitants, Charles City Census Schedules, 1810; James Roane, Charles City County Personal Property Tax Lists, 1794–1815; Bill of Complaint of Anne Royall against James Roane and Wife, August 1822, Box 235; Kulikoff, *Tobacco and Slaves*, 263–67.

33. The *Roane v. Royall et al.* court case cited "Anne Royall, widow of William Royal decd., Newton Gardner and Malvina his wife, William Archer and James Wylie." Throughout the notes I have cited the documents as they appear in the originals. These were not consistent in the way they named the defendants, in part because during the proceedings, Anne's niece Anna Malvina Cowan (sometimes just named Malvina) married Newton Gardner. The marriage took place on July 17, 1814, after the Roanes filed their complaint but before the depositions were taken. Gardner became a party to the complaint on his marriage to Anna Malvina since, as a married woman, her legal identity was subsumed under that of her husband. Poor communications meant that it would have taken the Roanes some time to hear of Anna Malvina's marriage.

34. The Commonwealth against William R. Roane, Monroe County Superior Court Order Book, 1809–14, 188; Separate Answer of Anne Royall, October 3, 1814, Box 235.

35. The Commonwealth against William R. Roane, Monroe County Superior Court Order Book, 1809–14, 188.

36. Wood, *Masterful Women*, 62–63.

37. Ibid.; Bardaglio, *Reconstructing the Household*, 24–34; Brown, *Good Wives, Nasty Wenches*, 324. See the comments contained in the Testimony of John Lewis, July 15, 1815, and the Affidavit of William R. Roane, July 23, 1814, both Box 235.

38. Bill of Complaint of James Roane and Wife, June 20, 1814, Box 235; Subpoena to Anne Royall, Anna Malvina Cowan, William Archer, and James Wylie, at Staunton, July 27, 1814, Box 235. On equity proceedings, see Alexander, *Notorious Woman*, 141–42.

39. Separate Answer of Anne Royall, October 3, 1814, Box 235; Separate Answer of William S. Archer, October 2, 1815, Box 235; Separate Answer of Anna Malvina Gardner by Her Husband Newton Gardner, October 1814, Box 235; Separate Answer of James Wylie, April 8, 1816, Box 235.

40. Separate Answer of Anne Royall, October 3, 1814, Box 235.

41. Ibid.

42. Alexander, *Notorious Woman,* 141–42.

43. Several of the witness depositions in Box 235 are annotated as being "excepted to being a mere affidavit taken without authority." See, for instance, Affidavit of Oliver Towle, Jr., May 23, 1814, Box 235.

44. Box 235 contains a number of depositions relating to the case of *Roane vs. Royall et al.,* though it is probable that others were taken which no longer survive.

45. Bill of Complaint of James Roane and Wife Elizabeth of Charles City, June 20, 1814, Box 235.

46. Deposition of John Lewis, July 15, 1814, Box 235, endorsed "excepted to being without . . . inadmissible."

47. Deposition of Dr. Charles W. Lewis, July 12, 1814, Box 235, endorsed "excepted to being a mere affidavit taken without any legal authority"; Depositions of Elizabeth Shawver, Jacob Shawver, and Sally Shawver, July 15, 1814, Box 235. The nose-tweaking incident was reported in Affidavit of James Thompson, July 27, 1814, Box 235, endorsed "excepted as taken without any authority." Patricia Cline Cohen notes that nose-tweaking was a contemptuous gesture among gentleman by the 1830s. Cohen, *Murder of Helen Jewett,* 92–93.

48. Affidavit of James Thompson, July 27, 1814, Box 235.

49. Deposition of James L. Linton, July 15, 1814, Box 235.

50. Affidavit of William R. Roane, July 23, 1814, Box 235.

51. Deposition of Christopher Shawver, September 5, 1815, Box 235; Deposition of Hugh Caperton, July 12, 1814, Box 235, endorsed "excepted because no authority."

52. Deposition of Mary Butler, July 12, 1815, Box 235.

53. Deposition of Christopher Shawver, September 5, 1815, Box 235; Deposition of Hugh Caperton, July 12, 1814, Box 235; Deposition of Mary Butler, September 6, 1815, Box 235.

54. Kierner, *Beyond the Household,* 199–201.

55. Brown, *Good Wives, Nasty Wenches,* 324; Doyle, "The Randolph Scandal."

56. Wood, *Masterful Women,* 62–63, 73–74.

57. List of Hearings in Case of *Roane v. Royall et al.,* Box 235; *Roane and Wife v. Royal etc.,* on an Issue from Chancery, April 10, 1815, Monroe County Superior Court Minute Book, 1814–21. A number of the depositions in Box 235 are dated late 1815. See also "Our Exceptions to the Opinion of the Court," Box 235, on the question of the trial of issues before a jury. On chancery courts, see

Sturtz, *Within Her Power,* 20–21, and Salmon, *Women and the Law of Property, passim.* On the recent reforms in the Virginia court system, see Roeber, *Faithful Magistrates and Republican Lawyers,* chap. 6. Costs of Continuance by Both Roane and Royall et al. Noted on Copy Trial of Issues, *Royall et al. v. Roane et ux,* May 26, 1817, Royall Family Papers.

58. Roeber, *Faithful Magistrates and Republican Lawyers,* 222–25.

59. Bardaglio, *Reconstructing the Household,* 7–17; Kierner, *Scandal at Bizarre,* 42–44; Roeber, *Faithful Magistrates and Republican Lawyers,* chap. 6.

60. Kierner, *Scandal at Bizarre,* 42–45; Bardaglio, *Reconstructing the Household,* 11–12.

61. Copy Trial of Issues, *Royall et al. v. Roane et ux,* May 26, 1817, Royall Family Papers; April 12, 1817, Botetourt County Circuit Court Order Book, Common Law, 1809–23, 262–63.

62. Lerner, "Transformation of the American Civil Trial"; Copy Trial of Issues, *Royall et al. v. Roane et ux,* May 26, 1817, Royall Family Papers; April 12, 1817, Botetourt County Circuit Court Order Book, Common Law, 1809–23, 262–63.

63. Complaint of James Roane, May 29, 1817, before William Mumford, Magistrate for Richmond City, Box 235.

64. Monroe County had been formed out of Botetourt County in 1799. The surviving evidence against Mrs. Royall has been collected in Box 235.

65. April 10–11, 1818, Botetourt County Circuit Court Order Book, Common Law, 1809–23, 301–2; September 10–12, 1818, Botetourt County Circuit Court Order Book, Common Law, 1809–23, 313, 315–16; April 7, 1819, Botetourt County Circuit Court Order Book, Common Law, 1809–23, 329.

66. June 9–11, 1819, Botetourt County Circuit Court Order Book, Common Law, 1809–23, 335–38; *Roane v. Royall,* Trial of Issues, Box 235.

67. "Our Exceptions to the Opinion of the Court," Box 235.

68. *Roane v. Royall* Decree, July 1819, Box 235.

69. Ibid.

70. Bill of Complaint of James Roane and Wife Elizabeth of Charles City, June 20, 1814, Box 235.

71. Separate Answer of Anne Royall, October 30, 1814, Box 235.

72. Edwards, "Law, Domestic Violence."

73. Separate Answer of William S. Archer, October 2, 1815, Box 235; *Roane v. Royall* Decree, July 1819, Box 235. The summary of hearings only lists Archer as being in attendance for the hearing in July 1815.

74. "William S. Archer," *Biographical Directory of the United States Congress.*

75. *Ann Royall v. Roane,* Bill of Complaint, August 1822, Box 235; "Mrs. Ann Royall," *Western Virginia and Kanawha County Gazette,* September 20, 1826; Wood, *Masterful Women,* 73–74.

76. Affidavit of Oliver Towle, Jr., May 23, 1814, Box 235.

77. Mann, *Republic of Debtors, passim.*

78. *A. and G. Beirne v. A. Royall and Gardner, a bond,* Royall Family Papers; November 11, 1817, Kenawha County Supreme Court Minute Book, 1814–19.

79. "Mrs. Ann Royall," *Western Virginia and Kanawha County Gazette,* September 20, 1826.

80. Dunaway, *African American Family,* 46–47.

81. Royall, *Letters from Alabama,* 77–79; M. Dunbar's Affidavit, May 22, 1820, Box 235; *Gardner v. Roane,* November 25, 1821, Box 235; *Gardner v. Roane* Depositions, Sealed June 18, 1825, Box 235.

82. Dunaway, *African American Family,* 24, 46–47; Tadman, *Speculators and Slaves;* Collins, *Domestic Slave Trade,* 28–32.

83. Royall, *Southern Tour,* 1:39.

84. Deposition of James Wiley in Case of *Wiley v. Roane,* March 25, 1820, Box 235; Memorandum of Agreement, September 13, 1819, between James Roane and Newton Gardner, Box 235; Bill of Complaint of Anne Royall, November 15, 1822, Box 235.

85. *Roane v. Royall* Decree, July 1819, Box 235; Distrainer, April 21, 1820, Box 235. Roane's bond as curator was set at $5,000, although his duties were suspended until he secured the bond in February 1820. *Roane v. Royall* Curator's Bond, November 27, 1819, and Petition of James Roane to John Brown, Judge of Chancery District Court at Staunton, December 30, 1819, Box 235.

86. See *Roane v. Royall* Decree, July 1819, Box 235; *Roane v. Gardner,* Memorandum of Agreement, September 13, 1819, Box 235; and Deposition of James Wiley, *Wiley v. Roane,* March 25, 1820, Box 235.

87. Copy Order for a Commissioner, August 13, 1830, Box 235, notes James Roane's death in 1830 and the need to appoint a commissioner to settle the case.

88. Bill of Anne Royall to Hon. John Brown of Superior Court of Chancery, November 15, 1822, Box 235.

89. Draft Court's Decision, December 16, 1822, Box 235; Second Report of Master Commissioner, Samuel Clark, Box 235; Defendant's Exceptions to Final Statement of Master Commissioner, Box 235.

90. It is almost impossible to convert this sum into modern-day values. It was certainly a hefty one. Draft Court's Decision, December 16, 1822, Box 235. The value of the whole estate when apportioned between Anne Royall and James Roane proved to be considerably less than it had been valued at for probate in 1813. Besides the slaves, the item of greatest value in the inventory of Royall's personal estate had been a bond due to William Royall by the Messrs. Ford for almost $5,000. As executrix, Anne had been unable to collect the bond, and it became clear when the commissioners produced their second report that the Fords were insolvent. The matter became a source of further dispute in drawing up the final division between Roane and Royall. A number of debts incurred during William Royall's lifetime, which became the subject of court cases, imposed costs on the estate, as did the litigation necessary to regain control of lands

belonging to the estate from tenants whose leases had expired. Even before the will case was decided against Anne, it had become clear that the expenses incurred in settling the estate were mounting and further diminishing its value. See Inventory of William Royall's Property, March 22, 1813, Monroe County Will Book 1, 1799–1817, 269–73; "Anne Royall Executrix a/c with the Estate," Kenawha, November 10, 1818, Monroe County Will Book 2, 1818–29, 27–32; Exceptions to Second Report of the Master Commissioner, Samuel Clark, Box 235; and Defendant's Exceptions for the Final Statement of the Master Commissioner, Box 235.

91. *Roane v. Royall* Supplemental Bill, June 18, 1821, Box 235; *Ann Royall v. Roane* Bill of Complaint, November 15, 1822, Box 235; Commissioners' Report, May 10, 1820, Box 235; Distrainer, April 21, 1820, Box 235.

92. "Mrs. Ann Royall," *Western Virginia and Kanawha County Gazette,* September 20, 1826.

3. Making Her Way Through Writing

1. On the growing restrictions for married women working outside the home, see Boydston, *Home and Work,* and Kierner, *Beyond the Household,* 17–25.

2. Kierner, *Beyond the Household,* 108–10. For a much wider discussion of the impact of women's education, see Kelley, *Learning to Stand and Speak.*

3. Coultrap-McQuin, *Doing Literary Business,* 12–15; Kelley, *Learning to Stand and Speak;* Mary Kelley, "Introduction: Section IV: Gendering Authorship and Audiences," in Gross and Kelley, eds., *History of the Book,* 2:347–49; Joanne Dobson and Sandra A. Zagarell, "Women Writing in the Early Republic," in Gross and Kelley, eds., *History of the Book,* 2:364–81.

4. Royall, *Letters from Alabama,* 69, 80–89.

5. Anne Royall to Mathew Carey, February 12, 1824, Anne Newport Royall Collection, Manuscript Division, Library of Congress (hereafter ANR Collection); Anne Royall to Carey and Lea, June 19, 1824, Case 7, Box 20, Notable American Women, Gratz Collection, Historical Society of Pennsylvania (hereafter NAW Collection). Just at the point that Anne Royall sought advice from Mathew Carey, he was in the process of handing over his business to his son Henry. Hence Royall wrote variously to Mathew Carey, Henry Carey, and to another incarnation of the business, Carey and Lea.

6. She refers to her correspondent only as "Matt," though it is clear from other references that this was the lawyer Matthew Dunbar. On Dunbar, see "Judge Matthew Dunbar," quoted in George W. Atkinson, *History of Kanawha County* (Charleston, WV, 1876), 298–99.

7. Anne Royall to Carey and Lea, June 19, 1824, NAW Collection; Anne Royall to Mathew Carey, February 12, 1824, ANR Collection. On the audiences for travel narratives, see Smith, "Travel Narratives," 94.

8. "Introduction," in Robert, ed., *New Year in Cuba,* 20; Gilmore, *Reading*

Becomes a Necessity of Life, 131–32; John, *Spreading the News;* Anne Royall to Carey and Lea, June 19, 1824, NAW Collection; Anne Royall to Mathew Carey, February 12, 1824, ANR Collection; Royall, *Letters from Alabama,* 141–42.

9. For instance, in the first letter, Royall gave Dunbar advice about his health and told him to avoid playing cards: Royall, *Letters from Alabama,* 5–6.

10. Ibid., 80.

11. Ibid., 156–58.

12. Ibid., 107–8, 115.

13. Ibid., 89–90; Davidson, *Revolution and the Word,* 71–72; Baym, *Woman's Fiction,* 22–23.

14. Anne Royall to Mathew Carey, February 12, 1824, ANR Collection; Royall, *Letters from Alabama,* 141–42.

15. Royall, *Letters from Alabama,* 141–42.

16. Anne Royall to Mathew Carey, February 12, 1824, ANR Collection.

17. Royall traveled to Richmond in spring 1824, though she did not explain her purpose there in either *Sketches,* 120–21, or *Black Book,* 1:150–51.

18. Anne Royall to Mathew Carey, February 12, 1824, ANR Collection.

19. Royall, *Sketches,* 112.

20. Gilmore, *Reading Becomes a Necessity of Life;* Zboray, *Fictive People;* Kelley, *Private Woman, Public Stage,* 7–9; Davidson, *Revolution and the Word,* 17–19.

21. Davidson, *Revolution and the Word,* 17–19; Kelley, *Private Woman, Public Stage,* 7–8.

22. Davidson, *Revolution and the Word,* 16–19; Kelley, *Private Woman, Public Stage,* 7–8; Alice D. Schreyer, "Copyright and Books in Nineteenth-Century America," in Hackenberg, ed., *Getting the Books Out,* 121–36.

23. Royall, *Black Book,* 1:131.

24. Remer, "Preachers, Peddlers, and Publishers"; Zboray, *Fictive People,* 19–66; Davidson, *Revolution and the Word,* 20–24; James N. Green, "From Printer to Publisher: Mathew Carey and the Origins of Nineteenth-Century Book Publishing," in Hackenberg, ed., *Getting the Books Out,* 26–44; Michael H. Harris, "'Spiritual Cakes upon the Waters': The Church as a Disseminator of the Printed Word on the Ohio Valley Frontier to 1850," in Hackenberg, ed., *Getting the Books Out,* 98–120.

25. On these changes, see Kelley, *Private Woman, Public Stage,* 7–8, and Zboray, *Fictive People,* 55–66.

26. Royall complained constantly about the way these items flooded the American market to the exclusion of works by American authors. On religious publishing, see Sellers, *Market Revolution,* 369–72; Harris, "'Spiritual Cakes'"; and David Paul Nord, "Benevolent Books: Printing, Religion, and Reform," in Gross and Kelley, eds., *History of the Book,* 2:221–46.

27. Bruccoli, ed., *Profession of Authorship,* 6; Okker, *Our Sister Editors,* 85–86; Coultrap-McQuin, *Doing Literary Business,* 13–14.

28. Rosemarie Zagarri, "The Postcolonial Culture of Early American Women's Writing," in Bauer and Gould, eds., *Cambridge Companion,* 19–37; Kelley, *Learning to Stand and Speak.*

29. Zagarri, "Postcolonial Culture," 19.

30. Ibid.; Kelley, *Learning to Stand and Speak,* 56–65; Kerber, *Women of the Republic.*

31. Coultrap-McQuin, *Doing Literary Business,* 12–15; Okker, *Our Sister Editors,* 84–109; Kelley, *Private Woman, Public Stage,* 8, 124–29.

32. Baym, *American Women Writers,* 1–4; Zagarri, "Postcolonial Culture"; Kelley, *Learning to Stand and Speak,* 56–57. Royall commented herself on the increasing numbers of novels on the market. Royall, *Letters from Alabama,* 89–90.

33. Kelley, "Introduction," 347–49; Dobson and Zagarell, "Women Writing in the Early Republic."

34. Kelley, *Private Woman, Public Stage,* 144–46.

35. Royall, *Black Book,* 1:140–41.

36. Ibid. The City Hotel was also known as Gadsby's Tavern.

37. Anne Royall to Mathew Carey, February 12, 1824, ANR Collection.

38. Ibid.; Anne Royall to Carey and Lea, June 19, 1824, NAW Collection. On Mathew Carey, see Remer, "Preachers, Peddlers, and Publishers"; Remer, *Printers and Men of Capital;* Green, "From Printer to Publisher"; Kelley, *Private Woman, Public Stage,* 7; Cathy N. Davidson, "The Life and Times of *Charlotte Temple:* The Biography of a Book," in Davidson, ed., *Reading in America,* 158–62; and Boynton, *Annals of American Bookselling,* 127–28, 148.

39. Royall, *Letters from Alabama,* 29–30.

40. Anne Royall to Carey and Lea, June 19, 1824, NAW Collection.

41. Anne Royall to Henry Carey and Co., April 26, 1824, folder 8451, Clifton Waller Barrett Collection, Albert and Shirley Small Special Collections Library, University of Virginia (hereafter CWB Collection); Anne Royall to Mathew Carey, February 12, 1824, ANR Collection; Anne Royall to Carey and Lea, June 19, 1824, NAW Collection.

42. Royall, *Black Book,* 1:133; Anne Royall to Henry Carey and Co., April 26, 1824, CWB Collection, is marked "Rec'd April 28; Ansn. April 29." Since Carey's replies do not seem to have survived, it is difficult to know what advice he gave her. Davidson, *Revolution and the Word,* 23–24; Remer, "Preachers, Peddlers, and Publishers," 504–5.

43. Royall, *Black Book,* 1:3. Wiley seems to have been Charles Wiley, a prominent New York bookseller, and the publisher of James Fennimore Cooper's first book. Boynton, *Annals of American Bookselling,* 155–64.

44. Tebbel, *History of Book Publishing,* 1:210–11; Boynton, *Annals of American Bookselling,* 155–65. Some of Royall's business dealings with her printers are revealed in two letters: Anne Royall to Durrie and Peck, June 23, 1826, Miscellaneous Papers: Anne Royall, Manuscripts and Archives Division, New

York Public Library (hereafter NYPL Collection); and Anne Royall to Durrie and Peck, September 27, 1826, ANR Collection.

45. Royall, *Black Book,* 1:4; Royall, *Sketches,* 1. On the practice of authors paying for their works to be published, see James N. Green, "The Rise of Book Publishing," in Gross and Kelley, eds., *History of the Book in America,* 104–5.

46. Anne Royall to Stephen Van Rensselaer, December 17, 1826, Case 6, Box 34, Gratz Collection, Historical Society of Pennsylvania. See the title pages of Royall's books for publication details.

47. Green, "From Printer to Publisher"; Wosh, *Spreading the Word,* 62–88.

48. Anne Royall to Thomas Jefferson, June 20, 1824, reel 54, Jefferson Papers.

49. Anne Royall to William Cary, September 16, 1826, Container 1, Cary-Mathews Family Correspondence, 1825–30, Papers of the Feamster Family, Manuscript Division, Library of Congress; Kelley, *Private Woman, Public Stage,* 124–33; "Sketches of Life and Manners in the United States. By a Traveller," *Literary Cadet and Saturday Evening Bulletin,* 17 June 1826.

50. Anne Royall to Thomas Jefferson, June 20, 1824, reel 54, Jefferson Papers.

51. Anne Royall to Henry Carey and Co., April 26, 1824, CWB Collection; Resch, *Suffering Soldiers;* Purcell, *Sealed with Blood,* 171–73.

52. Fabian, *Unvarnished Truth.*

53. Ibid., 42–48; Dorsey, *Reforming Men and Women,* 56–63.

54. See Royall, *Black Book,* 2:232; 3:33–35.

55. Anne Royall to William Cary, September 16, 1826, Cary-Mathews Family Correspondence, 1825–30, Papers of the Feamster Family.

56. It is not clear when (or if) Royall met General Lafayette, but their paths may well have crossed on his visit to Washington and Alexandria during 1824. See Royall, *Sketches,* 175–78, and Royall, *Black Book,* 1:108, 150, 162.

57. Royall, *Black Book,* 2:12, 57, 117; Advertisement for New Theatre, Chatham Gardens, *New York American,* February 26, 1825, February 28, 1825. Although these advertisements do not mention Royall by name, the references in the *Black Book* would suggest that she is the "Widow of a Masonic Brother" mentioned in them. Bullock, *Revolutionary Brotherhood,* 186–98; Goodman, *Towards a Christian Republic,* 38–41.

58. See Royall, *Black Book,* 2:12–13, 117, 325, and Royall, *Pennsylvania,* 1:221.

59. Royall, *Black Book,* 1:75, 150, 2:12–13; Royall, *Pennsylvania,* 1:86–91.

60. On the methods of traveling salesmen and Bible agents, see Remer, "Preachers, Peddlers, and Publishers," and Wosh, *Spreading the Word,* 70–71. Patricia Cline Cohen describes one encounter with Royall in *Murder of Helen Jewett,* 176–80.

61. See Royall, *Southern Tour,* 1:57–62.

62. Wosh, *Spreading the Word,* 70–71; Royall, *Black Book,* 3:33; Royall,

Southern Tour, 1:20, 32; "Mrs. Royal Again," *United States Telegraph,* March 6, 1827; *Middlesex Gazette,* May 7, 1828.

63. *United States Gazette,* January 23, 1827, February 17, 1827; *National Advocate,* January 24, 1827; *Boston Commercial Gazette,* March 8, 1827, June 5, 1828; Tebbel, *History of Book Publishing,* 1:210–11.

64. "Mrs. Royall's Pennsylvania," *United States Gazette,* August 31, 1829.

65. See Remer, "Preachers, Peddlers, and Publishers"; Cohen, "Women at Large"; and Thomas, "'There Is Nothing So Effective,'" 140–55, for examples of later female book agents.

66. "Mrs. Royal," *Niles' Register,* July 18, 1829.

67. Hill, ed., "The Diary of Isaiah Thomas," entry for June 13, 1826, 237; Royall, *Black Book,* 2:117–19; *Southern Patriot,* March 15, 1830; Allgor, *Parlor Politics,* 120–24; Kasson, *Rudeness and Civility,* 173–74.

68. See Royall, *Black Book,* 1:130–35, and Royall, *Pennsylvania,* 1:5–8, 49–52, 94.

69. Royall, *Pennsylvania,* 1:5.

70. Anne Royall to Mr. Backus, May 13, 1828, Case 6, Box 23, Gratz Collection; Anne Royall to Little and Co., on back of Anne Royall to Jo. Cole, May 18, 1831, Case 6, Box 34, Gratz Collection.

71. Anne Royall to James Martin Bell, October 4, 1829, James Martin Bell Papers, David M. Rubinstein Rare Book and Manuscript Library, Duke University; Anne Royall to Mr. Peck, June 12, 1826, File 6, Anne Royall, Bertha Overbury Collection, Barnard College Library.

72. *Southern Patriot,* March 19, 1830; Anne Royall to Hon. A. Ward, February 2, 1829, Correspondence of A. Ward, 1813–33, folder 328, Manuscript Collection, Boston Public Library.

73. Anne Royall to Durrie and Peck, September 27, 1826, ANR Collection. In a similar vein, see her earlier letters to Durrie and Peck, June 23, 1826, NYPL Collection, and July 1, 1826, Reel 48, Manuscript Collection, Morristown National Historical Park.

74. Anne Royall to Durrie and Peck, June 23, 1826, NYPL Collection.

75. Davidson, *Revolution and the Word,* 15–37; Kelley, *Private Woman, Public Stage,* 7–9; Zboray, *Fictive People,* 55–66.

76. Coultrap-McQuin, *Doing Literary Business,* 42–43, 51, 86.

77. Anne Royall to Durrie and Peck, June 23, 1826, NYPL Collection. Similarly, in a letter to Durrie and Peck later in the year, she revealed problems with distribution: Anne Royall to Durrie and Peck, September 27, 1826, ANR Collection, and to Durrie and Peck, October 5, 1826, Manuscript Collection, Morristown Historical Park; Promissory Note to Durrie and Peck from Anne Royall, February 14, 1827, Box 3, folder U, Bills, Receipts, Promissory Notes, 1826–34, Durrie and Peck Papers, Whitney Library, New Haven Museum.

78. Royall, *Pennsylvania,* 1:91.

79. Anne Royall to Charles Ingersoll, June 17, 1826, Coles Collection, Albert

and Shirley Small Special Collections Library, University of Virginia; Anne Royall to Jared Sparks, June 30, 1826, MS Sparks 153, Jared Sparks Manuscripts, Houghton Library, Harvard University; Anne Royall to General Lafayette, May 31, 1827, CWB Collection.

80. Royall, *Pennsylvania,* 1:255.

81. Ibid.

82. Royall, *Black Book,* 3:224; Royall, *Pennsylvania,* 1:90–91.

83. Royall, *Pennsylvania,* 2: appendix, 1; Bushman, *Refinement of America,* 238–79. It is not easy to ascertain Royall's income level, however, since she was reticent in talking about it.

84. Kelley, *Private Woman, Public Stage,* 11–12, 145–46; Coultrap-McQuin, *Doing Literary Business,* 23–24.

85. Coultrap-McQuin, *Doing Literary Business, passim.* An example of another woman who marketed her own books may be found in Davidson, *Revolution and the Word,* 33.

86. Patricia Cleary, "'Who Shall Say We Have Not Equal Abilitys with the Men When Girls of 18 Years of Age Discover Such Great Capacitys?' Women of Commerce in Boston, 1750–1776," in Wright and Viens, eds., *Entrepreneurs,* 39–61; Wood, "'Strongest Ties That Bind'"; Wilson, *Life after Death, passim;* Lebsock, *Free Women of Petersburg,* 37–42, 120–25.

4. MRS. ROYALL'S TRAVELS

1. Royall, *Black Book,* 1:89.

2. See the introduction to Kilcup, ed., *From Beacon Hill,* 32–33.

3. Royall, *Sketches,* 13.

4. The high literary style Royall sought to emulate is discussed in chapter 3. Bruccoli, ed., *Profession of Authorship,* 6; Okker, *Our Sister Editors,* 85–86; Coultrap-McQuin, *Doing Literary Business,* 13–14.

5. Royall, *Letters from Alabama,* 141–42; Anne Royall to Mathew Carey, February 12, 1824, ANR Collection.

6. Anne Royall to Carey and Lea, June 19, 1824, NAW Collection; Royall, *Tennessean,* 372.

7. Royall outlined to Matt Dunbar what she has read recently in Royall, *Letters from Alabama,* 69, 89–90, though this is the only place in her books where she discussed her reading in any detail. The inventory of William Royall's estate lists the sermons and Smollett, as well as other "old books." Inventory of William Royall's Property, March 22, 1813, Monroe County Will Book 1, 1799–1817, 269–73. Anne's writings reflect a familiarity with Enlightenment ideas and interests. References to Buffon and Voltaire appear in Royall, *Letters from Alabama,* 89–90.

8. On attitudes toward novels, see Zagarri, "Postcolonial Culture," 30–31.

9. Smith, "Travel Narratives." Royall, *Pennsylvania,* 1:109, and Royall, *Letters*

from Alabama, 29, mention her familiarity with La Rochefoucauld-Liancourt, John Ledyard, and Isaac Weld, the first two of whom wrote journals about their travels in the United States. On women's engagement with their reading in their own writing, see "Introduction," in Kilcup, ed., *From Beacon Hill,* 32–33.

10. Other women who were traveling and writing in the United States at much the same time included the Englishwomen Frances Wright, Mrs. Basil Hall, Frances Trollope, and Harriet Martineau. There were also a number of American women travelers, as discussed in Imbarrato, *Traveling Women.*

11. Batten, *Pleasurable Instruction, passim.*

12. Schriber, ed., *Telling Tales,* xxiii; Royall, *Sketches,* 13; Smith, "Travel Narratives."

13. Hamalian, ed., *Ladies on the Loose,* includes some of the journals of earlier women travelers.

14. Patricia Cline Cohen, "Safety and Danger: Women on American Public Transport, 1750–1850," in Helly and Reverby, eds., *Gendered Domains,* 112–14; Cohen, "Women at Large."

15. Cohen, "Women at Large"; Kierner, *Beyond the Household,* 169–70; Chambers, *Drinking the Waters.*

16. Wood, *Masterful Women,* 93; Cohen, "Safety and Danger," 109–22. For Royall's comments, see *Letters from Alabama,* 23–24, 30–31.

17. Brekus, *Strangers and Pilgrims,* 253–54; Cohen, "Safety and Danger," 109–11.

18. Cohen, "Safety and Danger," 109–22.

19. Brown, *Inventing New England,* 16–20.

20. Brown suggests that more than seventy such works were published in the last decades of the eighteenth century alone. Ibid., 18.

21. Sarjent Bush, Jr., "Introduction to the Journal of Madam Knight," in Andrews, ed., *Journeys in New Worlds,* 79–80; Imbarrato, *Traveling Women,* 32–33; Day, "'The History of Every One of Us,'" 75–76; Kelley, *Private Woman, Public Stage,* 7–8.

22. Brown, *Inventing New England,* 16–20. The idea was popularized by Davison, *Fashionable Tour.*

23. *Royall v. Gardner and Wife,* November 8, 1823, Chancery Order Book, 1823, 395, Greenbrier County Court House; Anne Royall to William Cary, September 16, 1826, Cary-Mathews Family Correspondence, 1825–30, Papers of the Feamster Family; "Mrs. Anne Royall," *Western Virginia and Kanawha County Gazette,* September 20, 1826. Her own feelings about the treatment she received in Kanawha are reflected in Royall, *Sketches,* 47, and *Black Book,* 1:140–41.

24. Royall, *Sketches,* preface.

25. She makes this clear in the prefaces to several of her volumes, in particular those to *Pennsylvania,* vol. 1, and *Southern Tour,* vol. 1.

26. "Mrs. Royall," *Harrisburg Argus,* November 8, 1828; Royall, *Black Book,* 1:6–7.

27. Royall, *Black Book,* 2:38.

28. Royall, *Sketches,* preface.

29. Ibid., *passim;* Baym, *American Women Writers,* 131.

30. Royall, *Pennsylvania,* 1:3–4; Royall, *Southern Tour,* 1:frontispiece.

31. Royall, *Sketches, passim.* On other travelers, see Martineau, *Retrospect of Western Travel,* and Trollope, *Domestic Manners of the Americans.*

32. Royall, *Black Book,* 1:36. The term "fashionable tour" had been popularized by Gideon Davison in *Fashionable Tour.*

33. Royall, *Pennsylvania,* 1:3. On her reception, see *Portsmouth Journal and Rockingham Gazette,* January 31, 1829, and *New Hampshire Sentinel,* February 13, 1829.

34. Royall, *Pennsylvania,* 2:257–68. The tour lasted from September 1828 to late January 1829. It was reported in the newspapers, which noted the crowds who came to meet Royall. See "Mrs. Royal," *Saturday Evening Post,* January 24, 1829, and "Mrs. Royall," *New-Hampshire Gazette,* February 10, 1829.

35. Royall, *Southern Tour,* 2:137.

36. Ibid., 3:132–33.

37. Royall, *Black Book,* 1:52.

38. Ibid., 1:52–53. On the growth of Niagara Falls as a tourist attraction, see Sears, *Sacred Places,* 3–6, 12–30.

39. Royall, *Black Book,* 2:358.

40. Ibid., 2:380. She noted that the mountains had already been immortalized by the "chaste and elegant pen" of Mrs. Hemans of Europe. Ibid., 2:385. On the use of the sublime in describing natural wonders, see introduction in Kilcup, ed., *From Beacon Hill,* 32–33, and Imbarrato, *Traveling Women,* 35–46. Brown examines the development of the White Mountains as a tourist destination in *Inventing New England,* 41–74.

41. Royall, *Southern Tour,* 3:60.

42. Royall, *Pennsylvania,* 2:90. On the gendered nature of travel writing, see Foster, *Across New Worlds,* 18–19, and Imbarrato, *Traveling Women, passim.*

43. Imbarrato, *Traveling Women,* 53–88. Examples may be found in the texts reprinted in Andrews, ed., *Journeys in New Worlds,* 91, 107, 205, 207.

44. For example, Royall, *Black Book,* 1:275; Royall, *Pennsylvania,* 2:27–28; Royall, *Southern Tour,* 1:142–45.

45. Royall, *Black Book,* 2:81, 43.

46. Royall, *Southern Tour,* 2:107.

47. Ibid., 2:53.

48. "Mrs. Royall," *Providence Patriot and Columbian Phenix,* November 21, 1829.

49. Royall, *Black Book,* 1:102–3. She made similar remarks about the "convention bonnets" in Richmond. Royall, *Southern Tour,* 1:36.

50. Royall, *Black Book,* 1:81.

51. Ibid., 1:7–8.

52. Royall, *Letters from Alabama,* 97.

53. Ibid., 97–100.

54. Brown, *Inventing New England,* 18–21.

55. Royall, *Pennsylvania,* 2:59.

56. Royall, *Black Book,* 2:37.

57. Royall, *Sketches,* 150.

58. Royall, *Pennsylvania,* 2:34–35; 1:42.

59. Ibid., 2:150–63.

60. Ibid., 2:185–86.

61. Royall, *Black Book,* 2:388. On the debates over women's education in the new republic, see Kierner, *Beyond the Household,* 108–10; Kerber, *Women of the Republic,* 193–204; and Kelley, *Learning to Stand and Speak.*

62. Royall, *Southern Tour,* 1:36.

63. Royall, *Sketches,* 286. On the beginnings of women's education, see Linda K. Kerber, "'Why Should Girls Be Learn'd and Wise?' The Unfinished Work of Alice Mary Baldwin," in Kerber, *Toward an Intellectual History,* 224–58, and Kelley, *Learning to Stand and Speak.* Emma Willard's Troy Academy was established in 1821, Catharine Beecher's two years later. Feller, *Jacksonian Promise,* 156–57.

64. Sellers, *Market Revolution,* 90–91; Watson, *Liberty and Power,* 105; William G. McLoughlin, "Cherokee Anomie, 1794–1810: New Roles for Red Men, Red Women, and Black Slaves," in Mancall and Merrell, eds., *American Encounters,* 455–56.

65. Royall, *Letters from Alabama,* 54–55.

66. Berkhofer, *White Man's Indian,* 88.

67. Royall, *Letters from Alabama,* 54–56.

68. Ibid., 54–56.

69. Ibid., 77.

70. Royall, *Black Book,* 1:61–62, 2:188–90, 306; Royall, *Southern Tour,* 2:141–48; Royall, *Letters from Alabama,* 80.

71. Royall, *Letters from Alabama,* 79–80.

72. Royall, *Southern Tour,* 2:142.

73. On the petition campaigns, see Hershberger, "Mobilizing Women, Anticipating Abolition," and Portnoy, *Their Right to Speak.*

74. Royall, *Black Book,* 1:62; Royall, *Southern Tour,* 2:142; Berkhofer, *White Man's Indian, passim;* McLoughlin, "Cherokee Anomie," 453–76.

75. Portnoy, *Their Right to Speak,* 52–55.

76. Royall, *Letters from Alabama,* 64. This outburst might have been ad-

dressed only to Dunbar, but she did not edit it out when she prepared the letters for publication.

77. Ibid., 164–65.

78. Royall, *Sketches,* 100–101.

79. Royall, *Southern Tour,* 2:80–81.

80. See, for instance, Royall, *Sketches,* 169.

81. Ibid., 157.

82. Royall, *Black Book,* 3:184–85. On Lundy's campaign, see Zaeske, *Signatures of Citizenship,* 33.

83. Royall, *Black Book,* 3:180–85.

84. See her explanation for the widespread distress she encountered in Washington. Ibid.

85. See Trollope, *Domestic Manners of the Americans,* 161–62.

86. Bush, "Introduction to the Journal of Madam Knight," 79–80; Day, "'History of Every One of Us,'" 75–76. Far from being critical of some of the European accounts of the United States, Royall praised the work of Frances Trollope: *Paul Pry,* 2 June 1832, 7 July 1832, and *Southern Tour,* 2:190. Royall noted that Basil Hall had used the riverboat on which she was traveling, but she had not read his work.

87. Royall, *Sketches,* 121–24.

88. Royall, *Black Book,* 2:313; Royall, *Pennsylvania,* 1:255; Royall, *Southern Tour,* 2:57–58.

89. Royall, *Sketches,* 40–41.

90. Royall, *Southern Tour,* 2:98–99.

91. Royall, *Pennsylvania,* 1:185.

5. A Virago Errant in Enchanted Armor

1. Royall, *Southern Tour,* 3:114.

2. Ibid., 3:115.

3. Ibid., 3:114.

4. Ibid., 3:117 22.

5. Ibid., 3:125.

6. William Stewart Bodley to Virginia Amoreux, June 1, 1830, Bodley Family Papers, The Filson Historical Society.

7. Ibid.

8. Royall, *Black Book,* 3:110–11.

9. John Tyler to Mary Tyler, May 13, 1830, in Lyon G. Tyler, *The Letters and Times of the Tylers,* 2 vols. (Richmond, VA, 1854), 1:550.

10. Royall, *Sketches,* 352.

11. Royall, *Black Book,* 1:5.

12. See, for instance, her comment on Noah Webster: Royall, *Sketches,* 388.

13. Bushman, *Refinement of America, passim;* Hemphill, *Bowing to Necessities,* 129–59, 179–212.

14. John Quincy Adams, diary entry for August 9, 1827, in Adams, *Memoirs of John Quincy Adams,* 7:321.

15. J. G. Meem to Colonel David Campbell, February 14, 1830, Campbell Family Papers, David M. Rubinstein Rare Book and Manuscript Library, Duke University.

16. "Correspondence," *National Advocate,* January 24, 1827.

17. "From the New-York Commercial Advertiser," *Connecticut Courant,* August 14, 1826.

18. See, for instance, "Mrs. Royall," *National Advocate,* June 4, 1827; *Democratic Press,* May 1827, 2; and *Southern Patriot,* March 15, 1830.

19. "Mrs. Anne Royall's Black Book," *The Ariel,* October 18, 1828.

20. "Fashionable Movements," *New England Galaxy,* September 15, 1826.

21. Gilmore, *Reading Becomes a Necessity of Life,* 20–24; Steffen, "Newspapers for Free"; John, *Spreading the News.* On the importance of this new print culture in disseminating political scandals, see Basch, "Marriage, Morals, and Politics," 892–93.

22. "Mrs. Royall," *Harrisburg Argus,* November 8, 1828; *Southern Patriot,* March 15, 1830.

23. Young, *Masquerade,* 167–224.

24. Royall, *Pennsylvania,* 1:3, 2:257–68; *Portsmouth Journal and Rockingham Gazette,* January 31, 1829; *New Hampshire Sentinel,* February 13, 1829.

25. *The Watch Tower,* June 30, 1828; *Providence Patriot and Columbian Phenix,* July 28, 1827.

26. Royall, *Southern Tour,* 1:86–97.

27. Ibid., 1:91–92.

28. "Misc.," *Virginia Free Press,* March 3, 1830.

29. Royall, *Black Book,* 1:260.

30. Butler, *Awash in a Sea of Faith,* 273–78.

31. Hatch, *Democratization of American Christianity;* Howe, "Evangelical Movement and Political Culture," 1216–18; Ginzberg, "Hearts of Your Readers," 196–99.

32. Howe, "Evangelical Movement and Political Culture"; Carwardine, *Evangelicals and Politics,* 97–132; Bodo, *Protestant Clergy and Public Issues,* 9–18; Butler, *Awash in a Sea of Faith,* 273–79.

33. Several of the letters she exchanged with Dunbar contain discussions of religion. Royall, *Letters from Alabama,* 32–35, 136–37; Ginzberg, "Hearts of Your Readers," 196–201.

34. Royall, *Letters from Alabama,* 32–33.

35. Ibid., 32–35.

36. Ibid., 6, 126–28.

37. Royall, *Black Book,* 1:95.

38. Ibid., 1:20.
39. Ibid., 2:361.
40. Ibid., 1:163.
41. Ibid., 1:163.
42. Ibid., 1:219.
43. Ibid., 2:158.
44. Royall, *Southern Tour,* 2:111.
45. Royall, *Black Book,* 3:202.
46. Ibid., 1:180.
47. Royall, *Pennsylvania,* 1:200, 194–95.
48. Royall, *Black Book,* 1:171.
49. Ibid., 1:180; 3:202.
50. Ibid., 1:163–245; Ryan, *Cradle of the Middle Classes,* 60–104; Cott, *Bonds of Womanhood;* Bloch, "American Feminine Ideals"; Welter, "Cult of True Womanhood"; Howe, "Evangelical Movement and Political Culture," 1216–18; Ginzberg, "Hearts of Your Readers," 197–98.
51. Hewitt, *Women's Activism and Social Change;* Ginzberg, *Women and the Work of Benevolence.*
52. Ginzberg, "Hearts of Your Readers," 197–200; Ginzberg, *Untidy Origins,* 36–38; Boylan, *Origins of Women's Activism.*
53. Royall, *Pennsylvania,* 1:194–95, 200; Ginzberg, "Hearts of Your Readers." Royall reported the insults thrown at her in many of her books, and these are confirmed in some of the newspaper comments. See "Mrs. Royall," *Literary Cadet and Rhode Island Statesman,* July 28, 1827, and "Madam Royall," *Cincinnati American,* September 9, 1830.
54. Royall, *Pennsylvania,* 2:174. The two women did not meet, though Royall had hoped to hear Wright speak in Wheeling. Wright left the town a couple of days before Royall arrived. Ibid., 2:164–65, 174.
55. "Miss Wright and Mrs. Royall," *The Ariel,* September 19, 1829; Ginzberg, "Hearts of Your Readers."
56. Royall, *Black Book,* 3:34–35; Anne Royall to Captain Hall (usually called Yankee Hall), May 3, 1828, CWB Collection. Royall was by this time almost sixty years old.
57. Anne Royall to Captain Hall, May 3, 1828, CWB Collection; Royall, *Black Book,* 3:36–42.
58. *New England Galaxy,* January 25, 1828.
59. "Mrs. Royall," *Saturday Evening Post,* February 2, 1828. See also "Hung Be the Skies in Black," *Middlesex Gazette,* January 30, 1828, and "Mrs. Royall," *Salem Gazette,* January 25, 1828.
60. Royall, *Black Book,* 3:38.
61. Ibid., 3:186.
62. Royall, *Pennsylvania,* 1:190.
63. Royall, *Black Book,* 1:225.

64. Ibid., 1:226.

65. Feller, *Jacksonian Promise,* 116, 178–79; Carwardine, *Evangelicals and Politics,* 97–132; Bodo, *Protestant Clergy and Public Issues,* 9–18.

66. Royall, *Pennsylvania,* 1:89; Royall, *Black Book,* 3:196.

67. See, particularly, Royall, *Black Book,* 1:164–247; 3:185–97.

68. Royall, *Pennsylvania,* 1:3, 190.

69. Butler, *Awash in a Sea of Faith,* 218–24; Ginzberg, "Hearts of Your Readers," 200–208.

70. John, "Taking Sabbatarianism Seriously," 550–60.

71. Hatch, *Democratization of American Christianity,* 170–75; John, "Taking Sabbatarianism Seriously," 554–55.

72. Howe, "Evangelical Movement and Political Culture," 1226–28; Bodo, *Protestant Clergy and Public Issues,* 23–26; Carwardine, *Evangelicals and Politics,* 100–111.

73. Royall, *Pennsylvania,* 2:133.

74. Verhoeven, "Case for Sunday Mails"; Rohrer, "Sunday Mails and the Church-State Theme"; John, "Taking Sabbatarianism Seriously," 548–56.

75. Verhoeven, "Case for Sunday Mails," 82–85.

76. Royall, *Black Book,* 3:230–34.

77. Royall, *Southern Tour,* 1:119.

78. Verhoeven, "Case for Sunday Mails," 77–85. See Petition from the Inhabitants of Portsmouth, New Hampshire, January 1830, *American State Papers,* Post Office Department, 1:238; Petition from the Inhabitants of Philadelphia, Pennsylvania, January 1830, *American State Papers,* Post Office Department, 1:239.

79. Howe, "Evangelical Movement and Political Culture," 1216; Bodo, *Protestant Clergy and Public Issues,* 35–41; Carwardine, *Evangelicals and Politics,* 99–100; John, "Taking Sabbatarianism Seriously," 564–67.

80. Royall, *Black Book,* 1:163–247; Royall, *Pennsylvania,* 1:270.

81. Royall, *Black Book,* 2:232.

82. Ginzberg has suggested that Frances Wright posed a still more potent threat. "Hearts of Your Readers."

83. "Mrs. Royall," *Morning Courier,* June 4, 1828; "Miss Wright and Mrs. Royall," *The Ariel,* September 19, 1829; "Original," *The Ariel,* January 9, 1829; Address of the Carriers of the Newburyport Herald, January 1, 1830, Manuscript Division, Brown University Library, Providence, Rhode Island.

84. Royall, *Black Book,* 1:26. John Quincy Adams also noted this assumption on Royall's part in his diary. Diary entry for August 9, 1827, in Adams, *Memoirs of John Quincy Adams,* 7:321.

6. A Political Woman and Common Scold

1. "Domestic News," *New York Observer,* July 11, 1829.

2. Ginzberg, *Women and the Work of Benevolence,* 25–35; Ginzberg, "Hearts of Your Readers"; Hershberger, "Mobilizing Women, Anticipating Abolition."

3. Zagarri, "Gender and the First Party System"; John, "Taking Sabbatarianism Seriously." Royall's concern was also shared by Freethinkers; see Ginzberg, "Hearts of Your Readers."

4. Royall, *Black Book,* 2:4–5.

5. Royall, *Letters from Alabama,* 16–17.

6. Ibid., 39, 16–19.

7. Watson, *Liberty and Power,* 48–49.

8. Royall, *Letters from Alabama,* 115–20.

9. Several newspapers labeled her a "Jackson Man." See, for instance, *New Hampshire Sentinel,* August 17, 1827. On her admiration for Jackson, see Royall, *Letters from Alabama,* 69–70, 115–20.

10. Feller, *Jacksonian Promise,* 116, 178–79; Carwardine, *Evangelicals and Politics,* 97–132; Bodo, *Protestant Clergy and Public Issues,* 9–18.

11. Royall, *Letters from Alabama,* appendix, 169–74; Royall, *Black Book,* 2:*passim;* "Mrs. Royall," *National Advocate,* June 4, 1827; Feller, *Jacksonian Promise,* 185–94.

12. "Mrs. Royal," *Essex Register,* August 20, 1827. On the election of 1828, see Basch, "Marriage, Morals, and Politics."

13. Royall, *Pennsylvania,* 2:270.

14. Watson, *Liberty and Power,* 11–12, 48; Zagarri, *Revolutionary Backlash.*

15. Branson, *These Fiery Frenchified Dames;* Allgor, *Parlor Politics;* Varon, *We Mean to Be Counted;* Sacher, "'Ladies Are Moving Everywhere'"; Royall, *Southern Tour,* 1:36–39; Royall, *Letters from Alabama,* appendix, 169–74.

16. Zagarri, *Revolutionary Backlash,* 160–61.

17. Zagarri, "Gender and the First Party System"; Varon, *We Mean to Be Counted;* Varon, "Tippecanoe and the Ladies, Too"; Zboray and Zboray, "Whig Women, Politics and Culture"; Zboray and Zboray, *Voices without Votes;* Wood, "'One Woman So Dangerous.'"

18. Jeanne Boydston, "Making Gender in the Early Republic: Judith Sargent Murray and the Revolution of 1800," in Horn et al., eds., *The Revolution of 1800,* 241–46; Zagarri, *Revolutionary Backlash,* 68–75. See also Klinghoffer and Elkis, "'The Petticoat Electors.'"

19. Zagarri, *Revolutionary Backlash,* 75–81.

20. Boydston, "Making Gender in the Early Republic," 240–66; Klinghoffer and Elkis, "'The Petticoat Electors'"; Zagarri, "Gender and the First Party System."

21. Zagarri, *Revolutionary Backlash, passim;* Rosemarie Zagarri, "Women

and Party Conflict in the Early Republic," in Pasley et al., eds., *Beyond the Founders,* 107–28.

22. Zagarri, *Revolutionary Backlash.*

23. Varon, "Tippecanoe and the Ladies, Too," 518; Basch, "Marriage, Morals, and Politics," 914–18; Zagarri, "Gender and the First Party System."

24. Wood, "'One Woman So Dangerous,'" 272–75; Allgor, *Parlor Politics,* 190–238.

25. "Mrs. Royall," *Essex Gazette,* July 28, 1827; "Mrs. Royal," *Essex Register,* August 20, 1827; Zagarri, *Revolutionary Backlash,* 148–80.

26. Royall, *Pennsylvania,* 2: appendix, 1–24.

27. Ibid., 2: appendix, 19n.

28. Ibid., 2: appendix, 2; 1:264–65.

29. "Letter from Washington, No. LVIII, Washington, July 6, 1829," *United States Gazette,* July 10, 1829; Statement by Andrew Way, Foreman, *U.S. v. Royall* (hereafter File U.S. v. Royall).

30. "Mrs. Royall's Case," *Richmond Whig,* July 31, 1829.

31. Ginzberg, *Women and the Work of Benevolence,* 23–26.

32. Statement by Andrew Way, Foreman, File U.S. v. Royall; Ryan, *Women in Public,* 68–76.

33. Royall, *Pennsylvania,* 2: appendix, 1–8.

34. Anne Royall to Mr. Sloan [Swann?], undated. On the back is a note signed by the clerk of the court, July 31, 1829, noting that Anne Royall had sworn to the foregoing note. File marked Circuit DC Criminal Apps. 129, File U.S. v. Royall.

35. *Newport Mercury,* June 27, 1829; *Farmers' Cabinet,* June 27, 1829; *New Bedford Mercury,* July 17, 1829. The tone of these newspapers suggests their editors supported the evangelical cause.

36. "Letter from Washington, No. LVIII, Washington, July 6, 1829," *United States Gazette,* July 10, 1829.

37. "Mrs. Royall in Trouble," *Morning Courier,* June 18, 1829.

38. "Letter from Washington, No. LVIII, Washington, July 6, 1829," *United States Gazette,* July 10, 1829.

39. *Essex Gazette,* July 18, 1829.

40. Indictment of the Grand Jury, File U.S. v. Royall.

41. "Mrs. Royall in Trouble," *Morning Courier,* June 18, 1829; "Mrs. Royall in Trouble," *Northern Sentinel,* July 3, 1829; "Mrs. Royall," *Pittsfield Sun,* July 23, 1829; "Mrs. Royall," *Morning Courier and New York Enquirer,* June 30, 1829; "From Our Correspondent," *Morning Courier and New York Enquirer,* July 17, 1829.

42. "Mrs. Royall. Washington D.C., July 18," *National Gazette and Literary Register,* July 20, 1829; "Mrs. Royall," *Daily National Journal,* July 18, 1829; Cranch, *Reports of Cases,* 3:618–20.

43. See Tucker, *Blackstone's Commentaries,* 5:168, and Cranch, *Reports of Cases,* 3:620.

44. Thomas, *Religion and the Decline of Magic,* 528–29; Case of *James v. Commonwealth,* Philadelphia, January 3, 1825, in Sergeant and Rawle, *Reports of Cases Adjudged,* 12:225; "Remarks on Scolding," *United States Gazette,* January 20, 1825.

45. D. E. Underdown, "The Taming of the Scold: The Enforcement of Patriarchal Authority in Early Modern England," in Fletcher and Stevenson, eds., *Order and Disorder in Early Modern England,* 119; Thomas, *Religion and the Decline of Magic,* 528–30.

46. Underdown, "The Taming of the Scold," 120; Brown, *Good Wives, Nasty Wenches,* 29.

47. Brown, *Good Wives, Nasty Wenches,* 29–32; Kamensky, "Talk Like a Man."

48. Case of *James v. Commonwealth,* Philadelphia, January 3, 1825, in Sergeant and Rawle, *Reports of Cases Adjudged,* 12:223.

49. Ibid., 12:220–36.

50. Cranch, *Reports of Cases,* 3:620–28.

51. "Common Scold," *Constitutional Whig,* May 11, 1827. Similar remarks were made about Royall.

52. "Trial of a Scold"; "For the United States Gazette," *United States Gazette,* January 13, 1825; "Common Scold," *Constitutional Whig,* May 11, 1827. There was also a case in New York in 1819; see Lawyer's Co-Operative, comp., *Abbott's New York Digest Consolidated Edition* (Rochester, NY: Lawyer's Co-operative Publishing, 1929), 7:881. *United States Gazette,* November 1, 1824, refers to a case in Boston.

53. Royall, *Pennsylvania,* 2: appendix, 11.

54. Cranch, *Reports of Cases,* 3:618–20, as the demurrers against the two other indictments had shown.

55. Royall, *Pennsylvania,* 2: appendix, 9.

56. Freedman, *Their Sisters' Keepers,* 11–14.

57. Bynum, *Unruly Women,* 14.

58. Case 118, Indictment of the Grand Jury, Bundle: Criminal Appearances, File U.S. v. Royall; "Mrs. Royall's Case," *Richmond Whig,* July 31, 1829.

59. "Mrs. Royall," *Daily National Journal,* July 20, 1829; "Mrs. Royall," *Daily Commercial Gazette,* July 29, 1829.

60. "Mrs. Royall," *Daily Commercial Gazette,* July 29, 1829.

61. "Mrs. Royall's Case," *Richmond Whig,* July 31, 1829.

62. *Newport Mercury,* June 27, 1829; *Farmers' Cabinet,* June 27, 1829.

63. *United States Gazette,* July 24, 1829; Royall, *Pennsylvania,* 2: appendix, 8, 21. *United States Telegraph,* June 12, 1829, mentions George Watterstone's dismissal. He had been Librarian of Congress, and some editors believed that he had been rotated out of office because of his strong support for John Quincy Adams.

64. "Mrs. Royall's Case," *Richmond Whig,* July 31, 1829; "Mrs. Royall," *New*

England Galaxy, July 31, 1829. Reports of the trial and witnesses appear in *Commercial Advertiser,* July 22, 1829, and *Daily National Intelligencer,* July 20, 1829, among others. Royall's account appears in Royall, *Pennsylvania,* 2: appendix, 10–16.

65. *United States Gazette,* July 24, 1829; *Richmond Whig,* July 31, 1829; Royall, *Pennsylvania,* 2: appendix, 19. On the opposition charges of immorality against Andrew Jackson, see Basch, "Marriage, Morals, and Politics." Royall suggested that the attacks on her were part of a campaign against the women of the Jackson circle. Royall, *Pennsylvania,* 2: appendix, 19n.

66. Statement of Andrew Way, Foreman, File U.S. v. Royall.

67. "Mrs. Royall's Case," *Richmond Whig,* July 31, 1829. The same account appears in "Mrs. Royall," *New England Galaxy,* July 31, 1829.

68. "Mrs. Royall," *Daily Commercial Gazette,* July 29, 1829.

69. "Mrs. Royall's Case," *Richmond Whig,* July 31, 1829.

70. "Letter from Washington, No. LIX, Washington, July 11, 1829," *United States Gazette,* July 14, 1829; *Daily National Intelligencer,* July 31, 1829.

71. "From Our Correspondent, Washington, July 22," *Commercial Advertiser,* July 25, 1829. The speech is also reported in "Mrs. Royall's Case," *Richmond Whig,* July 31, 1829.

72. "From Our Correspondent, Washington, July 22," *Commercial Advertiser,* July 25, 1829.

73. In other words, cowards. The Battle of Bladensburg in 1814 had seen the rout of the American army in just half an hour by the British troops attacking Washington, much to the anger and humiliation of many in Washington. See Constance McLaughlin Green, *Washington: Village and Capital, 1800–1878* (Princeton, NJ: Princeton University Press, 1962), 61, and Royall, *Sketches,* 171–74.

74. "Mrs. Royall," *Daily National Journal,* July 20, 1829; "From the National Journal of July 29," *Commercial Advertiser,* July 31, 1829.

75. "Mrs. Royall," *New England Galaxy,* July 31, 1829.

76. Royall, *Pennsylvania,* 2: appendix, 21.

77. "Mrs. Royall," *Virginia Advocate,* August 7, 1829. For another summary of Cranch's opinion see "United States vs. Ann Royall," *Niles' Register,* August 8, 1829, and the argument in full, "United States vs. Ann Royall," in Cranch, *Reports of Cases,* 3:620–28.

78. Royall, *Pennsylvania,* 2: appendix, 1–22.

79. "Letter from Washington, LXVI, July 31, 1829," *United States Gazette,* August 3, 1829; "Mrs. Royall," *National Gazette and Literary Register,* August 3, 1829. The legal complaints are in a file marked Circuit DC Criminal Apps. 129, File U.S. v. Royall.

80. "From Our Correspondent, Washington, July 31, 1829," *Commercial Advertiser,* August 3, 1829; "Mrs. Royall," *National Intelligencer,* August 1, 1829.

81. *Pittsfield Sun,* July 30, 1829.

82. "Mrs. Royal," *Providence Patriot and Columbian Phenix,* July 25, 1829.

83. "From the National Gazette," *United States Telegraph,* August 21, 1829; "From Our Correspondent, Washington, July 31, 1829," *Commercial Advertiser,* August 3, 1829; "Mrs. Royall," *Commercial Advertiser,* August 17, 1829.

84. "From Our Correspondent, Washington, July 31, 1829," *Commercial Advertiser,* August 3, 1829; Royall, *Pennsylvania,* 2: appendix, 17.

85. "Mrs. Royall's Pennsylvania," advertisement in *United States Telegraph,* August 31, 1829, and on subsequent occasions. The account is also mentioned in Anne Royall to Hon. Dretee Pearce, September 14, 1829, Case 6, Box 10, Gratz Manuscripts. Royall's account of the trial appears in Royall, *Pennsylvania,* 2: appendix. On newspaper speculation about Royall's silence, see "Something Mysterious," *United States Gazette,* August 6, 1829, and "Mrs. Royall," *Saturday Evening Post,* August 22, 1829.

86. Royall, *Pennsylvania,* 2: appendix, 21.

87. Royall, *Black Book,* 1:163–247; "From Our Correspondent, Washington, July 22," *Commercial Advertiser,* July 25, 1829; "Mrs. Royall's Case," *Richmond Whig,* July 31, 1829; Royall, *Pennsylvania,* 2: appendix.

88. Royall, *Pennsylvania,* 2:21–24.

89. Wood, "'One Woman So Dangerous.'"

90. As quoted in *United States Gazette,* July 24, 1829. On respectability, see Cohen, "Respectability of Rebecca Reed."

91. "Mrs. Royal," *Providence Patriot and Columbian Phenix,* July 25, 1829.

92. Cohen, "Respectability of Rebecca Reed"; Teute, "Roman Matron on the Banks," 90–94; Kasson, *Rudeness and Civility.* There are also parallels in Coryell, *Neither Heroine nor Fool,* and Coryell, "Superseding Gender."

7. THE FEMALE POLITICO AS NEWSPAPER EDITOR

1. Coryell, "Superseding Gender," 102.

2. See Boylan, *Origins of Women's Activism;* Ginzberg, *Women and the Work of Benevolence;* and Zagarri, *Revolutionary Backlash,* 140–47.

3. Coryell, "Superseding Gender"; Zagarri, *Revolutionary Backlash,* 155–64.

4. *Paul Pry,* December 3, 1831; Coryell, "Superseding Gender."

5. *New Hampshire Patriot and State Gazette,* April 22, 1833. For comments on the value of Royall's newspapers, see "All the Decency," *Richmond Enquirer,* December 10, 1831, and "Summary," *Vermont Chronicle,* February 3, 1832.

6. *Paul Pry,* December 3, 1831.

7. Royall, *Southern Tour,* 2:56–57.

8. Ibid., 3:144–61.

9. Royall mentions the assault on her in Pittsburgh in ibid., 1: appendix, 9–10. For other accounts, see "Mrs. Ann Royal," *Cincinnati American,* November 18, 1830, and "Anne Royall to the Courier and Enquirer," *Morning Courier and New York Enquirer,* November 12, 1830.

10. Royall, *Southern Tour,* 3:57. On the tactics of the evangelicals in dealing with those they saw as threats to their cause, see Ginzberg, "Hearts of Your Readers."

11. "Card," *Paul Pry,* December 10, 1831; Anne Royall to Jo. Cole, May 18, 1831, Case 6, Box 34, Gratz Manuscripts; Anne Royall to Mr. E. Little, April 18, [1832?], Bertha Overbury Collection.

12. Royall, *Southern Tour,* 2:209.

13. Sellers, *Market Revolution,* 370; John, *Spreading the News,* 4, 38. See also Pasley, *"Tyranny of Printers,"* appendix, 1, and Steffen, "Newspapers for Free."

14. Remer, *Printers and Men of Capital,* 24–38. Remer notes the uncertainty of newspaper publishing, particularly in the 1790s. Royall frequently catalogued the appearance of new newspapers and the disappearance of others. See also Freeman, *Affairs of Honor,* 124.

15. Lehuu, *Carnival on the Page,* 14–35; Cohen, *Murder of Helen Jewett,* 25–26.

16. Zagarri, "Postcolonial Culture," 19–20.

17. Ibid., 19–37; Okker, *Our Sister Editors.*

18. Writers have mistakenly claimed that Royall was unique and a pioneer for women's rights in becoming a newspaper editor. The evidence suggests otherwise. On the suggestion that Royall was a pioneer, see "Edited Her Own Paper: Eccentric Mrs. Royall, First of Woman Suffragists," *Washington Post,* April 12, 1899; "First Woman Editor: Anne Royall Pioneer in Yellow Journalism," *Washington Post,* October 6, 1901; Beasley, "Anne Royall"; and Jackson, *Uncommon Scold.*

19. For instance, see Martha J. King, "'What Providence Has Brought Them to Be': Widows, Work, and Print Culture in Colonial Charleston," in Eldridge, ed., *Women and Freedom,* 147–66; Olsen, "'Molly Pitcher'"; Blackwell, "Meddling in Politics"; and Beasley, "Anne Royall," 32.

20. "Congressional Printing," *The Huntress,* January 11, 1840.

21. Okker, *Our Sister Editors, passim.*

22. Olsen, "'Molly Pitcher'"; Blackwell, "Meddling in Politics."

23. Olsen, "'Molly Pitcher,'" 247.

24. Coryell, "Superseding Gender." See also Blackwell, "Meddling in Politics." The term "Domestic Feminism" has been used by historians to describe the rhetoric used by women reformers to justify their entry into the public sphere of reform. These female reformers insisted that they did so as mothers and as the nation's moral force, and that partisan politics was too corrupt for any respectable woman to become involved in it. Coryell, "Superseding Gender," 85; Baker, "Domestication of Politics."

25. See Zagarri, *Revolutionary Backlash,* 75–81, 115–47.

26. *Paul Pry,* December 3, 1831. On her earlier stance, see Royall, *Black Book,* 2:4–5.

27. *Paul Pry,* December 3, 1831.

28. The first advertisements appeared in the edition for December 17, 1831.

29. *Paul Pry*, December 10, 1831.

30. *Paul Pry*, December 31, 1831.

31. "Mrs. Royal," *Middlesex Gazette*, July 11, 1827; *Western Monthly Review*, May 1827; *Pittsfield Sun*, February 7, 1828.

32. The *New York Enquirer* published a number of letters, supposedly from Royall. See "Anne Royall to the Courier and Enquirer," *Morning Courier and New York Enquirer*, November 12, 1830. This paper underwent a number of changes in editor and ownership, resulting in changes of title.

33. *Paul Pry*, December 17, 1831. Royall was uncertain, or unwilling, to say whether the communication was from Stone, Noah, or someone else.

34. *Paul Pry*, December 3, 1831; *Paul Pry*, December 24, 1831.

35. *New Hampshire Sentinel*, December 16, 1831.

36. Pasley, "Minnows, Spies, and Aristocrats."

37. *Baltimore Patriot*, December 10, 1831.

38. *Paul Pry*, December 3, 1831.

39. Pasley, *"Tyranny of Printers,"* 392–94.

40. Ibid., 392–99; *Paul Pry*, December 3, 1831.

41. *Paul Pry*, February 11, 1832. The men she refers to are Louis McLane, Jackson's secretary of the treasury, and Mordecai Noah, editor of the New York *Courier and Enquirer.*

42. Watson, *Liberty and Power*, 138–41; Feller, *Jacksonian Promise*, 169–75.

43. Royall, *Southern Tour*, 3:122–23, 239–40. On the issue of bank loans to editors, see Wilentz, *Rise of American Democracy*, 366–67.

44. *Paul Pry*, February 18, 1832. Noah's objections were reprinted in *Paul Pry*, March 3, 1832. Watson, *Liberty and Power*, 140–41.

45. See *Paul Pry*, March 24, 1832; April 21, 1832.

46. "The Veto of the Bank Bill," *Paul Pry*, July 21, 1832.

47. "U.S. Bank," *Paul Pry*, October 12, 1833.

48. "United States Bank," *Paul Pry*, December 21, 1833; "U.S. Bank," *Paul Pry*, January 25, 1834; *Paul Pry*, May 3, 1834, and *passim;* Feller, *Jacksonian Promise*, 132–34, 169–75; Wilentz, *Rise of American Democracy*, 392–403.

49. "Georgia and the Nullifiers," *Paul Pry*, January 4, 1834.

50. "Matters and Things in General," *Paul Pry*, June 14, 1834.

51. Quoted in Sellers, *Market Revolution*, 302.

52. Wilentz, *Rise of American Democracy*, 314–15; Sellers, *Market Revolution*, 301–3; Pessen, *Jacksonian America*, 313–17.

53. Wilentz, *Rise of American Democracy*, 315–16; Pasley, "Minnows, Spies, and Aristocrats," 616–17. See also John, *Spreading the News*, 221–32, on Post Office officeholders.

54. *Paul Pry*, September 8, 1832, November 10, 1832; Pasley, "Minnows, Spies, and Aristocrats," 608–12.

55. *Paul Pry,* March 23, 1833, May 4, 1833, May 11, 1833; "Paul Pry," *Nashville Banner and Nashville Whig,* March 6, 1835.

56. "The Next President," *Paul Pry,* August 10, 1833; "The Next President," *Paul Pry,* October 26, 1833; Feller, *Jacksonian Promise,* 185–89; Wilentz, *Rise of American Democracy,* 446–55.

57. *Essex Gazette,* May 4, 1833; *Paul Pry,* December 7, 1833

58. "The War Begun," *Paul Pry,* August 17, 1833. On the consolidation of the Democratic Party, see Feller, *Jacksonian Promise,* 183–94, and Watson, *Liberty and Power, passim.*

59. John, *Spreading the News,* 206–56; "Judge Barry's Defence," *Paul Pry,* July 19, 1834; "Remarks of Judge Barry's Defence Concluded," *Paul Pry,* July 26, 1834.

60. *Paul Pry,* January 22, 1833, June 28, 1834; "Our Country," *Paul Pry,* September 27, 1834.

61. "The President and the Post Office," *Paul Pry,* November 22, 1834.

62. "Ohio Elections," *Paul Pry,* November 15, 1834; *Paul Pry,* December 27, 1834; "Judge White," *Paul Pry,* January 3, 1835.

63. "Judge White," *Paul Pry,* January 3, 1835.

64. Ibid.

65. *Paul Pry,* February 7, 1835; "A Brief Review of Parties," *Paul Pry,* April 25, 1835; *Paul Pry,* May 23, 1834; *Paul Pry,* July 2, 1836. On the Whigs, see Holt, *Rise and Fall of the American Whig Party,* 37–38.

66. Zagarri, "Women and Party Conflict," 120–24; Zagarri, *Revolutionary Backlash,* 124–47.

67. "Mrs. Royall," *United States Telegraph,* April 23, 1835. Royall was "married off" to various public men at different times, much to her annoyance. See *New-Hampshire Gazette,* December 24, 1833; "Amalgamation," *Portsmouth Journal of Literature and Politics,* October 10, 1835; and *Vermont Watchman and State Gazette,* November 10, 1835.

68. Olsen, "'Molly Pitcher'"; Pasley, *"Tyranny of Printers,"* 392–94.

69. *Vermont Gazette,* August 23, 1836. Similar comments were printed in other papers; see "Van Buren Demolished," *New Hampshire Patriot and State Gazette,* August 29, 1836, and "Petticoats," *The Globe,* September 26, 1836.

70. *Ithaca Herald,* November 9, 1836. The use of gendered slurs in elections is explored in Zboray and Zboray, "Gender Slurs."

71. "Harrisburg Reporter," *Paul Pry,* October 1, 1836.

72. "General Harrison," *Paul Pry,* June 25, 1836; Zboray and Zboray, "Gender Slurs," 413–18.

73. "Ohio Elections," *Paul Pry,* November 15, 1834; Howe, *Political Culture of the American Whigs,* 23–42; Howe, "Evangelical Movement and Political Culture"; Holt, *Rise and Fall of the American Whig Party,* 60–70.

74. "Who Has Changed?" *Paul Pry,* September 10, 1836; *Paul Pry,* October 8, 1836; "Eulogy to the 'Paul Pry,'" *Paul Pry,* November 19, 1836.

75. *Paul Pry,* November 5, 1836.

76. John Poole, *Paul Pry: A Comedy in Three Acts* (London, 1825); Porter, *Life and Times of Anne Royall,* 149–50.

77. "The Huntress," *The Huntress,* December 3, 1836. The dates appearing on the masthead of *The Huntress* are often inconsistent with the dates at the head of the editorial column. Where these are contradictory, I have used the date in the editorial column, which seems to be more regular.

78. "The Huntress," *The Huntress,* December 31, 1836.

79. "A Prospectus for the Huntress," *The Huntress,* December 3, 1836.

80. "Church and State," *The Huntress,* December 3, 1836, December 10, 1836; "The President Elect," *The Huntress,* December 17, 1836; "The New President," *The Huntress,* March 11, 1837.

81. "Ourself and the Administration Party," *The Huntress,* July 4, 1840; "Colonel Croghan and Gen. Harrison," *The Huntress,* October 31, 1840; "The Presidential Election," *The Huntress,* November 14, 1840.

82. Coryell, "Superseding Gender," 85–87; Zagarri, *Revolutionary Backlash,* 1–10, 163, 181–86; Zboray and Zboray, "Whig Women, Politics and Culture"; Zboray and Zboray, *Voices without Votes,* 79–97; Varon, "Tippecanoe and the Ladies, Too"; Zboray and Zboray, "Gender Slurs," 417–19.

83. "Scenes from the Gallery, No. 6," *The Huntress,* September 26, 1840; "The Presidential Election," *The Huntress,* November 14, 1840.

84. "Retrenchment and Reform," *The Huntress,* January 29, 1842.

85. Kelley, *Learning to Stand and Speak,* 5.

86. Ibid.; Zagarri, *Revolutionary Backlash,* 7–9; Hewitt, *Women's Activism and Social Change;* Ginzberg, *Women and the Work of Benevolence.* Moral reform referred to campaigns to eradicate prostitution and ostracize men who seduced young women, forcing them into prostitution.

87. Royall, *Black Book,* 1:172–73, 3:202–3; Royall, *Southern Tour,* 1:7–8.

88. Ginzberg, *Women and the Work of Benevolence,* 25–27, 67; Boydston et al., eds., *Limits of Sisterhood,* 118, 236.

89. Catharine Beecher does not appear to have commented on Royall, at least in her published writings.

90. *Paul Pry,* December 3, 1831.

91. *The Huntress,* November 3, 1838; *The Huntress,* February 25, 1843.

92. Similar tactics were used by Catharine Beecher to criticize abolitionist women like the Grimké sisters. See Catharine Beecher, "Essay on Slavery and Abolitionism," in Boydston et al., eds., *Limits of Sisterhood,* 125–29.

93. "From the Herald," *The Huntress,* January 6, 1849; *The Huntress,* February 25, 1843.

94. "Gen. Chaplin and Ladies of Western New York," *The Huntress,* October 5, 1850.

95. "The Bloomer or New Costume," *The Huntress,* June 28, 1851; "The New Costume," *The Huntress,* July 12, 1850; "The Bloomers," *The Huntress,* October 11, 1851.

96. Zagarri, *Revolutionary Backlash,* 170–71.

97. "Our Own Independent Ticket," *New England Weekly Review,* October 24, 1840.

98. *Morning News,* November 10, 1847.

99. Thurner, "'Better Citizens without the Ballot'"; Zagarri, *Revolutionary Backlash,* 75–81.

100. "167th Metropolitan Epistle, March 2, 1843," *Ohio Statesman,* March 18, 1843; Coryell, "Superseding Gender," 85–86.

8. The Widow of a Revolutionary War Officer

1. Speech of Peter Silvester, July 1, 1848, *Congressional Globe,* 30th Cong., 1st sess., Appendix, 932.

2. The appellation is from Petition of Anne Royall, December 19, 1844, Anne Royall's Pension Claim.

3. See, for instance, her claim that she was "the widow of one of your revolutionary worthys" in her letter to Thomas Jefferson, June 20, 1825, Jefferson Papers.

4. Royall, *Southern Tour,* 2:209.

5. Kelley, *Private Woman, Public Stage,* 11–12; Coultrap-McQuin, *Doing Literary Business,* 23–24.

6. Royall, *Southern Tour,* 2:209.

7. Rockman, *Scraping By.* On material goods as markers of the middle class, see Bushman, *Refinement of America.*

8. Anne Royall to Jo. Cole, May 18, 1831, Case 6, Box 34, Gratz Manuscripts.

9. Anne Royall to Little and Co., May 1831, Case 6, Box 34, Gratz Manuscripts. See also "Dreadful Literary Calamity," *Niles' Weekly Register,* June 25, 1831.

10. "Dreadful Literary Calamity," *Salem Gazette,* June 24, 1831, reprinted from *Camden Journal.*

11. Anne Royall to Stephen Van Rensselaer, December 26, 1833, folder 8451, CWB Collection.

12. See, for instance, *Paul Pry,* November 3, 1832, November 10, 1832; *The Huntress,* March 18, 1837, June 23, 1838.

13. Anne Royall to Mr. Sanderson, October 25, 1833, Am. Prose, vol. 7, item 97:2, 61, Dreer Collection, Historical Society of Pennsylvania.

14. Royall, *Black Book,* 3:110. For another version of events, see "Mrs. Ann Royal," *Macon Weekly Telegraph,* March 21, 1843.

15. As suggested by Smith-Rosenberg, "Female World of Love," 1–29, and Wilson, *Life after Death,* 66–67.

16. *The Huntress,* December 16, 1843.

17. The requests were often bluntly expressed. See, for instance, Anne Royall to Hon. Gideon Lee and others, March 1, 1839, File 3589, Graff Collection,

Special Collections, Newberry Library. Sometimes this was to the disgust of those from whom she sought aid; see Stickney, ed., *Autobiography of Amos Kendall*, 306–7.

18. Fragment addressed to Peter Force, February 9, 1835, File 3588, Graff Collection; Anne Royall to Mr. Holiday, January 19, 1849, Department of Special Collections, University of Wisconsin, Madison; "The Huntress," *The Huntress*, January 7, 1843.

19. "Removals from Office," *The Huntress*, March 20, 1841; "Postmasters at Their Old Tricks," *The Huntress*, October 8, 1842; "Notice to Our Subscribers," *The Huntress*, October 22, 1842; Steffen, "Newspapers for Free."

20. "Address to the Citizens of Washington," *The Huntress*, July 28, 1838; "Ourself," *The Huntress*, September 9, 1837.

21. Purcell, *Sealed with Blood;* Resch, *Suffering Soldiers;* Schulz, "Revolutionary War Pension Applications."

22. Jensen, *Patriots, Settlers*, 50–53; Resch, *Suffering Soldiers*, 2.

23. Teipe, *America's First Veterans*, 11–15.

24. Ibid., 16–17; Jensen, *Patriots, Settlers*, 57–58.

25. Resch, *Suffering Soldiers*, 208–9; Teipe, *America's First Veterans*, 31–32, 133–34; Jensen, *Patriots, Settlers*, 58–59.

26. Resch, *Suffering Soldiers*, 1–2, 208–9; Jensen, *Patriots, Settlers*, 59–63.

27. Jensen, *Patriots, Settlers*, 67.

28. Ibid., 67–69; Resch, *Suffering Soldiers*, 208–9.

29. Resch, *Suffering Soldiers*, 65–92.

30. Ibid.; Resch, "Politics and Public Culture."

31. Jensen, *Patriots, Settlers*, 3, 85–86, 224.

32. Resch, *Suffering Soldiers*, 150–51; Purcell, *Sealed with Blood*, 170; Cray, "Major John André."

33. Jensen, *Patriots, Settlers*, 85–86; Teipe, *America's First Veterans*, 28, 133–34.

34. See *Congressional Debates*, 19th Cong., 2nd sess., 655–713.

35. Jensen, *Patriots, Settlers*, 46–47; Zaeske, *Signatures of Citizenship*, 3.

36. Zaeske, *Signatures of Citizenship*, 3–5.

37. Teipe, *America's First Veterans*, 22; Jensen, *Patriots, Settlers*, 109; An Act for the Relief of Certain Surviving Officers and Soldiers of the Army of Revolution, May 15, 1828, *Congressional Debates*, 20th Cong., 1st sess., Appendix, xv.

38. Royall had previously reprinted Johnson's report on the Sunday mails in *Black Book*, 3:230–34.

39. *House Journal*, 21st Cong., 1st sess., May 3, 1830, 597; *List of Private Claims Presented to the House of Representatives of the United States from the 1st to the 31st Congress* (Washington, DC, 1853), Index, 241. No petition seems to have survived.

40. Jensen, *Patriots, Settlers*, 113–14.

41. Anne Royall to Hon. Tristam Burges, June 26, 1832, A.L.S. Collection,

Albert and Shirley Small Special Collections Library, University of Virginia. On Burges, see *Biographical Directory of the United States Congress*. For Royall's description of him, see Royall, *Letters from Alabama,* appendix, 192.

42. Jensen, *Patriots, Settlers,* 111–16.

43. Zaeske, *Signatures of Citizenship,* 3–4.

44. *House Journal,* 22nd Cong., 2nd sess., January 16, 1833, 184; *House Journal,* 22nd Cong., 2nd sess., February 14, 1833, 331. On the committee structure, see Jensen, *Patriots, Settlers,* 67–69.

45. Report 100, 22nd Cong., 2nd sess., February 19, 1833, Record Group 217, Records of the Accounting Officers of the Department of the Treasury Third Auditor, Settled Accounts and Claims (hereafter RG 217).

46. Ibid.

47. *House Journal,* 22nd Cong., 2nd sess., February 19, 1833, 363. On concerns about fraud, see Resch, *Suffering Soldiers,* 121–28.

48. "Our Claim on Congress," *Paul Pry,* January 18, 1834.

49. *Senate Journal,* 23rd Cong., 1st sess., January 9, 1834, 87.

50. Petition of Elizabeth Roane and Accompanying Papers, File 2113, RG 217.

51. S. 305, 23rd Cong., 1st sess., April 25, 1834, RG 217.

52. Ibid. The testimony is held in File 2113, RG 217. On officials' willingness to accept such testimony, see Teipe, *America's First Veterans,* 139.

53. S. 305, 23rd Cong., 1st sess., April 25, 1834, RG 217; A Bill for the Relief of the Widow and Heirs of Captain William Royall Deceased, S. 156, 23rd Cong., 1st sess., April 25, 1834, RG 217; Peters, ed., *Public Statutes at Large,* 6:595; "Congress," *Paul Pry,* July 5, 1834.

54. "Ourself," *Paul Pry,* September 20, 1834.

55. "Congressional Summary," *Scioto Gazette,* March 9, 1843.

56. H.R. 436, 26th Cong., 1st sess., 60, RG 217. See also *Congressional Debates,* Senate, 24th Cong., 1st sess., July 4, 1836, 1936.

57. S. 174, 24th Cong., 1st sess., February 15, 1836, RG 217; "Revolutionary Widows," *The Huntress,* December 1, 1836.

58. "The Winters," *Paul Pry,* April 23, 1836.

59. Resch, *Suffering Soldiers, passim.*

60. "Revolutionary Widows," *The Huntress,* December 2, 1836. For the earlier private comments, see Anne Royall to Hon. Tristam Burges, June 26, 1832, A.L.S. Collection.

61. "Revolutionary Widows," *The Huntress,* December 2, 1836.

62. Boyer, *Urban Masses and Moral Order;* Wilson, *Life after Death,* 66–70.

63. Cott, *Bonds of Womanhood.*

64. "Revolutionary Widows," *The Huntress,* December 2, 1836.

65. "Congress and Our Bill," *The Huntress,* July 14, 1838.

66. *Congressional Debates,* 19th Cong., 2nd sess., January 13, 1827, 696.

67. See the comments in Report 100, 22nd Cong., 2nd sess., February 19, 1833, RG 217.

68. "Widows' Pensions," *New Bedford Mercury,* January 6, 1837.

69. "Congress," *The Huntress,* March 18, 1837.

70. "Congress—Ourself—Patriotism and Self-Love," *The Huntress,* April 18, 1840. The marriage was recorded as November 1797, though Royall claimed an earlier date.

71. "Congress and Our Bill," *The Huntress,* July 14, 1838.

72. "Congress—House of Representatives—Contingent Expenses—Runners, etc. etc.," *The Huntress,* February 11, 1837.

73. "Congress," *The Huntress,* February 11, 1837; "Congress," *The Huntress,* February 25, 1837.

74. "Note," *The Huntress,* July 28, 1838; "Congress," *The Huntress,* December 1, 1838.

75. "Congress," *The Huntress,* December 1, 1838.

76. "The Pension Law—Congress," *The Huntress,* January 12, 1839.

77. "Congressional: Pensions to Widows," *Daily National Intelligencer,* January 24, 1848.

78. Jensen, *Patriots, Settlers,* 87.

79. "Pensions to Widows," *New Hampshire Patriot and State Gazette,* July 30, 1838.

80. "The Widows of Revolutionary Soldiers," *Pennsylvania Inquirer and Daily Courier,* January 2, 1841.

81. "Revolutionary Widows," *Pennsylvania Inquirer and National Gazette,* March 7, 1843.

82. "The Congress," *The Huntress,* July 22, 1848; "Our Friends," *The Huntress,* September 23, 1848.

83. Petition of Anne Royall, 33rd Cong., 1st sess., Sen. 33A-H21, Records of the U.S. Senate, Record Group 46, National Archives and Records Administration; "Speeches of the Members—Three Robberies," *The Huntress,* April 22, 1854.

84. Letter Addressed to Hon. James Shields, undated, Accompanying Petition of Mrs. Anne Royall, 33rd Cong., 1st sess., Sen. 33A-H21, Records of the U.S. Senate, Record Group 46.

85. S. 220, April 18, 1854, 33rd Cong., 1st sess., RG 217.

CONCLUSION

1. *The Huntress* appeared regularly until the end of May 1854, when Royall announced she would no longer publish a newspaper but would relaunch the title in pamphlet form. Three issues of *The Huntress* were printed in pamphlet form before its final demise on July 24, 1854. *The Huntress,* May 27, 1854; "To

the Public," *Daily National Intelligencer,* June 6, 1854; "To Our Patrons," *The Huntress,* June 24, 1854; "Congress," *The Huntress,* July 24, 1854. See also Letter Addressed to Hon. James Shields, undated, Accompanying Petition of Mrs. Anne Royall, 33rd Cong., 1st sess., Sen. 33A-H21, Records of the U.S. Senate, Record Group 46.

2. "Royall," *National Intelligencer,* October 2, 1854.

3. "Death of Mrs. Royall," *Daily South Carolinian,* October 7, 1854; "Mrs. Anne Royall Dead," *Evening Star,* October 2, 1854; "Mrs. Ann Royall," *New York Times,* October 3, 1854; "Mrs. Ann Royall," *Fayetteville Observer,* October 9, 1854; "Mrs. Ann Royall," *Boston Investigator,* October 11, 1854.

4. "The Late Mrs. Anne Royall," *New Albany Daily Ledger,* October 14, 1854. Similar stories appeared in "Mrs. Anne Royall," *North American and United States Gazette,* October 4, 1854, and "The Late Mrs. Anne Royall," *Evening Star,* October 3, 1854.

5. "The Late Mrs. Anne Royall," *Evening Star,* October 3, 1854.

6. "Mrs. Ann Royall," *Fayetteville Observer,* October 9, 1854; *The Ripley Bee,* October 14, 1854.

7. "Mrs. Ann Royal Dead," *Bangor Daily Whig and Courier,* October 7, 1854.

8. Ginzberg, "Hearts of Your Readers," 195–200.

9. *The Huntress,* November 3, 1838; "General Chaplin and the Ladies of Western New York," *The Huntress,* October 5, 1850; Zagarri, *Revolutionary Backlash;* Coryell, "Superseding Gender," 102.

10. See, for instance, "The Original Washington Female Correspondent," *Daily Evening Bulletin* (San Francisco), May 20, 1876; "Mrs. Anne Royall," *Daily Inter Ocean* (Chicago), November 19, 1887; "A Scolding Newspaper Woman," *Bismarck Daily Tribune* (Bismarck, ND), March 30, 1893; and Colonel J. W. Forcey, "Two Famous Women," *Boston Daily Advertiser,* July 19, 1871.

11. "The First 'Interviewer': Old Mrs. Anne Royall, the Diana of the Early Press (From the Washington Post, Jan. 2)," *Boston Daily Advertiser,* January 5, 1878.

12. "She Was a Holy Terror," *Washington Post,* February 22, 1891.

13. "Edited Her Own Paper: Eccentric Mrs. Royall, First of Woman Suffragists," *Washington Post,* April 12, 1899.

14. "Told of Anne Royall: Not So Black as Painted, Declared Defender," *Washington Post,* May 13, 1906.

15. Vylla Poe Wilson, "Anne Royall, Pioneer Woman Publicist," *Washington Post,* May 10, 1931; "Anne Was 'Go Getter' Reporter; Here's Proof," *Washington Post,* August 30, 1933; Vylla Poe Wilson, "Party Planned for Woman Scribes by Mrs. Roosevelt Another Indication of Their Progress," *Washington Post,* December 2, 1934.

16. Bob Arnebeck, "The Scold: What Happens to a Woman Who Won't Hold Her Tongue?" *Washington Post,* June 6, 1976.

17. Old Time Radio Researchers Group, *Cavalcade of America.* The episodes

on Anne Royall were no. 175, "Anne Royall," broadcast on February 20, 1940; no. 277, "The Printer Was a Lady," broadcast on May 4, 1942; and no. 411, "Witness for the People," broadcast on November 27, 1944. The third was a repeat of the second but with a new cast. The plays starred respectively Ethel Barrymore, Lynn Fontanne, and Fay Bainter as Royall. The introduction to "Witness for the People" emphasized the continuing relevance of Royall's defense of freedom of speech and of the press in the light of Nazi book-burnings and Japanese censorship of the press.

18. Ross, *Ladies of the Press;* Marion Marzolf, *Up from the Footnote: A History of Women Journalists* (New York: Hastings House, 1977).

19. Richardson Wright, *Forgotten Ladies: Nine Portraits from the American Family Album* (Philadelphia: J. B. Lippincott, 1928), 178. The chapter on Royall is entitled "The Widow with the Serpent's Tongue."

20. Ross, *Ladies of the Press,* 27–30; Mary Ormsbee Whitton, *These Were the Women: USA, 1776–1860* (New York: Hastings, 1954), 63; Emily Taft Douglas, *Remember the Ladies: The Story of Great Women Who Helped Shape America* (New York: G. P. Putnam Sons, 1966), 54–57; Maxwell and Dunlevy, *Virago!*

21. Porter, *Life and Times of Anne Royall;* Jackson, *Uncommon Scold;* James, *Anne Royall's U.S.A.* The books by Porter and James were reported in the press. See "Told of Anne Royall: Not So Black as Painted, Declared Defender," *Washington Post,* March 13, 1906; "Anne Royall's Doings," *Washington Post,* May 3, 1909; and "Advocate of Literary Teamwork in Marriage," *Washington Post,* May 11, 1936. The first of the radio plays about Royall broadcast in the *Cavalcade of America* was based on James's biography.

22. See, for instance, Rick Brown, "Anne Royall: America's First Professional Female Journalist?" www.historybuff.com/library/refroyall.html, and "Anne Royall," Wikipedia: The Free Encyclopedia, http://en.wikipedia.org/wiki/Anne_Royall.

23. "Edited Her Own Paper: Eccentric Mrs. Royall, First of Woman Suffragists," *Washington Post,* April 12, 1899; "Congress," *The Huntress,* February 14, 1852; "The Abolitionists—Alias Free Democracy—Alias Church and State," *The Huntress,* January 15, 1853.

24. "Congress," *The Huntress,* February 14, 1852; "The Abolitionists—Alias Free Democracy—Alias Church and State," *The Huntress,* January 15, 1853.

25. "Prospectus," *The Huntress,* December 2, 1836.

26. "Mrs. Ann Royall," *Boston Evening Transcript,* July 3, 1843.

Bibliography

MANUSCRIPT COLLECTIONS

Barnard College Library, New York
Bertha Overbury Collection
Manuscript Collection, Boston Public Library
Correspondence of A. Ward, 1813–33
Manuscript Division, Brown University Library, Providence
Address of the Carriers of the *Newburyport Herald,* January 1, 1830
David M. Rubinstein Rare Book and Manuscript Library, Duke University, Durham, NC
James Martin Bell Papers
Campbell Family Papers
The Filson Historical Society, Louisville, KY
Bodley Family Papers
Historical Society of Pennsylvania, Philadelphia
Dreer Collection
Gratz Collection
Gratz Manuscripts
Notable American Women, Gratz Collection
Manuscript Division, Houghton Library, Harvard University, Cambridge, MA
Jared Sparks Manuscripts
Manuscript Division, Library of Congress, Washington, DC
Cary-Mathews Family Correspondence, 1825–30, Papers of the Feamster Family
Thomas Jefferson Papers microfilm
Anne Newport Royall Collection
Massachusetts Historical Society, Boston
Adams Family Papers microfilm

Morristown National Historical Park, Morristown, NJ
Manuscript Collection microfilm
National Archives and Records Administration, Washington, DC
Record Group 46, Records of the U.S. Senate
Special Collections, Newberry Library, Chicago
Graff Collection
Whitney Library, New Haven Museum, New Haven, CT
Durrie and Peck Papers
Manuscripts and Archives Division, New York Public Library
Miscellaneous Papers: Anne Royall
Pennsylvania State Archives, Harrisburg
Land Records
Albert and Shirley Small Special Collections Library, University of Virginia, Charlottesville
A.L.S. Collection
Anne Royall Papers, Clifton Waller Barrett Collection
Coles Collection
Archives Division, Virginia Polytechnic Institute and State University, Blacksburg
Royall Family Papers
Department of Special Collections, University of Wisconsin, Madison
Anne Royall to Mr. Holiday, January 19, 1849

COURT AND LEGAL RECORDS

Roane v. Royall et al., Box 235, Clerk's Office, Augusta County Circuit Court, Staunton, VA.

Anne Royall's Pension Claim, No. W8566, Revolutionary War Pension and Bounty-Land Warrant Application Files, M-804, R2095, National Archives and Records Administration (NARA), Washington, DC.

U.S. v. Royall, Box 158, Record Group 21, Circuit Court District of Columbia, Case Papers 1802–63, May Term 1829, NARA, Washington, DC.

Record Group 217, Records of the Accounting Officers of the Department of the Treasury Third Auditor, Settled Accounts and Claims, March 1817–December 1897, NARA, College Park, MD.

VIRGINIA COUNTY RECORDS (MICROFILM), LIBRARY OF VIRGINIA, RICHMOND

Amelia County Deed Book, 1768–69
Amelia County Will Books, 1771–80, 1780–86
Botetourt County Circuit Court Order Book, Common Law, 1809–23
Botetourt County Marriage Bonds, 1770–1815

Charles City County Deed Books, 1789–1802, 1803–16
Charles City County Personal Property Tax Lists, 1794–1815
Chesterfield County Deed Books, 1772–74, 1800–1802
Chesterfield County Order Book 6
Chesterfield County Will Book 4
Greenbrier County Court House, Chancery Order Book, 1823
Kanawha County Deed Books, 1812–17
Kenawha County Land Tax Lists, 1811–13
Kenawha County Supreme Court Minute Book, 1814–19
Monroe County Order Books, 1811–13, 1813–17
Monroe County Superior Court Minute Book, 1814–21
Monroe County Superior Court Order Book, 1809–14
Monroe County Will Books, 1799–1817, 1818–29
James Roane, List of Inhabitants, Charles City Census Schedules, 1810

Newspapers and Periodicals

The Ariel: A Semimonthly Literary and Miscellaneous Gazette
Arkansas Gazette
Aurora and Pennsylvania Gazette
Baltimore Patriot
Baltimore Sun
Bangor Daily Whig and Courier
Bismarck Daily Tribune
Boston Commercial Gazette
Boston Daily Advertiser
Boston Evening Transcript
Boston Investigator
Carolina Observer
Cincinnati American
Commercial Advertiser
Connecticut Courant
Constitutional Whig
Daily Commercial Gazette
Daily Evening Bulletin
Daily Inter-Ocean
Daily National Intelligencer
Daily National Journal
Daily South Carolinian
Democratic Press
Essex Gazette
Essex Register
Evening Star
Farmers' Cabinet
Fayetteville Observer
The Globe
Harrisburg Argus
The Huntress
Independent Gazetteer
Ithaca Herald
Literary Cadet and Rhode Island Statesman
Literary Cadet and Saturday Evening Bulletin
Macon Weekly Telegraph
Middlesex Gazette
Morning Courier
Morning Courier and New York Enquirer
Morning News
Nashville Banner and Nashville Whig
National Advocate
National Gazette and Literary Register
National Intelligencer
New Albany Daily Ledger
New Bedford Mercury
New England Galaxy

New England Weekly Review
New-Hampshire Gazette
New Hampshire Patriot and State Gazette
New Hampshire Sentinel
Newport Mercury
New York American
New York Enquirer
New York Observer
New York Spectator
New York Times
Niles' Register/Niles' Weekly Register
North American and United States Gazette
Northern Sentinel
Ohio Statesman
Paul Pry
Pennsylvania Inquirer and Daily Courier
Pennsylvania Inquirer and National Gazette
Pittsfield Sun
Portsmouth Journal and Rockingham Gazette
Portsmouth Journal of Literature and Politics
Providence Patriot and Columbian Phenix
Richmond Enquirer
Richmond Whig
Ripley Bee
Salem Gazette
Saturday Evening Post
Scioto Gazette
Southern Patriot
United States Gazette
United States Telegraph
Vermont Chronicle
Vermont Gazette
Vermont Watchman and State Gazette
Virginia Advocate
Virginia Free Press
Washington Post
The Watch Tower
Western Monthly Review
Western Virginia and Kenawha County Gazette

Primary Sources

Adams, John Quincy. *Memoirs of John Quincy Adams, Comprising Portions of His Diary from 1795 to 1848.* Edited by Charles Francis Adams. 12 vols. Philadelphia, 1875.

American State Papers. Century of Lawmaking, American Memory, Library of Congress. http://memory.loc.gov/ammem/amlaw.

Congressional Debates (Register of Debates). Century of Lawmaking, American Memory, Library of Congress. http://memory.loc.gov/ammem/amlaw.

Congressional Globe. Century of Lawmaking, American Memory, Library of Congress. http://memory.loc.gov/ammem/amlaw.

Cranch, William. *Reports of Cases Civil and Criminal in the United States Circuit Court of the District of Columbia: From 1801–1841.* 6 vols. New York, 1852–53.

Davison, Gideon. *Fashionable Tour; or, A Trip to the Springs, Niagara, Quebeck and Boston in the Summer of 1821.* Saratoga Springs, 1822.

Hazard, Samuel, ed. *Pennsylvania Archives: Selected and Arranged from the Original Documents. Series I.* Volume 9. Philadelphia, 1854.

House Journal. Century of Lawmaking, American Memory, Library of Congress. http://memory.loc.gov/ammem/amlaw.
Martineau, Harriet. *Retrospect of Western Travel.* Edited by Daniel Feller. Armonk: M. E. Sharpe, 2000.
Peters, Richard, ed. *The Public Statutes at Large of the United States of America.* Volume 6. Boston, 1846.
Royall, Anne. *The Black Book; or, A Continuation of Travels in the United States.* 3 vols. Washington, DC, 1828–29.
———. *Letters from Alabama on Various Subjects: To Which Is Added an Appendix Containing Remarks on Sundry Members of the 20th and 21st Congress and Other High Characters, etc. etc. at the Seat of Government.* Washington, DC, 1830.
———. *Mrs. Royall's Pennsylvania; or, Travels Continued in the United States.* 2 vols. Washington, DC, 1829.
———. *Mrs. Royall's Southern Tour; or, Second Series of the Black Book.* 3 vols. Washington, DC, 1830–31.
———. *Sketches of History, Life and Manners in the United States. By a Traveller.* New Haven, CT, 1826.
———. *The Tennessean: A Novel Founded on Facts.* New Haven, CT, 1827.
Senate Journal. Century of Lawmaking, American Memory, Library of Congress. http://memory.loc.gov/ammem/amlaw.
Sergeant, Thomas, and William Rawle, Jr. *Reports of Cases Adjudged in the Supreme Court of Pennsylvania.* Vol. 12. Philadelphia, 1874.
Stickney, William, ed. *Autobiography of Amos Kendall.* New York, 1872.
"Trial of a Scold: The Trial of Mrs. Elizabeth Bowlan." Boston: Nathaniel Coverly, Jr., 1813.
Trollope, Frances. *Domestic Manners of the Americans.* London, 1832. Reprint, New York: Knopf, 1949.
Tucker, St. George. *Blackstone's Commentaries with Notes of Reference to the Constitution and Laws of the Federal Government of the United States and the Commonwealth of Virginia.* 5 vols. Philadelphia, 1803.

Secondary Sources

Abernethy, Thomas Perkins. *Western Lands and the American Revolution.* Revised edition. New York: Russell and Russell, 1959.
Albert, George Dallas. *The Frontier Forts of Western Pennsylvania.* Harrisburg, PA, 1896.
Alexander, Elizabeth Urban. *Notorious Woman: The Celebrated Case of Myra Clark Gaines.* Baton Rouge: Louisiana State University Press, 2001.
Allgor, Catherine. *Parlor Politics: In Which the Ladies of Washington Help Build a City and a Government.* Charlottesville: University Press of Virginia, 2000.

Andrews, William L., ed. *Journeys in New Worlds: Early American Women's Narratives.* Madison: University of Wisconsin Press, 1990.

Baker, Paula. "The Domestication of Politics: Women and American Political Society, 1780–1920." *American Historical Review* 89 (June 1984): 620–47.

Bamberger, C. M. *A Short History of Westmoreland County: The First County West of the Appalachians.* Jeanette, PA: Jeanette Publishing, 1941.

Bardaglio, Peter W. *Reconstructing the Household: Families, Sex and the Law in the Nineteenth-Century South.* Chapel Hill: University of North Carolina Press, 1995.

Bartlett, Virginia K. *Keeping House: Women's Lives in Western Pennsylvania, 1790–1850.* Pittsburgh: University of Pittsburgh Press, 1994.

Basch, Norma. *In the Eyes of the Law: Women, Marriage and Property in Nineteenth-Century New York.* Ithaca, NY: Cornell University Press, 1982.

———. "Marriage, Morals, and Politics in the Election of 1828." *Journal of American History* 80 (December 1993): 890–918.

Batten, Charles L., Jr. *Pleasurable Instruction: Form and Convention in Eighteenth-Century Travel Literature.* Berkeley: University of California Press, 1978.

Bauer, Dale M., and Philip Gould, eds. *The Cambridge Companion to Nineteenth-Century American Women's Writing.* Cambridge: Cambridge University Press, 2001.

Baym, Nina. *American Women Writers and the Work of History, 1790–1860.* New Brunswick, NJ: Rutgers University Press, 1995.

———. *Woman's Fiction: A Guide to Novels by and about Women in America, 1820–1870.* Ithaca, NY: Cornell University Press, 1978.

Beasley, Maurine. "Anne Royall, Huntress with a Quill." *The Quill* 78 (May 1990): 32–36.

Ben-Atar, Doron, and Barbara Oberg, eds. *Federalists Reconsidered.* Charlottesville: University Press of Virginia, 1998.

Berkhofer, Robert F., Jr. *The White Man's Indian: Images of the American Indian from Columbus to the Present.* New York: Knopf, 1978.

Biographical Directory of the United States Congress, 1774–Present. http://bioguide.congress.gov/biosearch/biosearch.asp.

Blackwell, Marilyn Schultz. "Meddling in Politics: Clarina Howard Nichols and Antebellum Political Culture." *Journal of the Early Republic* 24 (Spring 2004): 27–63.

Bloch, Ruth J. "American Feminine Ideals in Transition: The Rise of the Moral Mother, 1785–1815." *Feminist Studies* 4 (June 1978): 101–26.

Block, Sharon. *Rape and Sexual Power in Early America.* Chapel Hill: University of North Carolina Press, 2006.

Bodo, John R. *The Protestant Clergy and Public Issues, 1812–1848.* Princeton, NJ: Princeton University Press, 1954.

Boucher, John N. *History of Westmoreland County, Pennsylvania.* 3 vols. New York and Chicago: The Lewis Publishing Company, 1906.

Boydston, Jeanne. *Home and Work: Housework, Wages and the Ideology of Labor in the Early Republic.* New York: Oxford University Press, 1990.

Boydston, Jeanne, Mary Kelley, and Anne Margolis, eds. *The Limits of Sisterhood: The Beecher Sisters on Women's Rights and Woman's Sphere.* Chapel Hill: University of North Carolina Press, 1988.

Boyer, Paul. *Urban Masses and Moral Order in America, 1820–1920.* Cambridge, MA: Harvard University Press, 1978.

Boylan, Anne M. *The Origins of Women's Activism: New York and Boston, 1797–1840.* Chapel Hill: University of North Carolina Press, 2002.

Boynton, Henry Walcott. *Annals of American Bookselling, 1638–1850.* New York: J. Wiley and Sons, 1932.

Branson, Susan. *These Fiery Frenchified Dames: Politics and Culture in Early National Philadelphia.* Philadelphia: University of Pennsylvania Press, 2001.

Brekus, Catherine. *Strangers and Pilgrims: Female Preaching in America, 1740–1845.* Chapel Hill: University of North Carolina Press, 1998.

Brown, Dona. *Inventing New England: Regional Tourism in the Nineteenth Century.* Washington, DC: Smithsonian Institution, 1995.

Brown, Kathleen M. *Good Wives, Nasty Wenches, and Anxious Patriarchs: Gender, Race and Power in Colonial Virginia.* Chapel Hill: University of North Carolina Press, 1996.

Bruccoli, Matthew J., ed. *The Profession of Authorship in America, 1800–1870: The Papers of William Charvat.* Columbus: Ohio State University Press, 1968.

Bullock, Stephen C. *Revolutionary Brotherhood: Freemasonry and the Transformation of the American Social Order.* Chapel Hill: University of North Carolina Press, 1996.

Bushman, Richard L. *The Refinement of America: Persons, Houses, Cities.* New York: Vintage Books, 1992.

Butler, Jon. *Awash in a Sea of Faith: Christianizing the American People.* Cambridge, MA: Harvard University Press, 1990.

Bynum, Victoria. *Unruly Women: The Politics of Social and Sexual Control in the Old South.* Chapel Hill: University of North Carolina Press, 1992.

Carr, Lois Green, and Lorena S. Walsh. "The Planter's Wife: The Experience of White Women in Seventeenth-Century Maryland." *William and Mary Quarterly,* 3rd ser., 34 (October 1977): 542–71.

Carwardine, Richard J. *Evangelicals and Politics in Antebellum America.* Revised edition. Knoxville: University of Tennessee Press, 1997.

Cashin, Joan E. *A Family Venture: Men and Women on the Southern Frontier.* Baltimore: Johns Hopkins University Press, 1991.

Chambers, Thomas A. *Drinking the Waters: Creating an American Leisure*

Class at Nineteenth-Century Mineral Springs. Washington, DC: Smithsonian Institution Press, 2002.

Cohen, Daniel A. "The Respectability of Rebecca Reed: Genteel Womanhood and Sectarian Conflict in Antebellum America." *Journal of the Early Republic* 16 (Fall 1996): 419–61.

Cohen, Patricia Cline. *The Murder of Helen Jewett: The Life and Death of a Prostitute in Nineteenth-Century New York*. New York: Vintage Books, 1998.

———. "Women at Large: Travel in Antebellum America." *History Today* 44 (December 1994): 44–50.

Collins, Winfield H. *The Domestic Slave Trade of the Southern States*. New York: Broadway Publishing, 1904.

Coryell, Janet L. *Neither Heroine nor Fool: Anna Ella Carroll of Maryland*. Kent, OH: Kent State University Press, 1990.

Coryell, Janet L., et al., eds. *Negotiating Boundaries of Southern Womanhood: Dealing with the Powers That Be*. Columbia: University of Missouri Press, 2000.

Cott, Nancy F. *The Bonds of Womanhood: "Woman's Sphere" in New England, 1780–1835*. New Haven: Yale University Press, 1977.

Coultrap-McQuin, Susan. *Doing Literary Business: American Women Writers in the Nineteenth Century*. Chapel Hill: University of North Carolina Press, 1990.

Cray, Robert E. "Major John André and the Three Captors: Class Dynamics and Revolutionary Memory Wars in the Early Republic, 1780–1831." *Journal of the Early Republic* 17 (Fall 1997): 371–98.

Davidson, Cathy N., ed. *Reading in America: Literature and Social History*. Baltimore: Johns Hopkins University Press, 1989.

———. *Revolution and the Word: The Rise of the Novel in America*. Expanded edition. New York: Oxford University Press, 2004.

Day, Laura A. "'The History of Every One of Us': A Gender Study of America's Antebellum Travel Writers." Ph.D. diss., Purdue University, 1988.

Dayton, Cornelia Hughes. *Women before the Bar: Gender, Law and Society in Connecticut, 1639–1789*. Chapel Hill: University of North Carolina Press, 1995.

Dorsey, Bruce. *Reforming Men and Women: Gender in the Antebellum City*. Ithaca, NY: Cornell University Press, 2002.

Doyle, Christopher L. "The Randolph Scandal in Early National Virginia, 1792–1815: New Voices in the 'Court of Honour.'" *Journal of Southern History* 69 (May 2003): 283–319.

Dunaway, Wilma A. *The African American Family in Slavery and Emancipation*. Cambridge: Cambridge University Press, 2003.

Earman, Cynthia. "An Uncommon Scold." *Library of Congress Information Bulletin* (January 2000), www.loc.gov/loc/lcib/0001/royall.html.

Edwards, Laura F. "Law, Domestic Violence, and the Limits of Patriarchal Authority in the Antebellum South." *Journal of Southern History* 65 (November 1999): 733–70.

Eldridge, Larry D., ed. *Women and Freedom in Early America.* New York: New York University Press, 1997.

Eslinger, Ellen, ed. *Running Mad for Kentucky: Frontier Travel Accounts.* Lexington: University Press of Kentucky, 2004.

Fabian, Ann. *The Unvarnished Truth: Personal Narratives in Nineteenth-Century America.* Berkeley: University of California Press, 2000.

Faragher, John Mack. *Daniel Boone: The Life and Legend of an American Pioneer.* New York: Henry Holt, 1992.

Feller, Daniel. *The Jacksonian Promise: America 1815–1840.* Baltimore: Johns Hopkins University Press, 1995.

Fletcher, Anthony, and John Stevenson, eds. *Order and Disorder in Early Modern England.* Cambridge: Cambridge University Press, 1985.

Foster, Shirley. *Across New Worlds: Nineteenth-Century Women Travellers and Their Writing.* London: Harvester Wheatsheaf, 1990.

Frantz, John B., and William Pencak, eds. *Beyond Philadelphia: The American Revolution in the Pennsylvania Hinterland.* University Park: Pennsylvania State University Press, 1998.

Freedman, Estelle B. *Their Sisters' Keepers: Women's Prison Reform in America, 1830–1930.* Ann Arbor: University of Michigan Press, 1981.

Freeman, Joanne B. *Affairs of Honor: National Politics in the New Republic.* New Haven, CT: Yale University Press, 2001.

Friend, Craig Thompson, ed. *The Buzzel about Kentuck: Settling the Promised Land.* Lexington: University Press of Kentucky, 1999.

Gilmore, William J. *Reading Becomes a Necessity of Life: Material and Cultural Life in Rural New England, 1780–1835.* Knoxville: University of Tennessee Press, 1989.

Ginzberg, Lori. "The Hearts of Your Readers Will Shudder: Fanny Wright, Infidelity, and American Freethought." *American Quarterly* 46 (June 1994): 195–226.

———. *Untidy Origins: A Story of Women's Rights in Antebellum New York.* Chapel Hill: University of North Carolina Press, 2005.

———. *Women and the Work of Benevolence: Morality, Class, and Benevolence in the Nineteenth-Century United States.* New Haven, CT: Yale University Press, 1990.

Goodman, Paul. *Towards a Christian Republic: Antimasonry and the Great Transition in New England, 1826–1836.* New York: Oxford University Press, 1988.

Griffin, Patrick. *American Leviathan: Empire, Nation, and Revolutionary Frontier.* New York: Hill and Wang, 2007.

Gross, Robert A., and Mary Kelley, eds. *A History of the Book in America,* volume 2, *An Extensive Republic: Print Culture and Society in the New Nation, 1790–1840.* Chapel Hill: University of North Carolina Press, 2010.

Gundersen, Joan, and Gwen Victor Gampel. "Married Women's Legal Status in Eighteenth-Century New York and Virginia." *William and Mary Quarterly,* 3rd ser., 33 (January 1982): 114–34.

Hackenberg, Michael, ed. *Getting the Books Out: Papers of the Chicago Conference on the Book in 19th Century America.* Washington, DC: Center for the Book, Library of Congress, 1989.

Hamalian, Leo, ed. *Ladies on the Loose: Women Travelers of the 18th and 19th Centuries.* New York: Dodd Mead, 1981.

Harris, John Royall. "The Colonial Royalls of Virginia: Chapter II." *Virginia Magazine of History and Biography* 32 (1924): 103–7.

Hatch, Nathan. *The Democratization of American Christianity.* New Haven, CT: Yale University Press, 1989.

Helly, Dorothy O., and Susan M. Reverby, eds. *Gendered Domains: Rethinking Public and Private in Women's History.* Ithaca, NY: Cornell University Press, 1992.

Hemphill, C. Dallett. *Bowing to Necessities: A History of Manners in America, 1620–1860.* New York: Oxford University Press, 1999.

Hershberger, Mary. "Mobilizing Women, Anticipating Abolition: The Struggle against Indian Removal in the 1830s." *Journal of American History* 86 (June 1999): 15–40.

Hewitt, Nancy, ed. *A Companion to American Women's History.* Oxford: Blackwell, 2002.

———. *Women's Activism and Social Change: Rochester, New York, 1822–1872.* Ithaca, NY: Cornell University Press, 1984.

Hill, Benjamin Thomas, ed. "The Diary of Isaiah Thomas 1805–1828. In Two Volumes. Volume II." *Transactions and Collections of the American Antiquarian Society.* Worcester: American Antiquarian Society, 1909.

Hinderaker, Eric, and Peter C. Mancall. *At the Edge of Empire: The Backcountry in British North America.* Baltimore: Johns Hopkins University Press, 2003.

Holt, Michael F. *The Rise and Fall of the American Whig Party: Jacksonian Politics and the Onset of the Civil War.* New York: Oxford University Press, 1999.

Horn, James, Jan Ellen Lewis, and Peter S. Onuf, eds. *The Revolution of 1800: Democracy, Race, and the New Republic.* Charlottesville: University of Virginia Press, 2002.

Howe, Daniel Walker. "The Evangelical Movement and Political Culture in the North during the Second Party System." *Journal of American History* 77 (March 1991): 1216–39.

———. *The Political Culture of the American Whigs.* Chicago: University of Chicago Press, 1979.

Imbarrato, Susan Clair. *Traveling Women: Narrative Visions of Early America.* Athens: Ohio University Press, 2006.

Isaac, Rhys. *The Transformation of Virginia, 1740–1790.* Chapel Hill: University of North Carolina Press, 1999.

Jackson, George Stuyvesant. *Uncommon Scold: The Story of Anne Royall.* Boston: Humphries, 1937.

James, Bessie Rowland. *Anne Royall's U.S.A.* New Brunswick, NJ: Rutgers University Press, 1972.

Jeffrey, Julie Roy. *The Great Silent Army of Abolition: Ordinary Women in the Anti-Slavery Movement.* Chapel Hill: University of North Carolina Press, 1998.

———. "Permeable Boundaries: Abolitionist Women and Separate Spheres." *Journal of the Early Republic* 21 (Spring 2001): 79–93.

Jensen, Laura. *Patriots, Settlers, and the Origins of American Social Policy.* Cambridge: Cambridge University Press, 2003.

John, Richard J. *Spreading the News: The American Postal System from Franklin to Morse.* Cambridge, MA: Harvard University Press, 1998.

———. "Taking Sabbatarianism Seriously: The Postal System, the Sabbath, and the Transformation of American Political Culture." *Journal of the Early Republic* 4 (Winter 1990): 517–67.

Kamensky, Jane. "Talk Like a Man: Speech, Power, and Masculinity in New England." *Gender and History* 8 (April 1996): 22–47.

Kasson, John F. *Rudeness and Civility: Manners in Nineteenth-Century Urban America.* New York: Farrar, Straus and Giroux, 1990.

Kelley, Mary. *Learning to Stand and Speak: Women, Education, and Public Life in America's Republic.* Chapel Hill: University of North Carolina Press, 2006.

———. *Private Woman, Public Stage: Literary Domesticity in Nineteenth-Century America.* New York: Oxford University Press, 1984.

Kennon, Donald R., ed. *A Republic of the Ages: The United States Capitol and the Political Culture of the Early Republic.* Charlottesville: University Press of Virginia, 1999.

Kerber, Linda K. "Separate Spheres, Female Worlds, Woman's Place: The Rhetoric of Women's History." *Journal of American History* 75 (June 1988): 9–39.

———. *Toward an Intellectual History of Women: Essays by Linda K. Kerber.* Chapel Hill: University of North Carolina Press, 1997.

———. *Women of the Republic: Intellect and Ideology in Revolutionary America.* New York: Norton, 1980.

Kierner, Cynthia. *Beyond the Household: Women's Place in the Early South, 1700–1830.* Ithaca, NY: Cornell University Press, 1998.

———. *Scandal at Bizarre: Rumor and Reputation in Jefferson's America.* New York: Palgrave Macmillan, 2004.

Kilcup, Karen L., ed. *From Beacon Hill to the Crystal Palace: The 1851 Travel Diary of a Working-Class Woman by Lorenza Stevens Berbineau.* Iowa City: University of Iowa Press, 2002.

Klinghoffer, Judith Apter, and Lois Elkis. "'The Petticoat Electors': Women's Suffrage in New Jersey, 1776–1807." *Journal of the Early Republic* 12 (Summer 1992): 159–93.

Kulikoff, Allan. *Tobacco and Slaves: The Development of Southern Cultures in the Chesapeake, 1680–1800.* Chapel Hill: University of North Carolina Press, 1986.

Lasser, Carol. "Beyond Separate Spheres: The Power of Public Opinion." *Journal of the Early Republic* 21 (Spring 2001): 115–24.

Lebsock, Suzanne. *The Free Women of Petersburg: Status and Culture in a Southern Town, 1784–1860.* New York: Norton, 1984.

Lehuu, Isabelle. *Carnival on the Page: Popular Print Media in Antebellum America.* Chapel Hill: University of North Carolina Press, 2000.

Lerner, Renee Letow. "The Transformation of the American Civil Trial: The Silent Judge." *William and Mary Law Review* 42 (2000): 195–264.

Lewis, Charlene M. Boyer. *Ladies and Gentlemen on Display: Planter Society at the Virginia Springs, 1790–1860.* Charlottesville: University Press of Virginia, 2001.

Main, Jackson T. "The One Hundred." *William and Mary Quarterly,* 3rd ser., 11 (July 1954): 354–84.

Mancall, Peter C., and James H. Merrell, eds. *American Encounters: Natives and Newcomers from European Contact to Indian Removal, 1500–1850.* New York: Psychology Press, 2000.

Mann, Bruce. *Republic of Debtors: Bankruptcy in the Age of American Independence.* Cambridge, MA: Harvard University Press, 2002.

Maxwell, Alice S., and Marion B. Dunlevy. *Virago! The Story of Anne Newport Royall (1769–1854).* Jefferson, NC: McFarland, 1985.

Morton, Oren F. *A History of Monroe County, West Virginia.* Dayton, VA: Ruebush-Elkins, 1916.

Munger, Donna Bingham. *Pennsylvania Land Records: A History and Guide for Research.* Wilmington: Scholarly Resources, 1991.

Nobles, Gregory H. "Breaking into the Backcountry: New Approaches to the Early American Frontier, 1750–1800." *William and Mary Quarterly,* 3rd ser., 46 (October 1989): 641–70.

Norton, Mary Beth. *Liberty's Daughters: The Revolutionary Experience of American Women, 1750–1800.* Ithaca, NY: Cornell University Press, 1980.

Okker, Patricia. *Our Sister Editors: Sarah J. Hale and the Tradition of Nineteenth-Century Women Editors.* Athens: University of Georgia Press, 1995.

Old Time Radio Researchers Group. *The Cavalcade of America: Single Episodes.* https://archive.org/details/OTTR_Cavalcade_of_America_Singles.

Olsen, Christopher J. "'Molly Pitcher' of the Mississippi Whigs: The Editorial Career of Mrs. Harriet N. Prewett." *Journal of Mississippi History* 58 (Fall 1996): 237–54.

Parker, Alison M., and Stephanie Cole, eds. *Women and the Unstable State in Nineteenth-Century America.* College Station: Texas A&M University Press, 2000.

Pasley, Jeffrey L. "Minnows, Spies, and Aristocrats: The Social Crisis of Congress in the Age of Martin Van Buren." *Journal of the Early Republic* 27 (Winter 2007): 599–653.

———. *"The Tyranny of Printers": Newspaper Politics in the Early Republic.* Charlottesville: University Press of Virginia, 2001.

Pasley, Jeffrey L., Andrew W. Robertson, and David Waldstreicher, eds. *Beyond the Founders: New Approaches to the Political History of the Early American Republic.* Chapel Hill: University of North Carolina Press, 2004.

Peavy, Linda, and Ursula Smith. *Women in Waiting in the Westward Movement: Life on the Home Frontier.* Norman: University of Oklahoma Press, 1994.

Pessen, Edward. *Jacksonian America: Society, Personality, and Politics.* Second edition. Urbana: University of Illinois Press, 1978.

Porter, Sarah Harvey. *The Life and Times of Anne Royall.* Cedar Rapids: Torch Press Book Shop, 1909.

Portnoy, Alisse. *Their Right to Speak: Women's Activism in the Indian and Slave Debates.* Cambridge, MA: Harvard University Press, 2005.

Purcell, Sarah J. *Sealed with Blood: War, Sacrifice, and Memory in Revolutionary America.* Philadelphia: University of Pennsylvania Press, 2002.

Remer, Rosalind. "Preachers, Peddlers, and Publishers: Philadelphia's Backcountry Book Trade, 1800–1830." *Journal of the Early Republic* 14 (Winter 1994): 497–522.

———. *Printers and Men of Capital: Philadelphia Book Publishers in the New Republic.* Philadelphia: University of Pennsylvania Press, 1996.

Resch, John. "Politics and Public Culture: The Revolutionary War Pension Act of 1818." *Journal of the Early Republic* 8 (Summer 1988): 139–58.

———. *Suffering Soldiers: Revolutionary War Veterans, Moral Sentiment and Political Culture in the Early Republic.* Amherst: University of Massachusetts Press, 1999.

Robert, Karen, ed. *New Year in Cuba: Mary Gardner Lowell's Travel Diary, 1831–1832.* Boston: Northeastern University Press, 2003.

Rockman, Seth. *Scraping By: Wage Labor, Slavery and Survival in Early Baltimore.* Baltimore: Johns Hopkins University Press, 2009.

Roeber, A. G. *Faithful Magistrates and Republican Lawyers: Creators of Virginia Legal Culture, 1680–1810.* Chapel Hill: University of North Carolina Press, 1981.

Rohrer, James R. "Sunday Mails and the Church-State Theme in Jacksonian America." *Journal of the Early Republic* 10 (Winter 1987): 55–73.

Ross, Ishbell. *Ladies of the Press: The Story of Women in Journalism by an Insider.* New York: Harper, 1936.

Ryan, Mary P. *The Cradle of the Middle Classes: The Family in Oneida County, New York, 1780–1865*. Cambridge: Cambridge University Press, 1981.

———. *Women in Public: Between Banners and Ballots, 1825–1880*. Baltimore: Johns Hopkins University Press, 1990.

Sacher, John. "'The Ladies Are Moving Everywhere': Louisiana Women and Antebellum Politics." *Louisiana History* 42 (Fall 2001): 439–57.

Salmon, Marylynn. *Women and the Law of Property in Early America*. Chapel Hill: University of North Carolina Press, 1986.

Schriber, Mary Suzanne, ed. *Telling Tales: Selected Writings by Nineteenth-Century American Women Abroad*. De Kalb: Northern Illinois University Press, 1995.

Schulz, Constance B. "Revolutionary War Pension Applications: A Neglected Source for Social and Family History." *Prologue* 25 (Summer 1993): 103–14.

Scott, Joan. "Gender as a Useful Category of Historical Analysis." *American Historical Review* 91 (December 1986): 1053–75.

Sears, John F. *Sacred Places: American Tourist Attractions in the Nineteenth Century*. New York: Oxford University Press, 1989.

Sellers, Charles. *The Market Revolution: Jacksonian America, 1815–1846*. New York: Oxford University Press, 1991.

Smith, Elizabeth Amy. "Travel Narratives and the Familiar Letter Form in the Mid-Eighteenth Century." *Studies in Philology* 95 (Winter 1998): 77–96.

Smith, Daniel Blake. *Inside the Great House: Planter Family Life in Eighteenth-Century Chesapeake Society*. Ithaca, NY: Cornell University Press, 1980.

Smith-Rosenberg, Carroll. "The Female World of Love and Ritual: Relations between Women in Nineteenth-Century America." *Signs* 1 (Autumn 1975): 1–29.

Snyder, Terri L. *Brabbling Women: Disorderly Speech and the Law in Early Virginia*. Ithaca, NY: Cornell University Press, 2003.

Stealey, John E., III. *The Antebellum Kanawha Salt Business and Western Markets*. Lexington: University of Kentucky Press, 1993.

Steffen, Charles G. "Newspapers for Free: The Economies of Newspaper Circulation in the Early Republic." *Journal of the Early Republic* 23 (Fall 2003): 381–419.

Sturtz, Linda L. *Within Her Power: Propertied Women in Colonial Virginia*. New York: Routledge, 2002.

Tadman, Michael. *Speculators and Slaves: Masters, Traders, and Slaves in the Old South*. Madison: University of Wisconsin Press, 1989.

Tebbel, John. *A History of Book Publishing in the United States*, volume 1, *The Creation of an Industry, 1630–1865*. New York: Bowker, 1972.

Teipe, Emily J. *America's First Veterans and the Revolutionary War Pensions*. Lewiston, NY: Edwin Mellen Press, 2002.

Thomas, Amy M. "'There Is Nothing So Effective as a Personal Canvass': Revaluing Nineteenth-Century American Subscription Books." *Book History* 1 (1998): 140–55.

Thomas, Keith. *Religion and the Decline of Magic: Studies in Popular Belief in Sixteenth and Seventeenth Century England.* Oxford: Oxford University Press, 1971.

Thurner, Manuela. "'Better Citizens without the Ballot': American AntiSuffrage Women and Their Rationale during the Progressive Era." *Journal of Women's History* 5 (Spring 1993): 33–60.

Ulrich, Laurel Thatcher. *A Midwife's Tale: The Life of Martha Ballard, Based on Her Diary, 1785–1812.* New York: Vintage Books, 1990.

Varon, Elizabeth. "Tippecanoe and the Ladies, Too: White Women and Party Politics in Antebellum Virginia." *Journal of American History* 82 (Summer 1995): 494–521.

———. *We Mean to Be Counted: White Women and Politics in Antebellum Virginia.* Chapel Hill: University of North Carolina Press, 1998.

Verhoeven, Tim. "The Case for Sunday Mails: Sabbath Laws and the Separation of Church and State in Jacksonian America." *Journal of Church and State* 55 (Winter 2012): 71–91.

Waddell, J. A. *Waddell's Annals of Augusta County, Virginia from 1726 to 1871.* 2nd ed. 1902. Reprint, Rockwood, TN: EagleRidge Technologies, 2006. www.roanetnhistory.org/waddellsannals.html.

Watson, Harry L. *Liberty and Power: The Politics of Jacksonian America.* New York: Hill and Wang, 1990.

Welter, Barbara. "The Cult of True Womanhood, 1820–1860." *American Quarterly* 18 (Summer 1966): 151–74.

Wilentz, Sean. *The Rise of American Democracy: Jefferson to Lincoln.* New York: Norton, 2005.

Wilson, Lisa. *Life after Death: Widows in Pennsylvania, 1750–1850.* Philadelphia: Temple University Press, 1992.

Wood, Kirsten E. *Masterful Women: Slaveholding Widows from the American Revolution through the Civil War.* Chapel Hill: University of North Carolina Press, 2004.

———. "'One Woman So Dangerous to Public Morals': Gender and Power in the Eaton Affair." *Journal of the Early Republic* 17 (Summer 1997): 237–75.

Wosh, Peter J. *Spreading the Word: The Bible Business in Nineteenth-Century America.* Ithaca, NY: Cornell University Press, 1994.

Wright, Conrad Edick, and Katheryn P. Viens, eds. *Entrepreneurs: The Boston Business Community, 1700–1850.* Boston: Massachusetts Historical Society, 1997.

Young, Alfred F. "George Robert Twelve Hewes (1742–1840): A Boston Shoemaker and the Memory of the American Revolution." *William and Mary Quarterly*, 3rd ser., 38 (October 1981): 561–623.

———. *Masquerade: The Life and Times of Deborah Sampson, Continental Soldier.* New York: Knopf, 2004.

Zaeske, Susan. *Signatures of Citizenship: Petitioning, Antislavery, and Women's Political Identity.* Chapel Hill: University of North Carolina Press, 2003.

Zagarri, Rosemarie. *Revolutionary Backlash: Women and Politics in the Early American Republic.* Philadelphia: University of Pennsylvania Press, 2007.

Zboray, Ronald J. *A Fictive People: Antebellum Economic Development and the American Reading Public.* New York: Oxford University Press, 1993.

Zboray, Ronald J., and Mary Saracino Zboray. "Gender Slurs in Boston's Partisan Press during the 1840s." *Journal of American Studies* 34 (December 2000): 413–46.

———. *Voices without Votes: Women and Politics in Antebellum New England.* Durham: New Hampshire University Press, 2010.

———. "Whig Women, Politics and Culture in the Campaign of 1840: Three Perspectives from Massachusetts." *Journal of the Early Republic* 17 (Summer 1997): 278–315.

Index

Note: "AR" and "WR" refer to Anne Royall and William Royall, respectively.